THE ENCYCLOPEDIA
OF THE
AMERICAN AUTOMOBILE

Exeter Books

NEW YORK

Title page photo : a 1960 Chrysler 300F, last of the 'thoroughbred' 300s and epitome of American cars of the period

AUTHORS
Buick, Cadillac, Chevrolet, Packard and Studebaker are by Karl Ludvigsen; Chrysler, Cord, Dodge, Duesenberg, Edsel ,General Motors, Lincoln, Nash, Oldsmobile, Pierce-Arrow, Plymouth, Pontiac, Rambler and Stutz are by David Burgess Wise; Auburn and Hudson are by Ronald Barker; Ford is by Graham Gauld; Mercury is by Mike Twite; revision and the introductory chapter are by Brian Laban.

PICTURE ACKNOWLEDGMENTS
Alisi; American Motors; Arman; Belli; Betti; Boschetti; Brooklyn Antique Auto Museum; L. J. Caddell; Chrysler; Coluzzi; Deler; J. Neal East; Farabola; Ford; Fox Photos; General Motors; G. Goddard; Hamilton; Robert Hunt Library; ICP; IMS; IPC; Keystone; London Art Tech; Ludvigsen; Marka; National Motor Museum, England; Papetti; C. Pocklington; Popperfoto; Quattroruote; J. G. Rettie; H. Shell; J. Spencer Smith; C. Burgess Wise; N. Wright.

© Quattroruote-Domus & IGDA 1972, 1973, 1974, 1975
© Orbis Publishing Limited 1974, 1975, 1976, 1977, 1979, 1982

First published in USA 1982
by Exeter Books
Distributed by Bookthrift
Exeter is a trademark of Simon & Schuster
Bookthrift is a registered trademark of Simon & Schuster
New York, New York

ISBN 0-89673-132-4

Printed in Italy

Contents

Shaping the Industry

A story of success and failure — built around the dreams of famous men

AMERICA AND THE STORY OF THE AUTOMOBILE are inseparable. Although Europe brought the motor car into the world, it was the American auto industry and its methods that brought motoring to the masses. From the turn of the century onwards the new world's spirit of free enterprise gave rise to a thousand would-be motor magnates, some destined for the pages of history, many for everlasting notoriety, most for instant obscurity.

While the European motor industry grew with frustrating slowness, the American industry forged ahead. The sprawling, oil-rich land of opportunity *needed* the automobile whereas in Europe manufacturers were held back by serving a small market with limited motoring needs, and also suffered from the effects of war in their own backyard at a critical time. Within a generation the automobile in the USA had become as much a way of life as the horse had been only a few years before and by the 1920s America was the world's biggest car producer. Into the 1980s that position had still to be challenged, but the beginnings were very humble.

There are many claimants for the title but America's first true, internal combustion motor vehicle was probably Schank's tricycle, exhibited, unsuccessfully, at the 1886 Ohio State Fair. Five years later, a more successful three-wheeler was shown off by one John Lambert, also of Ohio. At the same time Henry Nadig was to be seen around Allentown, Pennsylvania, in a four-wheeled, single-cylinder machine. As early as 1886 the Moto-cycle Company of Philadelphia had published a catalogue of motor vehicles but these were steam-powered tricycles and none was apparently ever sold.

Who was the first may be open to argument, but what is sure is that the first to make automobiles on a commercial basis in the USA were the brothers Frank and Charles Duryea, of Springfield, Massachusetts. From building their first vehicle, which took to the road in September 1893, the Duryeas attracted sufficient financial backing to float the Duryea Motor Wagon Company in 1895. On Thanksgiving Day of that year, a prototype Duryea won America's first motoring contest, the *Chicago Times-Herald* Race, contested by a motley assortment of just six vehicles. This particular motoring milestone should have been passed some weeks earlier, on 2 November, but as only two of the near one hundred promised entries turned up on that day the Duryea gave a 'demonstration contest' with a locally built Mueller-Benz—and lost.

Still, this was a time for pushing back the frontiers; no matter that the Duryea averaged only 6.66 mph, in atrocious weather conditions. Thousands of spectators had happily braved the bleak and muddy aftermath of a blizzard to catch their first glimpse of the new invention and now there would be no looking back. On 1 November 1895 the world's first motor club, The American Motor League, had been formed in Chicago —a few days ahead of the better-known claimant for that

(No Model.)   4 Sheets—Sheet 2.

C. E. DURYEA.
ROAD VEHICLE.

No. 540,648.   Patented June 11, 1895.

Fig. 2.

Witnesses:

Inventor:

distinction, the Automobile Club of France. Now all that was missing was the cars.

The first production Duryeas appeared the following year and thirteen of these Benz-inspired vehicles were built, one becoming a Barnum and Bailey circus star as a kind of freak attraction.

While the Duryeas argued about policy among themselves and headed for obscurity, 1896 also brought a more durable name to the new industry. For several years Ransom Eli Olds had been working with gasoline and steam engines and with steam buggies; in 1895 he had started work on his first gasoline buggy. The next year the car was a regular attraction running around the neighbourhood, and it brought backing for the Olds Motor Vehicle Company, working from a factory in Detroit, which at the time was America's fourteenth largest city and a rapidly growing industrial centre.

Just before the turn of the century there were well over fifty 'automobile companies' in the USA but it was Olds who set a trend by looking towards the low priced end of the market, and mass sales. At first, Olds had

Above: Frank (below) and Charles Duryea may not have built America's first car but they did found the country's first commercial automobile manufacturing company, in September 1895

Left: a page from the first Duryea patent bears Charles's name and signature, but most of the original design and fund raising had been done by younger brother Frank. Bitter recriminations led to the demise of the company in 1898

Facing page: Ford's Model T was the key to the future. This is a 1913 four-seat open tourer

Right: the motor car had arrived, but across most of America the roads were not ready for it. There was little organised lobbying for better roads until 1913

Below: part of Henry Ford's celebrated battle to discredit the Selden patent. Ford built this Lenoir-engined Model A to a patent of 1862, to show that a workable automobile could have pre-dated Selden's patent

concentrated on building his engines; after a while his company was taken over and turned into the Olds Motor Works, building luxury cars in tiny numbers and with Ransom as a not very committed figurehead President. After some early flops, Olds convinced the company to come up with an easy-to-drive, $650, single-cylinder runabout, the Curved Dash Oldsmobile. From the moment it went on sale, in 1901, it was a success. Some 600 Oldsmobiles rolled out that year and a sort of mass production had arrived, bringing the first thoughts of a car for the people and economies of scale. While others fell by the wayside, Oldsmobile endured— though not without its dramas—to become the first of the great American survivors. Olds' success was a foundation stone of the automobile industry; much of the Curved Dash, like much of many of its lesser-known contemporaries, was 'bought in' and thus was Detroit's component industry born.

The auto industry had been slow out of the starting gate but now there was no looking back. The would-be car builders came—and mostly went—thick and fast. Winton was one name that ultimately did not survive, although it was a Winton which made history with the first coast-to-coast crossing of the USA, from San Francisco to New York between May and July 1903. Some twenty days of that epic drive were spent on repairs, largely made necessary by the appalling conditions of the roads of the day, which were not keeping pace with the development of the car. It would not be until 1913 that the Lincoln Highway Association would be formed to lobby for a proper trans-continental highway across the country.

By the time the first decade of the twentieth century was half over, many of the great names in this history were already multi-million dollar operations—and where there is money there are lawyers. In the early days, most of those around the auto business were involved in a bizarre cottage industry where almost every manufacturer paid royalties on each vehicle to a man who had never even built a car, but who in 1879 had applied for a broad patent on the motor car which would virtually enslave the American automobile industry during its formative years.

The man was an attorney, by the name of George Baldwin Selden, and he published his 1879 patent in 1895 – just when it became most effective for the longest possible period. For a while he contested some individual 'infringements' himself and made a tolerable living. Then in 1899, with backing from the newly organised Electric Vehicle Company and with the support of some very dubious legal rulings, the Selden

Patent was given full rein. Royalties were demanded from anyone who built a car and almost all opposition was swept aside. In September 1902 the majority of manufacturers capitulated; the Association of Licenced Automobile Manufacturers (ALAM) was set up, taking a percentage royalty for the Electric Vehicle Company as owners of the patent, a similar sum for itself as administrators, and half of the same for Selden, on every vehicle sold by ALAM members. ALAM did have *some* plus points; it encouraged standardisation for many components for instance, encouraged exchange of technical information among members and to some extent formalised contracts, agreements and guarantees. ALAM also decided, however, *who* would be licenced, and hounded those who were not—which was restrictive practice. Most manufacturers simply toed the ALAM line, but in 1903 one came along who would

Above: the 1903 Winton team in Ireland for the Gordon Bennett Cup. On the left is Alexander Winton in the 80hp 'Bullet' and on the right Percy Owen's 40hp 'Baby Bullet'

Below: an apparently youthful George Selden on his fancifully dated automobile. The photo is heavily retouched, deepening the mystery!

not. His battle to smash the Selden Patent was the first in a series of personal crusades which would make him the very stuff of motoring legend. He was Henry Ford.

Following some earlier Ford enterprises, the Ford Motor Company was founded in 1903 and, after almost going broke within a few weeks, suddenly took off, selling a million dollars worth of cars within a year. Henry Ford saw the future of the motor industry in scale, in building cars for everyman. He wanted to sell a $500 automobile, and $500 simply could not include royalties to ALAM. In 1904 ALAM sued Ford, among others, for infringement and Ford fought back. The case dragged on until 1911, making over a million dollars for the lawyers, but Ford, after appealing a 1909 judgement against him, won the day, freeing the whole industry and guaranteeing his own future as a folk hero.

Nor had Henry done much in the meantime to damage his growing reputation as the industry's great innovator. By 1905 he was building 25 cars a day and then on 1 October 1908, after gaining total control of the company, he launched the Model T. In many ways the T was the key to the future of the auto industry. It caught on quickly and in a huge way. It was a basic, reliable workhorse: a viable alternative at last to the real thing. To satisfy demand, Henry had to develop new techniques of mass production. He began 'batch engineering' parts and in 1913 he brought the moving conveyor belt 'production line' (already pioneered in the clock and armament industries) to his factories. He applied the system first to magneto assembly, then to other built-up components, and within a year to the whole car. Eventually he brought chassis production time down from $12\frac{1}{2}$ to $1\frac{1}{2}$ hours, more than doubled daily pay to a record $5 a man (much to the horror of employers in general) and in 1913 sold 182,809 cars.

Where Ford led, others, not always willingly, would follow; but Henry did not have the new industry all to himself. Already the big names were on the scene and the whole intricate web, much of which survives today, was being spun.

In 1902 one of Ford's earlier backers, William Murphy, had formed the Cadillac Automobile Company (from the bones of a previous Ford company) and in 1904 it was reorganised as the Cadillac Motor Car Company, with one Henry Leland, erstwhile builder of gearboxes for Olds, as President. David Dunbar Buick founded his eponymous automobile company in 1903, and in 1904 William Crapo Durant, a millionaire carriage builder, bailed Buick out of a temporary crisis and took over financial control. In September 1908, Durant formed a new company, which he called General Motors, and, having narrowly failed to buy out Ford, he acquired Buick, Oldsmobile, Cadillac and Oakland for his new empire. He also acquired a chauffeur-cum-racing driver (for his Buick operation), by the name of Louis Chevrolet. Weighed down by less successful acquisitions, GM came close to collapse in 1910, and Durant was ousted by Charles Nash, who, with Walter Chrysler, dumped most of the GM dross and put the organisation back into profit. Durant meanwhile set Chevrolet to work to build a car to save the day and in 1911 the Chevrolet Motor Company was born. In 1913 a disillusioned Louis Chevrolet walked out and in 1915 Durant began to take over Chevrolet as the company's success grew. In 1918, mostly through exchange of now much sought after Chevrolet stock, Chevrolet became the fifth major, and ultimately most powerful, element of GM, regaining for Durant his former throne.

Other names, too, were already on the scene. Bicycle builders the Dodge brothers set up shop in Detroit, supplying engines and other components to many of the industry's leading names. In 1903 they became Ford's major supplier. For a while, John Dodge was Vice President of Ford, but in 1913 the Dodges put the money they had earned from Ford to work, to launch an auto-manufacturing company under their own name. By 1916 they were America's fourth biggest car producer and in 1920 their output was beaten only by the Model T.

Already American auto manufacturers were bringing innovation as well as mass production and skilful

Above: a 1904 Stanley steamer. The boiler is at the front under the famous 'coffin-nose' bonnet and the twin-cylinder engine is geared directly to the back axle – characteristic of all subsequent Stanleys. In 1906 a streamlined Stanley, driven by Fred Marriott, set a land-speed record of over 127 mph and this most successful of the many steam car manufacturers survived for more than a quarter of a century – until 1927

marketing to the industry. In 1907 the Chadwick company tried supercharging, but only briefly. In 1908 Cadillac had been awarded the British Dewar Trophy for standardisation of production parts. In 1912 the same company became the first to offer electric lighting and starting as a standard fitment and in 1915 they announced their V8 engine, forerunner of all subsequent American V8s. In 1916 Packard went four better, with the first production V12. Steam cars, too, were having their day, although the record annual production of the most successful of some 150 manufacturers—650 vehicles from Stanley during 1912—was very small beer. Nevertheless, even they were perhaps more relevant than the extraordinary, eight-wheeled gasoline-powered, Reeves Octo-Auto, which appeared in 1911.

However, it was a much more pressing need which now inspired engineering advances, for in 1914 Europe went to war and in 1917 America would follow. When private car production became restricted in that year, production of ambulances and trucks took over, the Peerless lorry chassis providing a popular base for armoured vehicles built for Europe. Ford was late in supporting the war efforts in the States, although his European factories had been supplying military equipment almost for the duration. Henry himself was a pacifist and it was not until America became directly involved in the conflict that his factories at home became military suppliers. They went on to produce ambulances, naval patrol boats, steel helmets and V8 and V12 Liberty aero-engines.

The first Liberties were built by the Lincoln company, founded in 1917 by Henry Leland after he resigned from Cadillac and eventually taken over by Ford in 1922. Leland was a man of great principle and had always intended Lincoln to be a luxury car builder. When the war ended, a little early for his best interests, he had to wait until the dawn of the 1920s before the first Lincoln car rolled out, into a very difficult future.

The immediate post-war years were very bad ones for the motor industry. Virtually everybody, Lincoln, Ford and General Motors included, was feeling the pinch. Many of the lesser names disappeared for ever and in 1920 even the mighty Durant was a victim, ousted once more, but this time never to return, as GM again faced collapse. In April 1920 automobile shares plummeted on the New York market, as sales were further hit by post-war credit restrictions, raw material shortages and soaring interest rates. Again it was Ford who made the breakthrough, slashing prices to pre-war levels, in order to get business, and stock, moving. Reluctantly, other survivors followed suit, but a brief sales boom soon gave way to an even more dramatic slump. By year's end, every major manufacturer had slashed workforces and closed plants 'for stocktaking'. Charles Nash, late of GM and a producer of cars under his own name since 1917 (as well as claiming, by the end of the war, to be 'the world's largest producer of trucks'), was one of the first to close. Unlike some, Nash would survive, eventually to become a foundation stone of the American Motors Corporation in the mid-1950s, along with Hudson.

Above: movie 'bad-man' Fred Kohler leers at the camera from his 1929 Oakland All-American Six. Oakland, billed for want of more exciting characteristics as 'the Car with a Conscience', was a foundation stone of General Motors. Quick drying lacquer paint was one of Oakland's few pioneering innovations and the name survived only until 1931

The Detroit payroll took a dive from 176,000 to 24,000 men; executives rolled up their sleeves to keep operations ticking over, as office staff were sacked and equipment sold off.

Ironically, the luxury car builders were enjoying a minor heyday, with fierce competition between the likes of Cadillac, Lincoln, Packard, Pierce-Arrow and the soon to be united Auburn, Cord and Duesenberg stables. Duesenberg even introduced the first production straight-eight engine and pioneered hydraulic brakes during 1920.

Then, with the new year, sales began to take off again. When Ford re-opened, he eased his cash-flow problems by having dealers pay for cars, which mostly came from existing stock, on delivery. That helped him to pay off an acutely embarassing $50,000,000, which he owed the banks and the Internal Revenue, largely without recourse to his own funds. It could not have been too damaging a policy; Ford had almost 60% of the market in 1921, although between 1919 and 1926 Buick remained the industry's top dollar earner. In 1922 Ford became the first automobile company to sell a million cars in a year. The following year they were the first to sell two million!

Competition again brought all manner of technical innovation. 1922 saw Trico introduce electric screen wipers, and leaded petrol was introduced in the same year, opening the way for more efficient, higher compression engines and ultimately for some very high-powered legislation. Nash 're-invented' rubber engine mountings in 1922 and Firestone pioneered 'balloon' tyres in 1923. Cadillac offered four-wheel brakes in 1923 and Buick the same in 1924, when Chrysler pitched in with the Chrysler Six. Also in 1924, duPont made a huge leap forward in one of the most trouble-some areas of manufacture by introducing quick drying enamel to the paint shop. In 1927 Oldsmobile offered another cosmetic first, pioneering chromium plating to replace the less durable nickel. It was simply not good enough to live on past glories any longer, sales had to be fought for and the customer always wanted something new.

Styling was becoming ever more important in the race for sales; this year's new engine could no longer be put into last year's bodywork. When Errett Lobban Cord, stylist-cum-supersalesman, took the reins at Auburn, and later at Duesenberg, a classic line was born. Another began with Henry's son, Edsel, moving from the Ford Presidency to Lincoln, where his eye for design gave the struggling company an elegant new image and a new lease of life—albeit not one totally appreciated by Henry Leland, who, cramped by Ford management methods, went his separate way. In 1926 Harley J. Earl became the first man in the industry to hold the official title 'stylist', when he joined GM to produce the 1927 303 La Salle, the world's first

production V16. In 1925, for the first time, closed cars outsold open ones in the USA.

The old order continued its gradual internecine shuffles. In 1924 the Chrysler Corporation was formed, with Walter P. Chrysler at the helm, and Chevrolet helped develop a new, small six for Oakland, which would be marketed as the Pontiac. By 1927 General Motors was one of ten US companies with assets valued at more than two billion dollars—and it was growing rapidly both at home and overseas.

An era ended in 1927, when Henry Ford finally accepted the reality that the ubiquitous Model T could not go on forever. When production ended, in May, over fifteen million Ts had been built. While Ford closed down to work on the launch of the T's successor, the Model A (which would come in October after a $250,000,000 development programme), Chevrolet usurped the role of number one seller. Chevy would win the position back in 1931 and then hold it for virtually every year until the present day.

In 1929 $27\frac{1}{2}$ million vehicles were registered in the USA. There was something for virtually every pocket, from the Model A (styled under the direction of Edsel Ford in the image of a diminutive Lincoln) at $385, to Cadillacs and real Lincolns at $6000 plus. Money being no object, the rapid and reliable Lincoln was popular with both gangsters and the law, but although the car used in the 1929 St Valentine's Day massacre was all dressed up as a police department Lincoln, it was in reality an even more up-market Packard.

The automobile industry was in no small way self-generating. Such was the demand for cars and associated services that work, and money, was abundant. In 1929 Ford alone employed over 162,000 people in the USA, and Chevrolet had its first million-sales year. Demand created jobs, jobs created money and money created demand—just as Henry had always decreed. 5,337,087 cars were built in America in 1929. In 1928 Chrysler had bought out Dodge, for some $175,000,000, and in July Chrysler launched another

contender for the mass market, a low-priced Chrysler-derivative going by the name of Plymouth. Plymouth would endure, and immediately set a record for first season sales for a new marque. By 1933 Chrysler would be at a zenith, taking second place in the sales league between Chevy and Ford, with Dodge bringing up fourth.

The technical advances still flowed. Packard introduced the hypoid axle in 1927 and Cadillac brought a new word into the language in 1928: synchromesh.

Such developments smoothed the progress of the cars themselves but there was precious little happening to do the same for the industry. The fall in sales at the beginning of the 1920s had been bad enough but the depression which saw out the end of that decade and reached its peak in 1930 was something else again. Between 1930 and 1932, the industry's output fell by an astonishing 75%, expenditure on automobiles falling by a similar amount as personal income went down by 42%.

Once again, though times were hard, the upper echelons of society weathered the storm better than most and competition between the luxury car builders reached new sybaritic peaks. The Model J Duesenberg, introduced in December 1928, sold around one a week throughout its life, at prices up to $25,000, and still ranks as one of the all-time classics. So, too, does its contemporary, the Twin-Six Packard, introduced in 1930. Almost 6000 would be built before 1939. Franklin, Lincoln and Pierce-Arrow also boasted V12s at the time, and Cadillac and Marmon both built V16s. Peerless, too, might have had a Murphy-bodied V16 had the depression not forced them to abandon car production altogether in 1931, to start a new career, when prohibition ended, as brewers of Carlings Ale.

Their change of product may have been a novelty, but the demise of one more auto manufacturer was not. At the beginning of 1929 there were 48 different makes on the US market; by 1932 there were only 35 and by 1941 there would be just 21.

At the opposite end of the scale from Peerless, things were just as tough. The American Austin Company, of Butler, Pennsylvania, was formed in 1930 to market the tiny British Austin Seven, fetchingly restyled by Count Alexis de Sahknoffsky (himself more used to clothing Peerless and Cord chassis). The American Austin was offered with 'free' motoring for the first year, if regularly serviced at approved garages, and it was heavily promoted. It was cheap but it was a flop. Even in the depths of depression, the American motorist, it seems, had firm ideas about what was a car and what was a joke. The company went into liquidation in 1934. Their successors designed the original Jeep but did not have the capacity to produce it in sufficient numbers— that plum being picked up by the Willys company and, inevitably, Ford.

Buick introduced a six in 1930, to compete with the Chevrolet and similar marques, but old Henry, meanwhile, could not see why only the luxury market should have eight-cylinder engines and made another giant leap with the introduction of the low-priced Ford V8 in 1932. Soon, all American Fords were V8s and the V8 engine eventually became the hallmark of the American automobile.

For those who survived the depression, the 1930s were a grey period. Having weathered the storm, few were prepared to become too adventurous. One of the first victims of the 1930s was the Oakland, manufactured first in 1907 by the Pontiac Buggy Company and finally killed off, in 1931, by the success of its own low-priced stablemate of that name. The latterday Pontiac had the distinction of being the only marque created, not acquired, by GM to stay the course.

For the rest, fortunes were mixed. In 1933 Buick sales were at rock bottom. It took the arrival, in 1934, of Harlow H. Curtice and Harley Earl, as President and stylist respectively, to drag the company back onto its feet. Ford's market share plummeted too, from 60% to around 30%, in spite of every outward sign of success— the millionth V8 left the lines in 1934 and the second million was reached in 1935.

In 1932 even the durable Billy Durant finally threw in the towel, as his Durant, Star, Locomobile and Flint conglomerate (formed in 1921 as Durant Motors) collapsed. Durant, next to Henry Ford probably the most charismatic of the industry pioneers, went into the supermarket business and faded into obscurity, to die a relatively poor and forgotten man in 1947.

In 1932 Nash was one of the only two auto companies trading in the black; the other was GM, which by 1937 would have 40% of the US and a remarkable 35% of world production. In 1937 Cadillac dropped the V12 and introduced a new V16, heralding a very successful period for the company.

For some, life was not so good. Auburn, Cord and Duesenberg, in spite of magnificent aberrations like the mighty Duesenberg SJ of 1932, the stunning Auburn V12 Speedsters of the same period and the enterprising, Buehrig-styled, Cord 810 of 1935, were dying from lack of sales. In 1932 Fred Duesenberg was killed (in an SJ). In 1934 Cord left, in frustration, for England, and by 1938 the three great marques had followed each other into oblivion. Having sold its soul to Studebaker in 1929, Pierce-Arrow bought it back in 1933, only to lose it to the receiver in 1938, three years after the demise of another great name: Stutz.

The 1930s were largely a time for consolidation and steady sales. Cars and engines generally grew a little larger and the former became better equipped. Most cars now had heaters and around one in three could boast a radio. 'All-steel' construction ousted wood frames and gave the freedom to build the 'streamline'

shapes which were a 1930s fad, but – witness the Chrysler Airflow—a sales disaster. Curved windscreens were the vogue, but most of the real advances came in suspension and transmission development. Overdrives, freewheels and column gearchanges (a Cadillac first, as was the umbrella handbrake in 1934) proliferated. In 1940 Oldsmobile introduced the first 'modern' automatic transmission: Hydramatic.

The US led the world in car ownership. In 1937 there was one car to every 66 people worldwide; France led Europe with 24.5 people per car; America had one car for every 5.6 of the population. Throughout the 1930s US car exports were around 9–13% of production. Exports of the future were also appearing. In 1934 the first drive-in cinema opened, in July the first parking meter was installed (in Oklahoma) and in 1937 the first drive-in bank appeared.

The end of the decade saw a successful new marque, Mercury (the sixth to bear the name) and a new model, the Continental, from the Ford and Lincoln stables. The first Mercury, essentially a rebodied Ford, intended to bridge the gap to Lincoln, appeared in November 1938; the Lincoln Continental, stylish brainchild of Edsel, followed in 1939—when Ford cars outsold General Motors by two to one. Cadillac, on the other hand, dropped the La Salle in favour of a lower priced, 'real' Cadillac.

Henry Ford was losing control of his empire to his enigmatic former bodyguard, Harry Bennett, and by 1941 Henry was a sick man. Another industry pioneer, Walter Chrysler, who had retired in 1935, died in 1940.

Europe went to war again in 1939 and the American industry almost immediately began to supply military equipment, although the war did not stop GM from supplying its 25 millionth car (a Chevy) in 1940. Henry Ford again took his pacifist stand, refusing, against Edsel's counsel, to build Merlin aero engines in America, although his European factories were building them apace. The Rolls-Royce-designed engines were subsequently built by Packard and played no small part in winning the war. Obtusely, Ford co-operated with GM to build Pratt & Whitney radial engines. Ford also collaborated on the Jeep, although the main output of the 1940, army-spec vehicle came from Willys, who at peak production were turning out a Jeep every one minute twenty seconds.

Car production continued through 1941 and sales held steady around the four million mark, then in 1942, after Pearl Harbour, America joined the war in earnest and car production was virtually halted. In 1943 industry output was just 139 cars; output of more essential items was staggering – the industry war effort produced more than four million engines, almost three

Above: industry war output was staggering. America produced almost three million tanks and trucks during the war, even though car production had continued until 1942. Here, Ford trucks and vans await shipment into action

million tanks and trucks, and some 27,000 aircraft. Henry again took control of his company (Edsel having died in 1943) and extended the art of mass production to Liberator bombers which, by 1944, were leaving the Willow Run plant (later acquired by Kaiser-Frazer) at the rate of three to four hundred a month.

When the war ended in 1945, raw materials were scarce but the industry was given permission to build 200,000 cars—with prices fixed at near pre-war levels by the government Price Administrator, Chester Bowles. Such prices were less than cost and less than popular with the industry, but the end of the war marked a new beginning. In 1946 the US industry celebrated its Golden Jubilee by honouring twelve of its pioneers, among them the ailing Henry Ford. In 1947 Henry died, but there was already another Henry at the helm, the old man's grandson, Henry II, having taken over in 1945.

The new cars reflected relief and exuberance; they began to become extroverts. A survey in 1945 showed that 75% of motorists wanted simple, four-door saloons, in black, dark blue or grey, and without ornament; the stylists knew better. The post-war models dripped chrome. Bigger, toothier grins were the order of the day. That, however, was more or less the extent of the market's sense of adventure, the same nuts and bolts in a flashier package. Even when it came to accepting conformity by a different name, buyers were intractably conservative; Kaiser-Frazer, set up in 1946, failed to break the establishment stranglehold. After their demise in the early 1950s, few other outsiders would ever try, although, strangely, the market was more welcoming to imports—especially those with a sporty flavour and an English name.

In 1948 the American industry built its one hundred millionth car, and Cadillac, of all people, gave the unsuspecting public the first (tiny) tail-fin, creating a monster that would grow through the 1950s to bizarre proportions and come to symbolise, for better or worse, the cars of the next decade.

Under the skin there was a fairly set pattern. The V8 was becoming almost universal, the 'economy' straight-six being the only widely available alternative. Cadillac's new 'high compression' V8 of 1949 had been, with 160 bhp, the most powerful engine of its day. In 1951 Chrysler usurped that position with its 'Hemi', and the horsepower race began. In general, suspension design lagged behind. Independent coil springs at the front were more a sop to the advertising man than to roadholding, and cart springs at the back were simply cheap and adequate. Most American drivers simply did not care about cornering power; their cars were more often headed into the blue yonder along endless rolling straights, and that is what they coped with best. Automatic transmission of a kind had been available for years, now it became a commonplace as the problems were ironed out, with Hydramatic, Powerglide, Dyna-flow and others appearing in the ad copy. For those who could be bothered to change gear of their own volition, steering column change eliminated most of the effort and almost all the precision.

The 1950s saw the beginning of the strange world of the 'dream car' styling exercises and excesses, often on fairly mundane chassis, ostensibly presaging the future

but more generally creating a centrepiece for another motor-show stand. In the early days the dream car was nearer to reality than it would become in the 1960s and perhaps more than anything it was an indicator to the big corporations of what the public might or might not eventually accept. Not surprisingly, Harley Earl was in the vanguard of the show-stoppers, with his Buick Y-Job of as early as 1939, and Buick were steady front runners in the dream car stakes. Their XP-300 of 1951 was more than cosmetic, boasting a hybrid engine, rear mounted automatic transmission, De Dion suspension and many other innovations. For all its novelty, it was notably less fanciful than its mechanically similar, Earl-designed contemporary, Le Sabre—a prime example of how designers then looked towards aircraft-inspired shapes, just as they would later look to rockets.

Fanciful the dream cars may have been, but their influence was soon felt. Cadillac, for instance, wasted no time in translating fancy into fact for the Eldorado and within the span of 1953 the glassfibre-bodied Chevrolet Corvette sports car had passed through the show and prototype stages to become a production reality.

There were other innovations; in 1954 GM sold its fifty millionth car and Chrysler produced a series of fifty, exerimental, gas turbine-engined cars, designated Plymouths, in a genuine effort to break new ground. Whether or not the dream cars ultimately had any influence on engineering, they certainly offered valuable exposure for styling ideas. General Motors' annual Motorama shows for example, with the design exercises as their centrepieces, could boast over two million visitors in a season. As well as showing just how much the public would stand, the dream cars also marked the beginning of a new, and occasionally fruitful, association between the manufacturers and the specialist styling houses.

As well as the dreams, there was a nightmare: the Edsel story. The Edsel, named after Henry Ford's late son, was intended to fill the gap just up-market from Ford, but instead it became the motor industry's most celebrated flop. By the time the cars were launched, in 1957, the gap no longer existed. Just two years and $300 million later, the Edsel disappeared. Ironically it had gained its few sales at the almost fatal expense of its own stablemate, Mercury.

In 1954 the fourth element of the present day 'big four' was born, as Nash, Hudson and Rambler became the bones of American Motors. The Hudson name disappeared in 1957 and Rambler took the ascendancy in AM. After a boom sales year in 1955 (when the whole industry sold some eight million cars) even Buick faced a sales slump that would last into the 1960s, and in 1958 the mighty Packard built its last vehicle.

In 1956 Ford became a public company and Semon E. Knudsen, son of Henry's one time right-hand man, became, at 43, GM's youngest ever manager—at Pontiac. From Pontiac, Knudsen would take the reins at Chevrolet—a progression later followed by his successors Pete Estes and John Z. DeLorean.

The wanton excess and rampant bad taste of the 1950s were simply another expression of the spirit of a decade, as much a reflection of social attitudes as of anything to do with engineering. As the 1950s gave way to the 1960s, attitudes were changing yet again.

Above: a 1949 Chrysler Town & Country Newport convertible – a touch of glamour in an otherwise dull range. For all its strictly decorative woodwork and dripping chrome ostentation, it has a certain elegant simplicity which was not the hallmark of the next decade

Although the world war had ended, there had been other conflicts throughout the 1940s and 1950s, America being drawn in particular into the middle eastern theatre in the face of communist expansionism. Oil had become a commodity of some strategic importance, rather than an inexhaustible outpouring from the Texas wells. Even America would eventually face an oil crisis, and oil meant gasoline. The Suez crisis of 1956 was a reminder of the West's vulnerability. Suddenly the gas-guzzling monsters of old were not the only option; small imports were gaining ground and the 'compact' was waiting in the wings.

America's idea of a compact in those days was still a long way from Europe's thoughts. The 3.5-litre, V8 Oldsmobile F85, for instance, at almost sixteen feet long, was a good two to three feet and one and a half litres bigger than many 'large' European cars. Ford's Falcon and the 'badge engineered' Dodge Lancer/Plymouth Valiant were the sort of cars designed to combat the imports' nearly 10% market share. They were largely successful and also provided a necessary cushion to the market before the gradual introduction of true small cars in the late 1970s. At much the same time, the horsepower race went on and American cars developed quite a sporty flavour. Ford, in particular, took motor sport very seriously, changing the face of Indianapolis racing in the early 1960s with the introduction of their V8 racing engine in the back of European-style chassis and actually beating the Europeans at their own game by dominating Le Mans and other long distance sports car races with the magnificent GT 40, so called because it was a 40 in high GT car. In 1963 Ford had tried to buy Ferrari; having failed to do so they built the GT40 as a Ferrari beater. In 1965 Ford commissioned the world-beating, Cosworth-designed V8 Grand Prix engine, another instant success.

In 1959 Chevrolet had further advanced its own sporty image with the introduction of the air-cooled, rear-engined, all-independently sprung Corvair—a car destined for infamy as the first target of consumer crusader Ralph Nader in his 1965 book *Unsafe at Any Speed*. Nader, for better or worse, initiated a new public

Left: pollution tinges the Los Angeles sky. Environmentalists pointed the accusing finger at the automobile, and government made the industry toe the line on reducing emissions

Below: Ford had a glorious sporting revival in the 1960s which included four consecutive victories at Le Mans with derivatives of the magnificent GT40. This is Dan Gurney in the Mark II at Le Mans in 1966. This car retired but another, driven by Chris Amon and Bruce McLaren, won, and Gurney was back with A.J. Foyt to score another Ford victory the following year

awareness of the darker sides of the auto industry, which would lead to sometimes worthy but often cripplingly repressive legislation. Had Nader's book been published a couple of years earlier, the Ford Mustang, first of the 'pony cars' and the most instantly successful all-new model in motoring history, might have been a very different car. The late 1960s were the last fling of the automobile built virtually without restriction. As the 1970s approached, legislation would become tougher and tougher. Engines would have to meet ever more stringent emission requirements, and chassis would have to be stronger and stronger to pass more and more demanding crash tests. The character of the automobile had changed yet again, with the car now virtually shaped by legislation.

The environmentalist lobby cited Los Angeles smogs as evidence of the sixty million tons of carbon monoxide, twelve million tons of hydrocarbons, and millions of tons of other assorted filth which, they claimed, cars disseminated annually. The legislators over-reacted, of course. Senator Ed Muskie put a bill before Congress proposing that exhaust emissions should be '95% clean'. Some cynics suggested this would mean cars putting out exhaust gases cleaner than the air they were breathing in. To add to the problems of the rising tide of Japanese imports (over a million cars a year by 1977) and of struggling European subsidiaries hit by the effects of the 1973 Arab-Israeli war and the subsequent oil embargoes, the industry now had to re-design its cars.

'De-toxing' strangled engines and reduced their efficiency, leading, ironically, to higher fuel consumption. Contemporary estimates saw oil supplies running out within thirty-five years and, even though 90% of the world's wells were in America, this caused considerable concern. In 1975 Congress decreed that each manufacturer must, by stages, reduce the average fuel consumption of all models built in any year to reach a figure of 27.5 mpg (US) by 1985. That was exactly double the 1974 average and had to be achieved by considerably 'cleaner' engines. At the same time cars were to be made safer and had to prove their mettle through staggeringly expensive crash-testing programmes. One of the more lamented victims of this purge was the convertible, rendered virtually extinct by the early 1970s. The cynics again had a point—cars were being designed to be safe to *crash* rather than safe to drive.

One obvious way to meet the requirements was to build smaller, and 'downsizing' now began in earnest, at last accepting lessons from Europe and Japan. In fact, the industry's achievements were admirable. In the late 1970s and early 1980s the ubiquitous V8 was supplanted by smaller and more efficient fours and V6s, often with fuel injection or turbocharging. Diesel engines, with their inherent fuel economy and potential emission advantages, became a real alternative, although experiments with the Wankel rotary engine came to naught in 1974 when GM cancelled plans to build Wankel-engined Vegas. The beginning of the 1980s saw front-wheel-drive, four-speed automatic transmissions (with 'automatic overdrive' top gears), high-pressure radial tyres and 'low-drag' brakes contributing to overall economy, but the biggest factor was a severe slimming programme. Oldsmobile's 1979 model Toronado, for instance, showed a weight saving of no less than 900 lb over its immediate predecessor and between 1979 and 1980 Ford improved the fuel consumption of the Thunderbird by 45%, which no doubt pleased the government watchdog, the Environmental Protection Agency. By 1980 Chevrolet saw half its $2\frac{1}{2}$ million projected output as being small cars. The Citation, introduced in 1979, confirmed the trend by returning the best-ever first season sales of any new GM model.

Fuel shortages, record interest rates and the severe recession at the end of the 1970s hit hard. The market was changing, families were smaller; by 1981, more than half of America's households had no more than two members and 30% of car buyers were single, favouring small, sporty cars. Ford even introduced a two-seater, the EXP, in 1981. Half the female population now worked, and made their own decisions when it came to buying cars. 40% of Ford's 1980 sales, for instance, were to women. It was no longer social suicide to buy small.

The change was reflected in the industry structure as well as in the cars. The mighty American motor industry could no longer exist in total isolation; the day of the 'world car' was drawing nearer. In the 1960s Western Europe had overtaken the USA as the biggest volume producer and by 1970 Japan was the second

Left: under the skin of the K-car. The transverse-engine, front-wheel-drive layout of the 1982 Chrysler family is typically new-generation American Automobile

biggest manufacturing nation. Japanese and European companies were also opening operations in the USA. Volkswagen established a manufacturing plant in 1978 and Honda took the first steps towards car manufacture by opening a motor cycle plant in 1979. As early as 1972, Chevrolet had begun importing utility vehicles built by the Japanese Isuzu company and a year earlier Dodge had cemented a deal with Mitsubishi to market Colt cars in America. The Colts were gradually Americanised until the launch of Dodge's own compact, Aspen, with 'Lean-Burn' engine, in 1976. The success of these smaller cars rescued Dodge from a very bleak future. In 1974 GM acquired 34% of Isuzu and a year later imported 60,000 Opel-replica Isuzus under the Oldsmobile banner. AMC's rescue plan worked in reverse, with European money, from Renault, giving the company a new lease of life. Initially Renault's $150 million investment made possible a new plant at Kenosha, Wisconsin, and AMC began to sell Le Car and 18i models along with their own lines. By 1980, after

further huge capital transfers, Renault owned 46.4% of AMC capital stock and there were more than 1300 AMC-Renault dealerships in the USA.

In 1979, AMC made its largest ever profit, but a year later it and the rest of the industry were again in the depths of depression. In that one year the industry overall lost some four billion dollars. In October 1981 the industry suffered its worst monthly sales for 23 years, with a loss of 26% over the previous season. Losses for the big three manufacturers, Ford, Chrysler and GM, were again expected to reach more than two billion dollars but, having accepted the message that it must adapt to survive, the industry dug in once again, as it had in the 1920s, the 1930s and the early 1960s, in order to forge its way out of its problems and reach out towards its centennial. Let nothing stand in the way.

Facing page, top: the four-rotor, Wankel-engined Corvette was dropped at the prototype stage

Facing page, centre: AMC is the smallest of the big four and, in spite of the success of cars like this 1982 Spirit, its survival was bought at the cost of commercial association with Renault

Facing page, bottom: Chrysler too has its foreign connections. The 1982 Plymouth Sapporo began life as the Japanese Colt

Left: the shape of cars to come? Ghia's diminutive Ford prototype was born in Europe, around Fiesta running gear, but does it point the way for America?

Auburn

Auburn cars were too advanced for the motoring public and too cheap to attract the sophisticated enthusiast

LIKE AN ACTOR who achieves ephemeral fame after long years on the boards in small parts, the Auburn is now remembered chiefly for the golden years that occupied less than a third of the company's span. Like many an actor it fell from public favour rather abruptly through, it seems, over-exposure and exploitation by a zealous manager more concerned with cashing in on the rich pickings of a short-term stardom than with securing the foundations for a more protracted, if less sensational, career. An over-simplification, perhaps, and not entirely fair comment.

In fact, Auburn was a true pioneer make dating back to 1900, when the infant US automobile industry's entire output was a little over 400 cars. Things were very different a quarter century later when Auburn suddenly began to receive star billing under the inspired promotion of a certain Erret Lobban Cord. Had he concentrated his talents on the Auburn enterprise and not diffused them on an empire-building spree, who can tell? Auburn might yet figure in today's very abbreviated roll of US car makers.

Very unlikely though, because had Cord not stepped in to revitalise Auburn when it was on its knees in 1924, the odds are that it would never have had a golden day, only a quiet funeral with scarcely a mourner.

But let's start at the beginning—at Auburn, Indiana, in 1900—with a single-cylinder engine beneath the seat, a tiller before it, wooden wheels shod with solid rubber tyres and two brothers full of optimism. These were Frank and Morris Eckhart, who were busy running the Eckhart Carriage Company (founded by their father in 1874) when the horseless carriage puttered on the scene. They were soon bitten by the automobile bug and in 1900 formed the Auburn Automobile Company.

By 1903 their little centre-engined, chain-driven, one-lunger was ready for marketing, a humble two-seat runabout with nothing but the basic essentials, although it did now ride on pneumatics. They took it to the Chicago Auto Show that year and, during 1904, some 50 were made. Next year came a slightly more ambitious twin-cylinder car which formed the backbone of production for the next five years. Clearly the tempo at Auburn, Indiana was very slow compared with the creative bustle in Detroit and, of course, Europe where fresh ideas spilled out so exuberantly in that first decade that few designs remained static for long.

However, the Eckharts stepped another rung up the social ladder in 1909 with a four-cylinder engine using a 'loose' (ie proprietary) powerplant, the 25–30 hp Rutenber. This was a well established make that sold to many customers through to the 1920s. Two-speed planetary transmission and centre-chain drive were primitive legacies retained, but you could have this model with enclosed bodywork.

By 1912 the Eckharts had advanced their thinking and pretensions considerably, as manifested in a handsome big six with bodies in full contemporary style behind Mercédès-like radiators. This 41 hp 6–50, also powered by Rutenber, even had electric lighting.

By 1916 Auburn were using three 'loose' engines from different sources—a four-cylinder Rutenber for the 4–38, a six-cylinder Teetor for the 6–38, and a big Continental engine for the 6–40. Two years later the four was dropped; the smaller six (6–39B) was rated at 25.35 hp (bore and stroke $3\frac{1}{4} \times 4\frac{1}{2}$ in) and there were four body styles—Chummy Roadster, 5-seat Touring, Sport Roadster and Touring Car with detachable winter top.

Facing page: the flowing lines of the 1935 Auburn 851 were achieved using a body which was hand built from 22 separate sections

Auburn's first production car, a single-cylinder, two-seater, chain-driven runabout, was introduced at the Chicago Motor Show in 1903

Frank and Morris Eckhart's first four-cylinder-engined car was the Auburn G, which used a 25–30 hp Rutenber motor. It was produced from 1909 until 1911

In 1913, Auburn further increased their range by offering the 33L, a full-four-seater, four-cylinder, open touring car

The Auburn 6–50 of 1914 used a six-cylinder Rutenber engine. One of the special features of this handsome and sophisticated machine was its fully electric lighting system

One of Auburn's biggest failures was the Beauty-Six which used a 25 hp Continental Red Seal engine. By 1924, daily output was down to a mere six cars

This last model was an ancestor of the convertible hardtop of recent years. In the summer months the full-length top could be hoisted to the garage roof, and in winter lowered onto the car to form a snug, eight-window sedan. For the larger chassis there was no Sport Roadster, but instead a seven-passenger Sedan; this model (6–44) had a motor with a bore and stroke of $3\frac{1}{2} \times 5\frac{1}{4}$ in and, in engineering content, both types followed the mainstream of conventional design for US automobiles of the period with, for instance, dry plate clutches, three-speed sliding-gear transmissions, electric starters and half-elliptic springs.

Prices ranged from $1345 to $2450, a shade higher than equivalent Buicks, but in 1918, when over a million cars were made in Detroit alone, one could become a Model T Ford owner for less than $400, buy a Chevrolet Roadster for $620 or, at the other extreme, pay up to $8000 for the most sybaritic of the Pierce-Arrow range. So the Auburns were inexpensive rather than cheap, and with nothing more to offer than many other rather dull but sound makes. The Eckharts needed a financial boost and the Auburn a face-lift, and in 1919 they sold out to a group of Chicago businessmen led by Ralph Bard, with Morris Eckhart retained as president.

The face-lift came, appropriately named the Beauty-Six, and for a time it seemed they would unstick from their backwater. The Beauty-Six had a 25.6 hp Continental 'Red Seal' engine ($3\frac{3}{4} \times 4\frac{1}{2}$ in), a somewhat flashy exterior and a wealth of attractive equipment, but it was no dynamic marvel. The sponsors' great expectations were briefly encouraged but not fulfilled. By 1924 daily output was down to a miserable six cars or so, 450 employees were draining resources for inadequate returns, and some 700 unclaimed Beauty-Sixes were losing their youthful bloom on the company parking lot when E. L. Cord appeared on the scene.

Cord has been called many things—super-salesman, empire-builder, master entrepreneur, but never an engineer. Yet you have only to remember the automobiles for which he was responsible to appreciate that he was not in love with them only for the money they could bring him. Auburn—Cord—Duesenberg, each today is revered as an American Classic. He knew a thing or two about public taste and what would magnetize a showroom, occasionally erring by stepping too far ahead of his potential customers. He also had

the courage to actively incite his engineers to think radical thoughts and put them into practice. But like many an over-ambitious entrepreneur he was never content to let well alone, to check the commercial foundations before building yet another floor.

Cord's first profitable activity had been as a teen-age revitalizer of decayed Model T Fords. He is said to have made and lost three substantial fortunes by the age of 21. By 1924 he had established a reputation as one of the country's top car salesmen after several years with a Chicago distributor for Moon cars.

Then came a rendezvous with Ralph Bard and the opportunity to move to Auburn as general manager on his own conditions—a share in the company and the opportunity to buy a controlling interest if he made

The flagging fortunes of Auburn were revitalised in 1924 when E. L. Cord became General Manager. Shortly afterwards, the famous Auburn 'eights' appeared, one of which was the 8–115. Several models were available, including the boat-tailed Speedster (*above*) and the convertible sedan-phaeton (*above, right*)

a go of it. The unsaleable stock was jazzed up and backed by a vigorous sales campaign and these cars sold. Cobwebs gathering in the machine shops and assembly lines were swept away by the new broom and Chief Engineer James Crawford was put to work designing a new car to carry a straight-eight, L-head Lycoming engine. In next to no time Cord was Vice-president and in 1926, at the age of 32, he became President.

The 'Eight-in-Line' appeared in early 1925 with $3\frac{1}{8}$ in bore and $4\frac{1}{4}$ in stroke, but for the New York Show displacement was increased to 276 cu in and the car named the 8-88, first of a famous line. Among the 61 makes present the Auburn was one of the top crowd-pullers. Behind a deeply cowled nickel radiator shell

were some of the handsomest bodies on the market, and customers began to line up. Particularly intriguing was the rumble-seat roadster by McFarlan, with a small side door to let a passenger enter and leave gracefully without having to clamber up and down steps on the rear fender.

The rest of the bodies were by the Limousine Body Company of Kalamazoo. As Auburn business expanded so too did the Cord empire—suddenly rather than progressively—for during 1926-7 he took over Duesenberg, together with the brothers Fred and August, with the ultimate aim of making the world's most super super-car. By absorbing Lycoming Motors he managed to sell engines to his competitors as well as to himself and, by adding the Limousine Body

Below: Auburn's legendary V-12 Speedster was a flop when introduced in 1932, in spite of its price of under one thousand dollars. The Speedster captured so many speed records, however, that it twice won the American Stock Car Speed Championship. These records included distances of up to 2000 km and speeds of up to 117 mph

Company he ensured that none of his automobiles would ever want for clothes.

He also bought two engineering plants in Connersville, Indiana, and by the time the Cord Corporation was founded, in June 1929, he doubtless imagined himself well on the way to becoming as big as GM— he was said already to control assets worth over $11 million.

1927 was notable for Auburn's first factory-sponsored engagement in endurance runs and stock car racing. Their chief test driver, Wade Morton, who was later to advance to the status of sales chief for Duesenberg, first took an 8–88 roadster to the Culver City Speedway, Los Angeles, and convincingly demonstrated its pace and reliability by covering 1000 miles in under 16 hours at an average of 63.4 mph. Then he entered stock car races in various parts of the country with fair success before breaking stock records up to 15,000 miles on the Atlantic City Speedway. The arch enemy then was Stutz, which he couldn't quite match; for example, two, or maybe three, Stutz cars bettered Morton's time up the arduous Pike's Peak Hill-Climb in Colorado.

New for 1928 was a power increase for the 8–88 motor, already enlarged since the original and now equipped with a twin-barrel updraught Stromberg; it was retermed the 8–115. To supplement it a new and smaller eight was added, the 8–77, with a small bore, long stroke, 24 hp motor ($2\frac{3}{4} \times 4\frac{3}{4}$ in). As we shall see later this engine, rather surprisingly, was destined to outlive the larger one. Apart from these, the range still included a six, the 6–66, but the four-cylinder unit had been dropped earlier. Other new engineering features included a redesigned chassis frame with deeper side members and extra cross-members, a change from mechanical to hydraulic brakes and the addition of centralised chassis lubrication operated from the driver's seat by a pedal under the dash.

There were also two new bodies available, a convertible sedan-phaeton that looked as though it had come out of a first-grade custom shop, and the first of the classic boat-tailed speedsters (styled by Count Alexis de Sakhnoffsky) which from that time were never absent from the Auburn family although the style evolved through several phases and changes.

One of the flashiest, most extrovert cars of the time, with bright duo-tone paint jobs emphasising the Auburn feature of sweeping the belt lines up and over the hood to meet at the radiator filler, the Speedster sported a steeply raked V-windshield, a long pointed tail and Dayton centre-lock wire wheels. All it needed to complete the effect was something more racy than the standard wings as fitted to the rest of the range, and they were to come later. The Speedster style was available on both eight-cylinder cars, and in each case the price tag was far below that of sporting machinery from any other source.

Wade Morton took a stock Speedster first to Daytona, where he bettered 108 mph over the measured mile, then paid a second visit to Atlantic City to see what he could put into 24 hours. This time it was 2033 miles at almost 85 mph, and the stock car records went tumbling. Probably Morton's greatest personal satisfaction that year occupied only 21 minutes 45 seconds—the time it took him to climb Pike's Peak, establish a new record for stock cars and, even more important, defeat Stutz. Now this was quite a feat, because the 8–115 Speedster was price tagged at $1895 and the Stutz Black Hawk, with its overhead-cam engine (oddly enough with the same cylinder

Above: Auburn's 'eight-in-line', L-head Lycoming engine was designed by James Crawford and inspired by E. L. Cord. It first appeared in 1925

Below: a 1935 851, with a supercharged 4585 cc engine giving a power output of 150 bhp and a top speed—via a two-speed rear axle—of 100 mph

dimensions as the Lycoming, but credited with no more power in its standard form) was more than 2½ times that.

From the sales viewpoint 1929 was to be the peak pre-depression year for Auburn with over 22,000 customers buying Auburn cars—let's remember, though, that the Ford plant at Dearborn could supply that number from about three days' production and that in 1929 over 27½ million road vehicles were registered in the US.

At the '28 shows Auburn had a three-model range as before, all uprated once more—the 20 hp 6–80, 26 hp 8–90 and 34 hp 120. Prices ranged from $995 for the 6-cylinder Sport Sedan to $2095 for a five-passenger Phaeton Sedan on the 120 chassis. Auburn

prices were still about the same as Buicks, but to quote the extremes again, the humblest buyer could get a Ford Model A Roadster for as little as $385 and a 2-door Sedan for $495, while a Roadster or five-seat Touring Chevvy cost him $525. For the very, very rich there was that strange dinosaur-like survivor of earlier days, the massive Locomobile '48' with a choice between no less than five body styles all priced at $12,500. The most sophisticated Cadillac was then the Imperial Phaeton Sedan at $5995, whereas Lincolns cost $4600–7300.

However, E. L. Cord was now almost ready with his super-car for those to whom the price of a Cadillac or Lincoln was chickenfeed—the Model J Duesenberg. Fred Duesenberg's masterpiece—at least on paper even if it did not quite come up to everyone's expectations in the metal—arrived at New York a little less complete than it looked, with the chassis alone marked at $8500, and you couldn't get even a simple phaeton body put on it for less than $2500. Thereafter both chassis and body prices rose so that by 1932 the least expensive was $13,500 and the supercharged SJ added a further $2250 to the chassis. A few special orders are known to have cost their purchasers $25,000—or more.

Also in 1929 Cord set in motion another grandiose project to go some way towards bridging the gap between his bargain basement Auburns and millionaire Duesenbergs. This was the L29 Cord with the 125 bhp Lycoming straight-eight engine driving the front wheels, these being united by a true de Dion axle tube.

It first appeared in late '29 but proved an abortive disaster for a number of reasons, primarily that it was quite immature when thrust upon the public. The major Achilles heel was a combination of primitive

side of the Atlantic.

Above: the 851s and 852s were the last Auburns from the Cord empire. They were dashing cars, but were somewhat impractical, seating only two and having no external access to the rear luggage compartment

universal joints in the drive shafts and poor traction through having too small a proportion of the all-up weight over the driven wheels. Its saving grace was stupendously racy styling with very low build.

The L29, however, was a lemon, with a dazzling peel but rotten inside. It also had the misfortune to enter the stage just as Wall Street was tumbling—Herbert Hoover's Utopian dream of 'two chickens in every pot and two cars in every garage' was not to be. Those who did buy L29s certainly needed another car in the garage. In three years of erratic production only 4429 of these cars were built.

So much for the Auburn relatives, but the Auburn family, too, had suffered a sad disappointment, a rather glorious failure. It was the Cabin Speedster on the 120 chassis. Now this really was a great car and it's a shame that the crowds that gathered wherever it appeared (initially at the 1928 New York Show) never went into a showroom and actually ordered one. The design was attributed to the irrepressible Wade Morton and it was the most rakish, racy thing imaginable to come from an American factory. There was a distinctly European look about it, accentuated by the snug-fitting cycle wings that moved with the front wheels, as fitted to contemporary Aston Martins and Lagondas in England. The dropped frame was special, rising over the front axle and underslung at the rear to lower the build and centre of gravity. Its belly was protected by a full underpan, and the streamlined body was panelled in aluminium. Inside were aviation-type lightweight wickerwork seats. With 125 bhp under the bonnet it was guaranteed to exceed the magic 100 mph—and all for $2195. No doubt Cord expected the young bloods, the movie stars and the football heroes to fall for the Cabin Speedster. They looked—and marvelled—and walked away. The US public has always proved strongly resistant to *avant-garde*, nonconformist concepts stemming from its own

So to 1930, and acute depression. Cord had too many irons in the fire and none of them hot. The lame duck L29 was not even warm, the Duesenburgs never had a hope of being money-spinners, and then even the faithful Auburn suddenly cooled off. Sales dropped to under 14,000 a year: ever resilient and never lacking the courage for a drastic move, Cord closed the Auburn ranks by dropping all existing models and bringing out a new medium-sized eight in a short-term, one-model policy. This was the 8-98, fitted with an enlarged derivative of the old 1927 long-stroke motor with bore stretched to 3 in. It gave a beefy 98 bhp at 3400 rpm.

By this time Auburn were recognised style-setters and were producing a body range every bit as handsome as the specialist coachbuilders could create for the individual customer on far more costly chassis. They were bold without being too ritzy or *nouveau-riche* and the engineering beneath was simple, but very sound. Auburns always had exceptionally stiff frames, but the 9-98 was given a brand new one with cruciform bracing, and a free-wheel to permit clutchless shifts was added to the three-speed transmission. Almost overnight the Auburn iron glowed cherry red again and sales that year, in the depths of the depression, were the highest ever at over 28,000.

Then there was another *faux-pas*, but surely by the marketing rather than the engineering department. Was it a wrong step psychologically for Auburn to try breaking into the luxury market with a cut-price offering? Were habitual Auburn owners too conservative to risk separation from the trusty eight and go flirting with a more complex, unknown V12? Or did the aristocracy perhaps avoid it because an Auburn was unfashionable?

It was a time of terrific rivalry between the class makes—Cadillac, Lincoln, Packard, Pierce-Arrow, Marmon, Franklin—to draw the old and new rich with ever more powerful but less mechanically obtrusive super-cars using huge V12 and V16 engines. Then a V12 Auburn suddenly jumped in, priced from under a thousand dollars. Designed by George Kublin of Auburn and, naturally, manufactured for them by Lycoming, the new engine had a swept volume of 391 cu in, the bore and stroke being $3\frac{1}{8} \times 4\frac{1}{4}$ in. The cylinder banks were set at 45° included angle, and a strange feature was Kublin's unique valve gear and combustion chamber arrangement. The valve stems were horizontal, actuated through rockers from a central camshaft, the chambers forming deep pockets above the cylinders which had individual removable water jackets that gave access to the valves without removing the heads. A two-speed axle by Columbia (yet another Cord subsidiary) with vacuum-controlled selection and giving six forward speeds overall was optional for both the eight and V12, typical alternative final-drive ratios being 4.55 and 3.04 to 1.

There was little to distinguish the V12 from the 8-100 (successor to the 8-98) except for a few extra inches in the wheelbase; as many parts as possible, including the bodies, were identical to keep the price down. And then there was a Speedster V12, which captured so many records that it won the American Stock Car Speed Championships in the first two years of its production, 1932-3. These included distances up to 2000 km and speeds up to 117 mph.

The fickle public took little notice and the V12 was little better than a flop. Moreover the eight, too, fell from grace so that 1932 ended with a near-miss from a million-dollar loss. The next year was far worse, with a wretched 6000 or so Auburn customers. Then, during 1934, an extraordinary thing happened; Cord suddenly uprooted and took his family to live in England, apparently because of threats to kidnap his children, but maybe too because the commercial climate around him was blowing a bit hot from several quarters. The Duesenberg president, Harold T. Ames, deputized at the Auburn plant and under his leadership two more seemingly palatable dishes were prepared, one aesthetic and the other mechanical.

That master styling engineer Gordon Buehrig, later to earn international repute with his futuristic 810 front-drive Cord, was asked completely to rehash the boat-tailed Speedster, which was then in its Phase Two style. At the same time Augie Duesenberg was commissioned to devise a supercharger installation for the straight-eight Lycoming which would be optional on the whole range.

Buehrig duly produced his Model 851 Speedster, a sort of schoolboy's dream come true—especially the supercharged version with four enormous flexible exhaust pipes sweeping from its bonnet side panel. A tiny cockpit behind the usual raked V-screen emphasised the length of the hood and downswept tail, and exhibitionist tear-shaped wings enclosed the wheels. A hinged metal panel concealed the top when lowered. It was extremely dashing and equally impractical, seating only two and having no external access to the baggage compartment, which was situated in the tail.

With its Schwitzer-Cummins centrifugal blower running at six times engine speed through an ingenious frictional planetary gear, the Lycoming gave about 150 bhp at 4000 rpm, compared with 115 at 3600 for the unblown car. Each 851 and the 852 of the following year carried a plaque on the dash panel to confirm that it had been tested at over 100 mph before delivery. Ab Jenkins (of 'Mormon Meteor' fame) took a supercharged one to the Bonneville Salt Flats in Utah, where he had already done great things for Pierce-Arrow, and among the figures he achieved was a 12-hour stint averaging just short of 103 mph—the first time a standard stock model had done better than 100 mph for that distance.

The writing was now clearly on the wall, though, for the Buehrig Speedsters were sold at a loss and orders for the rest of the cars, despite a Buehrig face-lift with new skirted wings and a bolder V-shaped grille with painted surround, were nowhere near sufficient to sustain the plant. After 1936 there were to be no more magic palliatives to keep the patient breathing another year.

The Cord empire was still not completely floored, however. Cord himself returned from England to unravel some of the tangles only to watch the sensational all-new, front-drive car bearing his name go the same way as the L29; the last of the 810s and 812s, 2320 in all, were made in 1937. The great Duesenberg had already made its last appearance at the New York Show in November 1936.

Auburn-Cord-Duesenberg—what bitter-sweet memories those names evoke! Each of them spawned automobiles that were aesthetically out of their contemporary world. Some failed that richly deserved to succeed, and even the most temperamental and irresponsible among them, the L29, is now remembered kindly for its handsome figure and paper promise, however unfulfilled. One can readily understand how the Duesenberg expired—prohibitive cost and a failure to advance with the times; like the dodo, it never evolved to keep pace with the changing scene around it. In retrospect, neither of the Cords really stood a chance. Even had front-drive engineering been ready for them, the public were not ready for it.

Even so, those who remember the Auburn tell us how strong and reliable it was, how comparatively fast, too; and we can see for ourselves that it was better looking than most. Maybe if the price tags had been a bit higher more folk might have bought it, on the supposition that a man's (and his family's) social status is often judged by the car he runs and every neighbour knew an Auburn was rather cheap—didn't the Auburn ads keep telling them so?

Below: extreme exaggeration of line distinguished the 1931 Auburn Speedster but, distinctive and elegant though the car was, it did little for the company's flagging fortunes

Buick

Buick is an important part of the largest automobile manufacturing corporation in the world

Above right: a Grosvenor-bodied Buick 15/18 hp of 1913

Left: a 1922 Buick 6. Note the narrow old-fashioned tyres

Above left: examples of early and more recent Buick badges

The Grosvenor Carriage Co Ltd
LONDON.

AT THE DAWN of this century, Flint, Michigan, was known as 'Vehicle City'—not for automobiles but for its role as the main producer of horse-drawn carriages in the United States. Each year 150,000 carriages rolled out of the factories of Flint, location of the world's largest maker of buggy whip sockets. Flint was the ideal and obvious location for the convention of blacksmiths that was called to order there in May 1903. On the nineteenth of that month the conferring smiths decided to spend $5000 on setting up a state college to teach the art of shoeing horses. On that very same day in May, an organization was founded that would have a lot to do with the eventual eclipse of the blacksmith: the Buick Motor Company.

In more than seventy years of existence, the Buick firm and its products have come to stand for many things. The Buick car is one of the best-known American automobiles in the world. It has a special *cachet* as a car of luxurious appointments and advanced and elegant style that is also priced within the reach of the average buyer. Equipped with overhead valves from the beginning, Buick cars have usually shunned radical design features, but have always been at the forefront of contemporary engineering. From Buick have come many gifted men who have made important contributions to the growth of the automobile industry. Buick's biggest contribution of all, however, was its role as the foundation stone on which the General Motors empire was built.

To David Dunbar Buick, the creation of the first Buick car was only a short phase in a long life of experimenting and inventing that ended with the Scots-born machinist virtually destitute. Two years after his birth in 1854, Buick's family went to the New World to settle in Detroit. After his apprenticeship, he became an innovator in the design of plumbing for

Centre, from left to right: a 1908 Buick type F, a 1909 Buick 10E and a 1912 type 35

Bottom, from left to right: a 1914 Buick B25, a 1915 type C37 and a type 44 roadster

indoor bathrooms. In Germany a method had been developed for applying an enamel finish to iron bathtubs but, as it was held entirely secret, Buick worked out his own way of doing it, which made a lot of money for his firm, Buick & Sherwood. He sold his interest in this company, together with some patent rights, in 1901, at the age of 47, for the then-handsome sum of $100,000. This allowed Buick to tinker to his heart's content, helped by his son Tom, in the shop at the rear of his home in Detroit.

First Buick made an engine which he sold to car makers, a horizontally opposed twin of L-head design. Then he changed the design to give the engine overhead valves, setting the pattern for all Buick's future power units. Engineers Walter Marr and Eugene Richard helped Buick complete a car in 1903 to carry this engine, and it was on the basis of this simple vehicle that the Buick Motor Company was formed that year with the financial backing of the Briscoe brothers, to whom David Buick also owed money. Before the year was out, however, the firm had been sold to a Flint wagon maker and moved to that city, north-west of Detroit. Walter Marr became the firm's chief engineer.

After building and testing a prototype, Buick and Marr sold the first production Buick automobile in August of 1904. Called the Model B, it used an opposed-

twin engine placed under the seat, developing about 20 horsepower from 2.6 litres. The drive line was a two-speed planetary transmission and a chain to the rear axle. It was a good little car, but it had taken so long (by the standards of those days) to get it ready for production that the investors had run out of time and money. So they appealed for help to one of Flint's millionaire carriage-builders, 43-year-old William Crapo Durant. That November, Durant took over financial control of Buick. During these several changes of ownership David Buick found his share of

Below left, from top to bottom: the open Buick Sport Tourer produced in 1923; the classic Buick Master Six of 1930; and the luxury Limousine of the 1930s

Right and below right: the Harley Earl-designed 66SR Sport Coupé used an 8-cylinder motor which produced 120 bhp at 3200 rpm. Note the flowing lines and the 'dickey seat'

the company amounting to less and less, and finally he was only a board member and employee. In 1908 he left the Buick Motor Company, never to return.

By then, the Buick car had become nationally famous, with 8800 cars built and sold, twice as many as in 1907. In addition to the two-cylinder model there were four other basic Buick types, powered by three different four-cylinder, in-line engines of 2.7, 4.2 and 5.5 litres. The smallest was used in the Model 10, new in 1908 and the most popular Buick, priced right in line with the new Model T Ford at $850. From that point onward, however, Fords became cheaper and Buicks more expensive. The small four-cylinder car remained an important part of the Buick line until 1924, the last year it was produced. None of the larger fours lasted through World War I.

Buick had grown so rapidly under super-salesman Durant that by 1908 it was one of the 'big four' of the US auto industry that also included Ford, Reo and Maxwell-Briscoe. Durant began thinking about merging his Buick with another firm to build an even larger combine, and, with that end in view, incorporated a new firm which he named 'General Motors' on 16 September 1908. Durant's General Motors Co took over the assets of Buick, and within a year had bought Oldsmobile, Cadillac and Oakland, which later became Pontiac. Through the troubled years that followed for Durant and the new-born General Motors, Buick's prosperity was a vital lifeline for the survival of the company that became the greatest in the world.

In its early years as the foundation of Durant's General Motors, Buick was fortunate to be managed by two men who later left GM to build cars under their own names: Charles Nash, from 1910 to 1912, and Walter Chrysler, from 1912 to 1920. Remaining chief engineer, Walter Marr introduced Buick's first six-cylinder car in 1914. The B55 was the first Buick to

Below left: compare the front views of the 1934 series 50 and the Viceroy model of five years later

Below: in America, it has always been customary to alter body styles from year to year. Our picture shows a 1937 Buick Century *(top)*; a 1940 Phaeton Roadmaster convertible *(centre)*; and a 1941 Business Coupé

Above and right: The 1941 Buick convertible. This year was the last full production year before the US entered World War II and was one of Buick's most successful with the company producing 377,428 models

Left: 1936 marked the beginning of a much needed revival in Buick's flagging sales, following the timely arrival of Harlow H. Curtice as general manager. This is the 1936 Roadmaster four-door convertible

good-looking Buicks had earned early in the export market. In 1907, an association began in Canada that eventually made the McLaughlin-Buick that country's most popular car. In London, assembly of Bedford-Buicks was under way in 1909 and later spread to other GM plants abroad. The first coast-to-coast crossing of South America by automobile was accomplished by a Buick in 1914. Buick dealers shepherded a single car on a round-the-world tour in 1925. In most countries overseas, the smaller, handier Buick—not the Cadillac—was the most desirable prestige car from America.

During the 1920s, the Buick was fitted into its now-traditional upper-medium-price bracket under Alfred P. Sloan's careful organization of the GM marketing structure. In 1924, it gained added stature with the addition of four-wheel brakes and the replacement of a rather bland radiator shape with a new one that some people—especially Packard—thought looked quite a lot like a Packard. It evolved from then until 1949 as a clearly recognizable Buick styling characteristic. From 1925 until 1930, during which a companion marque, the Marquette, was unsuccessfully marketed for two years, Buicks were powered by a bewildering variety of six-cylinder engines from 3.1 to 5.4 litres.

Through the 1930s and 1940s, Buick gained fame as one of the strongest apostles of the smooth, powerful and quiet straight-eight engine. The Buick conversion to in-line eights took place in 1931 with engines of 3.6, 4.5 and 5.7 litres. The 5.7-litre was the first production Buick engine producing more than 100 horsepower: 104 at 2800 rpm to be exact. GM men hoped the new model would spark Buick sales, which had been falling steadily due to the depression and also to the conservatism that had sapped the vigour of once-eager Buick. A 1929 experiment with styling that was a little too rounded (hardly noticeable today) led to the model being called the 'pregnant Buick' and scared the GM division's management away from any further experiments. By 1933, Buick sales had plummeted to only 40,620, and advertising spoke of the past.

The 1934 Buick line brought independent front suspension, new but hardly exciting styling, a lower-priced model, and a new general manager, Harlow H. Curtice. Wrote historian Beverly Rae Kimes, 'No more dynamic nor dominating personality had appeared on the Buick scene since Durant'. Curtice headed Buick until 1948 and kept a watchful eye on its fortunes through another ten years as GM's president.

Curtice enjoyed a specially close and fruitful friendship with GM's talented styling chief, Harley Earl. It began when Curtice was shown Earl's planned designs for the 1936 Buick. 'Harley,' said Curtice, 'would you want to be seen driving one of these cars?' Responded Earl, 'To be honest with you, no; these cars are designed for the Buick market'. Curtice quickly replied, 'Let's get this straight. There is no "Buick market". It has disappeared. Design me a Buick that *you* would like to own'. That's just what Earl did, and went on doing so as long as the two men worked together.

Curtice went after his engineers also, getting them to adopt aluminium pistons and hydraulic brakes. He hired a new advertising agency, and took the then-controversial step of giving names instead of numbers to each line of cars: Special, Century (for a car that could do 100 miles an hour), Roadmaster and Limited. Another line, the Super, was added in 1940. Buick's new 1936 models received a good reception, and in the same year a great car enthusiast, Charles A. Chayne, became the division's chief engineer. Sales kept on climbing until they reached 377,428 in 1941, the last full year before the USA entered World War II.

weigh more than 3000 pounds and the first with a wheelbase as long as 130 inches.

Around 1910, a young draftsman named Leo Goossen came to the attention of Walter Marr. During 1917 and 1918 Goossen worked closely with Marr in the design of two prototype engines and cars, an L-head V12 and a V6 version of the twelve. For health reasons, however, the young Goossen had to leave Buick in 1919 and travel west, where he was hired by racing-engine builder Harry Miller on the basis of the strong letter of recommendation Walter Chrysler had given him. Goossen became the designer of many great Miller engines and, indeed, of the Drake Offenhauser engine that, in turbocharged form, remained the engine to beat at Indianapolis in the 1970s.

Goossen's first exposure to auto racing had come at Buick, where a very successful team had been set up with such star drivers as Bob Burman and the Chevrolet brothers. Durant had, in fact, discovered Burman's talents at Buick, and by 1908 had set up an official Buick Racing Team. The next year a Buick advertisement stated, 'During the season of 1909, Buick cars won 166 firsts—90 per cent of the events entered. America's most important events won by Buicks'. The first race on the first day of competition at the new 2½-mile track at Indianapolis was won by a Buick driven by Arthur Chevrolet and Bob Burman, on 19 August 1909. Around 1912, however, Buicks began to fade from the US racing scene as Walter Chrysler concentrated on increasing production, to an amazing 124,834 cars in 1916. The one-millionth Buick was built in 1923, the first year in which production also exceeded 200,000 cars.

From 1919 to 1926, Buick's sales were the highest in the auto industry, in terms of dollar volume. This was helped by the fine reputation the durable and

Bugatti-owner Chayne gave the 1938 Buick torque-tube rear axle control and rear coil springs, and re-shaped the engine's pistons and combustion chambers for more turbulent combustion, allowing higher compression ratios. By 1941 the biggest 5.3-litre Buick eight was developing 165 bhp at 3800 rpm—respectable for the time in any company. A styling break-through came in 1942, with front fenders which flowed back, on some models, to join the rear fenders. This was considered so radical that GM's Fisher Body Division refused to supply the bodies with these fenders bolted to the doors. Buick had to add them to the cars in Flint.

Buick built aircraft engines and Hellcat gun-carriers during World War II, valued in all at more than a billion dollars. During the war its engineers worked with torque converter transmissions and, in 1948, Buick became the first American maker to offer a torque converter drive as an option, on the Roadmaster series. This was the famed Dynaflow, which became synonymous with both smoothness and 'looseness' of coupling between the engine and the road. It was used in a 1948 Buick which was the same in style as previous models, even though the big cars of the other GM divisions (which normally shared bodies with Buick) had gone to a new full-fendered style—which Curtice did not especially like and had declined. The new body was used by Buick in one year only, 1949, the first with the famed Ventiports or 'portholes' in the side, an inspiration of stylist Ned Nickles.

Missing from the line in 1949, the lower-priced Special came back in 1950 with a handsome new body and the toothy-looking combined bumper and grille, the first of its kind. Big Buicks featured a new body style that had been introduced in '49, the so-called hardtop convertible, officially known as the Road-master Riviera. This, of course, was the first of the hardtop models that the whole industry was to feature in twenty years to come. Buick built more than half a million cars in 1950 and moved up to third place in US car sales behind Chevrolet and Ford—an astonishing performance for a relatively costly car. Buick came to symbolize success to both car buyers and builders, success that Ford later tried to imitate with its famous failure, the Edsel.

In 1952, Buick introduced the first American four-barrel carburettor, invented by one of its own engineers, Adolph Braun. During 1953, the first Buick V8 engine appeared, an unusual design with pentroof combustion chambers, vertical valves and very over-square dimensions. The 1953 golden anniversary year also saw the first Skylark in production, a cleanly

Left: the 1950 Road-master Estate Wagon 79 featured wooden-finish estate-car panels and the famous bonnet 'ventiports', a typical Buick trademark

Left: convertibles have been very popular in America for many years and one of the most popular was the 1953 Buick Skylark. Note the wire wheels, whitewall tyres and toothy Buick grille

Left: this Buick was one of 781,296 sold in 1955, one of Buick's most successful years. Soon afterwards, however, Buick sales dropped and only in the 1970s achieved sales comparable to the 1955 figure

Below: in 1959, Buick trimmed the tail fins of their cars to a more reasonable size. This is the 2-door Electra coupé which is best known for its excellent brakes, featuring aluminium-finned front drums

customized Roadmaster convertible that Buick unfortunately chose to call a 'sports car'. A much more sporty machine arrived in 1954, with the return of the Century. It had a new 'small' body, with the 'big' 200 bhp engine and a top speed of 107 mph. With the new body came the controversial wrap-round windshield that became another industry trend-setter.

Offered with a new Dynaflow, in which the pitch of the torque converter stator blades was changed automatically, the 1955 Buick line was well received in a boom year; 781,296 were built in 1955—a level Buick took until the 1970s to reach again. Not all those '55 models were very well made, and in the last half of the decade of the 1950s Buicks lost their reputation for

high quality and long life. The low point was reached with the hideously ugly 1958 model, followed by the radically low, fin-tailed 1959 Buick, which gave up the traditional model names (to the regret of many Buick buyers) in favour of Invicta, Le Sabre and Electra. The best that could be said of these cars was that they had excellent brakes, with aluminium-finned front drums.

Early in 1959 a skilled production man, Edward Rollert, was put at the controls of Buick, to revive the ailing division whose production had dropped to less than a quarter-million cars a year. Rollert did an outstanding job, literally saving Buick. By 1961 he had revived the Special in the form of a charming compact car of quality, powered by an aluminium 3.5-litre V8

Left top: the Electra 225 of 1961 which, in a form, was still available into the late 1970s

Left centre: the Riviera, introduced in 1963, was intended as a competitor to Ford's Thunderbird. The Riviera's original styling later evolved into a shape that no longer stood out quite so prominently form, was still available into the late 1970s

Below: the GS-X of 1970 typified the design trends of the late sixties and early seventies, decked out with sports wheels and mirrors, aerofoils, spoilers and lashings of matt black paint. The American trend later swung away from the brash, 'boy-racer' image, to a more conservative approach, when it was realised that the public opinion might scorn the attitude that a car manufacturer would promote a faster, and therefore thirstier, image for its cars in a time when a severe petroleum shortage was forecast by many commentators

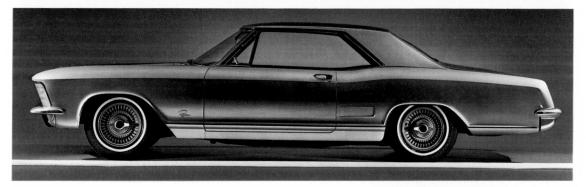

that has since become world-famous. Revised by Buick's Joseph Turlay from a GM Engineering Staff design, the little V8 powered Mickey Thompson's 1962 Indianapolis entry, won races in Bruce McLaren's first sports cars, formed the basis of the engine with which Jack Brabham and Denny Hulme won Grand Prix Championships in 1966 and 1967, and is now one of the better engines in the Leyland range of cars, in their Rover. A companion engine, a 90-degree V6 with a cast iron block, was introduced in the Special in 1962 and offered until 1967, after which it was replaced by an in-line six made for Buick by Chevrolet. The design of the subsequent, smaller cast-iron V8 was based on that of the little aluminium engine that—contrary to many reports—made a great deal of money for the division.

Then of 6.6 litres, Buick's big V8 engine was ideally displayed in 1963 in the Riviera, which was GM's long-awaited response to the success of Ford's four-passenger Thunderbird. The Riviera was a handsome car, the crisp inspiration of GM's new director of styling, William L. Mitchell, and it was also very nice to drive. A new and larger Riviera came along in 1966, extending a line that was further enlivened in 1971 with the introduction of the most controversial Riviera, a new model with a teardrop tail and sweeping fender line and a touch of Saoutchik style. With it, Bill Mitchell successfully broke away from the box-shape in which most contemporaries seemed captured. For

1974, the Riviera again reverted to a squared-off tail, and no longer stood out so prominently from the rest of the GM range, looking more like the run-of-the-mill cars than in previous years. For 1979 the Riviera underwent a total metamorphosis, becoming Buick's first front-wheel-drive car, with independent suspension all round and a 3.8-litre turbocharged V6 engine as standard. It indicated that at last great thought was being put into new automobile design after many years of very conventional engineering philosophy.

Buick's intermediate-size models, Specials and Skylarks, successfully kept pace with the performance race of the late 1960s, with models like the GS 400. In 1973 Buick again revived the Century name for its intermediates, styled with a flowing front fender line frankly reminiscent of the 1942–48 models. During the sixties, Buick engineers also continued to pioneer automatic transmission design, creating the basic three-speed-plus-torque-converter units which GM now uses in all its cars.

At the top end of the 1979 Buick range, the Electra 225 became established as a sound alternative for those to whom a Cadillac was too pretentious. The least costly big Buick was the Le Sabre. At the other, more basic end of the Buick range, 1979 saw the introduction of General Motors' first 'X-car', a sub-compact, front-wheel-drive range, which in its Buick incarnation was known as the Skylark. It replaced the Isuzu-built, Opel

Below: the Custom Electra 225 of 1971. Note the absence of the centre pillars, another popular American styling quirk

Bottom: the 1979 Riviera was Buick's first front-wheel-drive car. It was powered by a 3.8-litre V6 engine, turbocharged for a good blend of performance and economy

clones which had been imported and sold through Buick dealerships since the mid-1970s. It was announced at almost the same time that Buick would have its own 'world car' for 1982, rather than having to rely on further Isuzu-built imports. A sporty, 2+2 Buick was planned for the 1983 model year and Buick's sporting pretensions also showed up in the 1979 Roadhawk, a performance version of the short-lived Skyhawk, which was dropped early in 1980.

Autumn 1980 saw another milestone for Buick, the end of the occasionally illustrious line of Buick V8 petrol engines. Hereafter, in deference to the all-important EPA fuel consumption figures, fours would be the basic engines in many models, with various V6s at the top of the options list—although the 5.0-litre GM V8 and the 5.7-litre diesel V8 would still be available as options in certain models. The fuel-efficient V6 line included a 4.1-litre engine and a turbocharged version of the faithful 3.8.

Other car lines for 1981 were the virtually unchanged Skylark, an aerodynamically cleaner Regal, the Le Sabre and Electra (with GM's new four-speed, over-drive automatic transmission as standard, and offering no petrol V8 option) plus the latest version of the Riviera.

The Buick range was not undergoing any drastic changes at this time, as GM concentrated the much needed new models in divisions with more ephemeral customer tastes than the relatively staid Buick.

The 1982 model year saw the Skyhawk name revived, for the new 'world market' J-car, and another front-wheel-drive line was added with the introduction of a new version of the Century, in the A-car class. The Skylark continued as Buick's badge-engineered sister to the successful Chevrolet Citation, and the Regal, Electra and Le Sabre lines completed the 1982 offerings.

With magnificent new headquarters in Flint, nick-named the 'Taj Mahal', Buick was well equipped for a future it viewed with confidence. For this division of General Motors Corporation, life had begun at 70.

Below: the aerodynamically efficient, V6-engined Regal of 1981, a luxury car with sporting aspirations

Bottom: Buick's neat version of the X-car was the Skylark, a well-equipped, 2.5-litre front-wheel-drive car with the emphasis on economy

Cadillac

From the primitive, single-cylinder Type A, Cadillacs have evolved into cars fit for presidents to own and to give as gifts

CADILLAC WAS the branch of the early General Motors that led the way in the engineering and manufacturing fields, just as Buick led in production. Long before World War I, the Cadillac was well established as one of the finest cars built in America and, as the recipient of two Dewar Trophies, it had gained world-wide fame. Few cars have remained as true to their original purposes and traditions as has the Cadillac.

The Cadillac car can, in fact, be said to have added lustre to the name it was given. While a commissioned officer in the Royal French Army, Antoine de la Mothe Cadillac founded the city of Detroit, as a fur trading centre, in 1701. Cadillac was later honoured in several ways by his king, Louis XIV, which served to obscure his rather doubtful family origins in the small town in Gascony where he was born. The Cadillac family did have a coat of arms, however, dating from the 11th century, and it was adopted for the Cadillac

car. It remains the only coat of arms, of authentic origin, in use on any American car today.

Cadillac, of course, arrived in Detroit two hundred years too early to start an automobile company. His name was chosen for the company and the automobile, in 1902, by a well-to-do lumber merchant, William H. Murphy. Several years earlier, Murphy had backed a young mechanic, Henry Ford, in the founding of a new firm to produce cars to Ford's designs. Ford had differences with his backers, however, and left the company to go his own way. Murphy and his associates were planning to give up their car-building venture after this, but decided to consult with the company that was to make engines for their cars, the Leland and Faulconer Manufacturing Company of Detroit.

The guiding spirit of Leland and Faulconer was Henry Martyn Leland, a skilled and highly-principled

Above: one of Cadillac's earliest models was this 1906 4-seater tourer. It was almost carriage-like in appearance and used very narrow tyres

Above left: the Cadillac badge remains the only authentic coat-of-arms in use on any American car today

Facing page: a 1917 Cadillac model 55. This car used a 5.1-litre V8 engine

41

Above: the first Cadillac model made was this four-seater tourer introduced in 1903. It had a 1610 cc engine which produced 7 hp

Right: from their earliest days, Cadillacs have always been a symbol of luxury and elegance. This is the Cadillac 55 landaulet-coupé of 1917

Below right: the 1925 Cadillac Suburban was powered by a V8 engine. It was a four-door, four-seater tourer and its stylish body was in keeping with the Cadillac image

Top: a 1906 four-seater Cadillac tourer. This was one of the company's first four-cylinder cars

Above: a most unusual hardtop was featured on this 1904 Cadillac. The car used a single-cylinder motor producing 9 hp. Luggage was carried in the wicker baskets attached to the sides of the rear seats

motto: 'Craftsmanship a creed, accuracy a law'.

Leland wasn't present at the meeting on 22 August 1902 at which Murphy and his partners reorganised their motor car firm and named it the Cadillac Automobile Company. Two years later, when it was merged with Leland and Faulconer, it was again renamed the Cadillac Motor Car Company. Henry Leland then became Cadillac's president. The first Cadillac car, the prototype of the Model A, was completed on 17 October 1902, and was shown in January 1903 at the New York Automobile Show.

This first single-cylinder Cadillac was a primitive machine by the standards of the European cars of its day, but its simplicity, light weight and high ground clearance were just what America's atrocious roads required. As Models A, B, E, F, K, M, S and T, 16,126 examples of the single-cylinder Cadillac were sold between 1903 and 1908. With various body styles, their prices ranged from $750 to $1,400. Detail improvements in the 1610cc engine increased its output from 7 to 10 horsepower during its lifetime. Fitted with a copper water jacket, the engine rested underneath the front seat and drove through a two-speed planetary transmission.

The Model K, with a two-seater light runabout body, was the one that won Leland, Cadillac, and Frederick Bennett, England's importer of Cadillacs, their respective places in the motor industry hall of fame. They proved, with a dramatic demonstration at Brooklands, in March 1908, that Cadillac cars were

Above left: Cadillac's first V8 was introduced in 1914. It was a 5.1-litre engine and produced 70 bhp. Since then, not a single year has passed in which the company has not produced a V8 engine

Below left: General Pershing poses alongside his 1918 Cadillac Model 57

gunsmith and toolmaker. Born in Vermont in 1843, Leland was not a youngster at the turn of the century. Yet he had the vitality to suggest to Murphy that he push ahead with his car company, using a horizontal single-cylinder engine that had been designed at the Leland plant by Alanson P. Brush. Henry Leland entered the American motor industry almost by chance, rather than choice. It was to the young industry's great benefit that he did so, for Leland may have done more than any other individual to give this eager but untutored motor business a sense of responsibility toward fine engineering and high precision. From Leland's beliefs and practices came the Cadillac

made from parts that were entirely interchangeable—a claim that few, if any, other car makers could boast at that time. It was taken for granted in those days that a certain amount of hand-fitting would always be necessary when replacing old and worn parts of a car with new ones.

Prompted by Frederick Bennett, officials of Britain's Royal Automobile Club picked three new Cadillacs at random from the eight that were in stock in London at that time. They were driven to the Brooklands circuit, briefly tested to find out what their performance was, and then taken completely apart. The RAC men then mixed up all the parts and threw in some new pieces

Above: the 1934 Fleetwood V12 was part of a line produced alongside the legendary V16 from 1930 to 1937. The V12 models further enhanced Cadillac's reputation as great engineers

Above right: a close-up of the V8 engine used in the 335 model of 1931

Right: front and side views of the 1932 Cadillac 355 Sedan. The model was introduced as a competitor to the luxury Mercedes cars of the day

Below: a superb example of the V16-engined 452B of 1932, one of the American motor industry's legendary cars

taken from the spare parts supplies, for good measure. From these jumbled parts, two of Bennett's mechanics assembled three Model K Cadillacs again, the RAC representatives looking over their shoulders to make sure that they didn't hand-scrape the pieces to make them fit. Then all three of the completed Cadillacs ran 500 miles at Brooklands without the slightest trouble, and one of the three, picked again by the RAC, won its class in the 2000-mile Reliability Trial in June 1908. It was hardly surprising that the RAC awarded Cadillac the coveted Dewar Trophy for that year, recognising the greatest advance made then by any motor car.

Cadillac's growing reputation had attracted the attention of the legendary William Crapo Durant of Flint, Michigan. Durant chose Cadillac, along with Buick, Oldsmobile and Oakland, as a component of his General Motors Company in July 1909. Cadillac became a division of GM when the firm was reorganised as a corporation in 1916. This did not, however, mean that the high standards of Cadillac, set by Henry Leland and his son Wilfred, were lowered in any way by ace-salesman Durant. Cadillac remained an independent operation, perhaps the most independent of all the GM divisions, building what it called 'the most moderately priced strictly high-grade motor car in the world'.

Four-cylinder Cadillacs were produced, 67,167 of

Below: the V16 engine was used in a number of different models such as this 1931 sedan

Bottom: Cadillac's legendary V16 motor was an overhead valve unit of 7.4 litres, producing 165 bhp at 3400 rpm. The engine was designed by Ernest Seaholm, Cadillac's chief designer from 1923 to 1943

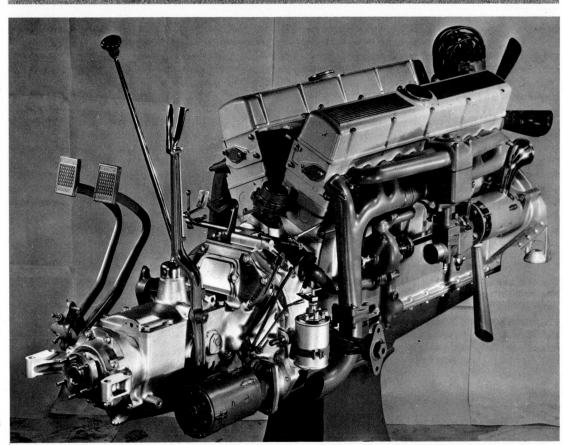

Right: the 1931 452A was another famous model to use the V8 engine

Below and bottom left: a splendid example of the coachbuilder's art is this pre-war Cadillac V16 Fleetwood sedan

Above right: another of Cadillac's coachbuilders was the Derham company who produced this pristine V8 landau

them in all, starting with the 5-litre Model D of 1905. A smaller four-cylinder car, the Model G, was launched in 1907 and continued until 1912. That was the year that Cadillac made motoring history again with the introduction of the Delco ignition, lighting and self-starting system. Though not the first self-starter, this system, the joint creation of Cadillac and Charles F. Kettering's Delco Laboratories, is recognised as being the first practical complete electrical system for a car, the forerunner of all those that have since been developed. This achievement won for

Cadillac another Dewar Trophy—the only time in history this great award has been given twice to the same manufacturer.

Charles Kettering was the catalyst in Cadillac's decision to take another step forward, to bypass the six-cylinder engine (there has never been a Cadillac six) and adopt the V8. Kettering and his associates built the V8-powered prototype car that convinced Henry Leland that this was the direction he should follow in the future. Announced in September 1914 as the standard Cadillac engine for 1915, the 5150 cc V8, developing 70 horsepower, came as an unpleasant surprise to the company's competitors and was both a technical and commercial success. In fact, since 1915 not a single year has passed in which automotive V8 engines were not being produced at Cadillac—war years included.

Engines, aero engines to be precise, were involved in the events that led to the Lelands' departure from Cadillac during World War I. The Lelands wanted Cadillac to convert to full production of the new Liberty aero engine, but Billy Durant wasn't so eager to bring car production to a full stop. Henry and Wilfred left Cadillac and set up a new company, the Lincoln Motor Company, from which has grown the most important modern competitor to Cadillac.

After the Armistice, Cadillac entered the auto market of the 1920s with a product of unsurpassed

1930s, fitted to various competitors' cars.

In 1925, Lawrence P. Fisher, one of the six famous coach-building Fisher brothers, became president of Cadillac. Fisher was to have a strong personal impact on Cadillac's future and one of the first steps he took to secure it was to carry out a five-million-dollar expansion programme that allowed the GM division to produce 47,420 cars in 1927, almost twice its previous record for one year. In 1928, a new 5.6-litre V8 engine was introduced, having side-by-side connecting rods instead of the earlier fork-and-blade construction. It retained an aluminium crankcase, however, with a separate cast-iron cylinder block for each row of four L-head cylinders.

This new V8 was first produced in a small-bore, 5-litre size in 1927 to power the La Salle, introduced then as a smaller companion car to the Cadillac. The

Below: a 1947 limousine. This car used the V8 power unit introduced in 1936 to replace the V12 and V16 engines. The cast-iron engine produced 150 bhp from 5.7 litres

reputation but undistinguished appearance: advanced and stylish bodywork was a rarity on all American cars of that period. The basic Cadillac was then built on a 132-inch wheelbase, weighed about 4200 pounds, and sold for around $3200. With the help of engineers from the GM research laboratories, Cadillac's V8 was given a new, dynamically-balanced, counterweighted two-plane crankshaft for the 1924 model year. This made the engine much smoother and fought off, as far as Cadillac was concerned, the attack of the straight-eight design that enjoyed such a vogue in the 1920s and

La Salle was especially significant as the car that prompted Lawrence Fisher to hire a young Californian car designer, Harley Earl, and bring him east to give some shape and style to the La Salle and Cadillac. Subsequently, of course, Earl established the profession of automobile styling and became its leading practitioner. Not even his flair could save the La Salle during the tough years of the depression, however. The last one was produced in 1940.

Other Cadillac changes during the 1920s included the adoption of four-wheel brakes, in 1923, and the

Above: front and side views of the 1947 V8 sedan. Note the famous 'egg-crate'-style grille, introduced in 1941 and used, in various forms, ever since

pioneering use of chrome plating over nickel trim surfaces, to prevent tarnishing, in 1928. Also in 1928, Cadillac became the first car maker in the world to offer a synchronized-shifting transmission, called Synchro-Mesh—a term that has since become part of the English language. Vacuum-boosted brakes were provided on the larger cars in 1932, and the change-over to hydraulic brakes was made in 1937.

Many of these changes were the work of Ernest Seaholm, Cadillac's brilliant chief engineer from 1923 to 1943. In January 1930, the world learned of the finest achievement of Seaholm and Cadillac: the model 452, the world's first V16 production car. If there had ever been any doubt about Cadillac's role as the premier luxury car of the United States, the fabulous V16 erased it. Hydraulically-silenced overhead valves were used in the 45-degree, 7.4-litre engine that developed 165 bhp at 3400 rpm and was carried in a special chassis on a 148-inch wheelbase. All coachwork was by Fleetwood, which had become an exclusive supplier to Cadillac in 1926, and prices ranged from $5350 to $9500.

In August 1930, Cadillac introduced a V12 model based on the architecture of the V16, but designed to use the chassis and bodywork of the V8 cars. These two beautiful engines were part of the Cadillac line until 1937. After that the V12 was dropped and the over-head-valve sixteen, of which 3863 had been built, was replaced by a radical new Seaholm V16 with half the number of parts. It was an L-head design with the cylinder banks at the unusually wide angle of 135 degrees. Only 511 of them were made between 1938 and 1940; since then, Cadillac has remained faithful to the V8.

1941 was a year of revolution for Cadillac. The foundation was laid then for the fantastic success the marque has since enjoyed. Planning for it began in 1934, when the shrewd German-born Nicholas Dreystadt was named as Cadillac's general manager. Under him a new V8 engine was introduced in 1936, a less costly power unit made entirely of cast iron. By 1941, it was producing a very respectable 150 horsepower from 5.7 litres, and it was used in all Cadillacs. Available as an option with it, in that year, was the Hydra-Matic transmission, the first fully-automatic drive offered in Cadillac's field.

For 1941, Dreystadt cut back the number of wheel-bases offered from five to three. By abandoning the La Salle, he was able to offer a true Cadillac, the Series 61, at an attractively low price: $1445. That year the Cadillac also appeared with a bold new grille design, the work of Harley Earl and the brilliant young head of the Cadillac Studio, William Mitchell. It was a horizontal, rectilinear egg-crate design that is the un-mistakable progenitor of all the Cadillac grille designs

For a number of years, the tail-fin-craze raged in America and these fins became bigger and bigger. *Above* is the 1955 Coupé de Ville while *below*, from top to bottom, are a 1958 Sedan de Ville, a 1957 Fleetwood Brougham and a Fleetwood Sixty Special of 1959

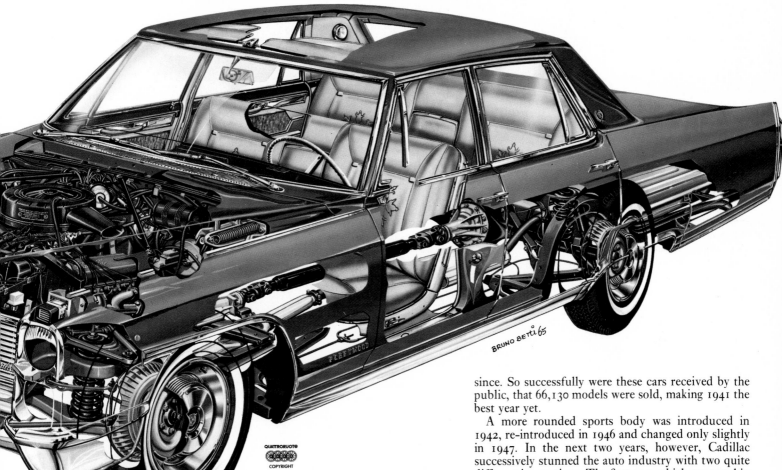

BRUNO BETTI 65

Below: a 1959 Cadillac
Eldorado hardtop

Bottom: 1964 Eldorado
convertible

since. So successfully were these cars received by the public, that 66,130 models were sold, making 1941 the best year yet.

A more rounded sports body was introduced in 1942, re-introduced in 1946 and changed only slightly in 1947. In the next two years, however, Cadillac successively stunned the auto industry with two quite different innovations. The first one, which appeared in 1948, was the tail fin. Those first fins were the direct result of a visit by Earl and his stylists to an airport near Detroit to see the impressive Lockheed Lightning interceptor, the twin-boom, twin-tail P38. Those first Cadillac fins look miniscule today, but of course they sent shock waves through the whole motor world at that time.

Cadillac's second startling step forward was under the bonnet: a high-compression overhead-valve V8 engine, introduced in 1949. It traced its beginnings back to 1937, when the engineers started experimenting with overhead valves and five main bearings (instead of three) as aids to the attainment of better efficiency from higher compression. The fruits of their labours were evident in the lighter weight and higher power of the 1949 engine, most powerful of the American cars of the time, with 160 horsepower from 5430 cc.

This widely copied engine established for Cadillac a new and unusual image, that of a performance car. 'Fordillacs' became popular—Fords fitted with the powerful Cadillac engines. Edward Cole was then chief engineer of Cadillac and he encouraged those who wanted to use these luxury cars in sporty ways. At Le Mans in 1950, a Cadillac-engined Allard was placed third, a basically standard Series 62 coupé was tenth and a special-bodied Series 62 finished eleventh. After 1951, however, the new hemispherical-head Chrysler V8 moved ahead of Cadillac's more durable design in power and sparked the beginning of the famous 'horsepower race'.

Cadillac followed Chrysler in offering power steer-

Top: this is the 1965 Fleetwood model, featured in the cutaway on the previous page

Above: the 1967 Eldorado model was the first Cadillac to feature front-wheel drive. Alongside stands the more conventional Fleetwood model of the same year

ing, making it standard equipment in 1954. The next year the premium Eldorado series was introduced, with 270 horsepower under the·bonnet and with ventilated, forged-aluminium wheels. Among the experimental cars shown by Cadillac in the mid 1950s, the heyday of the dream cars, was the Eldorado Brougham of 1955, a very handsome smaller car. It went into limited production at the end of 1956 with such, then-revolutionary, features as quadruple headlights and self-levelling air suspension. It was a cleanlined four-door car with a brushed-stainless-steel roof panel. A different kind of Eldorado Brougham was built in 1959 and 1960: a larger car with crisp lines, built in Turin by Pininfarina to GM designs, at the rate of only 75 a year.

The 1959 and 1960 standard Cadillacs marked the peak, both literally and figuratively, of the tail-fin craze. After that, the stylists, now led by Bill Mitchell, started trimming the fins back until they were blended into the wing again in the outstandingly crisp and formal 1965 model. Front-end cornering lights, coming on automatically when the turn signals are operated, were first offered by Cadillac. So, in 1964, was fully automatic Comfort Control, which either heats or cools the interior as needed to reach the temperature the occupants want. 1964 was the year that Cadillac produced its three-millionth car, at a time when the company said it was offering so many options that it could keep its production lines going for three years without having to build two identical cars.

The 1967 model year was the first in Cadillac history in which more than 200,000 cars were built. Contributing a little more than ten per cent of that total was a brand-new car with a familiar name, the Eldorado. This was a new kind of Eldorado, a close-coupled coupé with a long bonnet, that imitated the extravagance of the great V16, and front-wheel drive—the first and only Cadillac with this feature. It used the drive train developed for the 1966 Oldsmobile Toronado and was clothed in a razor-edged body that sold very well to buyers who were mainly aware that it was a 'sporty' Cadillac and who probably had no idea which

the Eldorado only, its stroke length was increased to bring the capacity to 8.2 litres, a round 500 cubic inches.

George R. Elges, a former manufacturing man, became General Manager of Cadillac in 1969 and led the division to new production peaks. 1972 was the first quarter-million-car model year, with a total of 267,787 Cadillacs produced. In the early seventies Cadillac's Chief Engineer, Robert Templin, was recruited to work on GM's Wankel rotary-engine project. Elges and his associates studied the increasing popularity of Mercedes-Benz cars in the United States and for-

Below: one of the most fabulous American cars of all time, the 1967 front-wheel drive Cadillac Eldorado

end it was driven by. The Eldorado has since passed through one very successful restyling, so much so that a 1972 model was chosen by US President Richard Nixon as a suitable gift to Soviet leader Leonid Brezhnev during his visit to Russia. In 1971, an Eldorado convertible was added, the only such model offered by any of the American luxury makes.

Engineering improvements in the normal Cadillacs were not overlooked. For example, variable-ratio power steering was pioneered by Cadillac, in the US, in 1966. For the 1968 model year, an extensively redesigned engine of 7.75 litres was introduced, simplified for easier service with ten per cent fewer parts and 25 per cent fewer gasketed joints. Its gross output was 375 bhp, with a peak torque of 525 lb ft. In 1970, for

mulated the policies which have led to the present trend of smaller, more economical models. The prime Cadillac example of the trend is the compact Seville. Introduced in 1975, in 1980 it was further 'down-sized' and received front-wheel-drive, which helped to preserve the roominess so important to luxury American cars while reducing the overall length. At the same time the Seville was also subjected to a very controversial restyling, which left it with a long nose and a short, sweeping tail—very 1930s British! In June the de Ville was given the 4.1-litre V6 as standard equipment in place of the 6.6-litre V8—it was already standard on the Electra. The market was now in the depths of recession, and the motor industry was particularly hard hit. Around 300,000 industry workers were laid off and

Above: the 1979 range included this Seville model, which was the company's interpretation of the smaller car trend precipitated by the fuel shortage of the early seventies

unemployment in Detroit was running at about the same level as in the Great Depression of the 1930s. Certainly, the line workers were not Cadillac's main customer group but the state of the motor industry has long been a reasonable yardstick of the general state of the economy. Even Cadillac had to adapt to the new realities and, fortunately, as part of GM, it was doing so. The decision was taken around autumn 1980 to go ahead with development of a new, small, Cadillac based on the sub-compact J-cars which would soon appear.

While Cadillac prepared to breach this section of the market, it had to make some more immediate moves but it could not be seen to be cheeseparing. For the 1981 range, Cadillac introduced a new engine which would be basic to all models. As befits a Cadillac, it had eight cylinders—a 6.0-litre V8. It was, however, a very special V8. By clever adaptation of the valve gear (carried out by the Eaton Corporation) and some equally clever electronics, the engine reacted to smaller demands by the driver or road conditions by cutting out two, or even four, cylinders, to run on six or four with substantial fuel savings. The de Ville, Fleetwood and Seville also offered the 4.1-litre V6 and the GM 5.7 diesel.

The V8-6-4, as it came to be known, was not an outstanding success, perhaps underlining again the age-old fact that the market really did not like too much

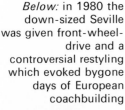

Below: in 1980 the down-sized Seville was given front-wheel-drive and a controversial restyling which evoked bygone days of European coachbuilding

mechanical hocus pocus. For 1982 Cadillac came up with an elegant, new, aluminium block, iron head, 4.1-litre V8, allied to the new generation four-speed overdrive automatic and saving some 210 lb over the older V8s. This engine was the base for Fleetwood and de Ville, Eldorado and Seville, while the 'modular displacement' engine was restricted to the limousine line. Otherwise, these cars were little changed; the big news was in the introduction of a completely new and very different Cadillac, the Cimarron. Introduced in September 1981, the Cimarron was a front-wheel-drive, typical J-car, powered by a 1.8-litre four-cylinder motor. It was a pretty little car, with very European lines combined with Cadillac refinement. Its major drawback was perhaps a lack of power and that was due to be countered sometime in 1982 by the availability of a new 2.0-litre four with a five-speed manual gearbox.

The Cimarron was a brave move for Cadillac, but then the company had plenty of those to show in its history—and most of them successful. While complying with the ever-increasing mountains of legislation which now govern all aspects of the American motor car, and with the pressures which are costing many cars their individuality, Cadillacs maintain their own high standards and their own unmistakable identity—true to the traditions of the man who started it all, Henry Leland.

Right: a big Cadillac, the 1981 Fleetwood Brougham. All the 1981 range featured the 6-litre 'modular displacement' V8-6-4 engine as standard, but use of the innovative engine was short-lived

Below: a small Cadillac, the Cimarron. Moving with the times, Cadillac introduced the attractive, 1.8-litre, front-wheel-drive Cimarron in September 1981, complete with traditional 'egg-crate' grille. It was almost immediately scheduled for uprating to a full two litres

Chevrolet

Chevrolet was formed at the instigation of Billy Durant, the General Motors founder, but Louis Chevrolet had his own ideas

Below: the first Chevy, the Classic 6, unveiled on 3 November 1911, was powered by a 4.9-litre, T-head six. 2999 of these cars were sold in 1912, although many people thought the model was somewhat overpriced at $2150

GENERAL MOTORS AND CHEVROLET; which is more dependent on the other today? It is so difficult to separate them that this question is unanswerable. In 1972, General Motors built 5,740,440 cars and trucks in the United States; more than half of these, 3,068,444 to be exact, carried the Chevrolet name. Many more vehicles bearing the Chevrolet name were produced by GM plants in Brazil, Mexico, South Africa and Argentina, and even by Isuzu in Japan. Chevrolet, the car named after a Swiss-born racing driver, is beyond doubt the vital backbone of General Motors.

Durant authorised them to go ahead with the six.

On 30 May 1911, the project was revealed in a release to the press: 'W. C. Durant of the General Motors company and racer Louis Chevrolet, one of the speed wonders of the day and a co-worker with Mr Durant in the manufacture and exploitation of fast cars, will establish a factory in Detroit for the manufacture of a new high-priced car.' The story went on to refer to the forthcoming new car as a 'Durant-Chevrolet.'

Billy Durant made good this promise on 3 November 1911, when he organized the Chevrolet Motor Company of Michigan. By that time Chevrolet and Planche had completed their first prototype cars, powered by a 4·9-litre T-head six. A large garage was rented on Detroit's West Grand Boulevard to begin assembly of the 1912 Chevrolet Classic 6 from purchased components. Priced at $2150, this first Chevrolet was indeed an expensive car for its day. Nevertheless, the small shop somehow managed to build and sell 2999 of these cars in 1912.

There were quite a few more twists and turns in the road travelled by the early Chevrolet car and company. Engines for the cars were made by another new Durant enterprise, the Mason Motor Company in Flint. Several former Buick employees were involved in both Mason and another new Flint firm, the Little Motor Car Company. Little entered the market in 1912 with a small roadster powered by a four-cylinder Mason engine and priced at $650. Production of Little cars got off to such a lively start that Durant decided to base Chevrolet manufacture in Flint too, instead of building a big Ford-style plant in Detroit. The necessary total production capacity was achieved by setting up assembly plants around the country.

Chevrolet manufacture was moved to Flint in August 1913 and put under the control of the executive who was running Little. Louis Chevrolet was overseas when some of these changes were made and on returning he saw that a merger between the Little and Chevrolet product lines seemed inevitable. Finding this not to his liking, he left the world of Billy Durant in December 1913 to pursue his own interests.

The 1914 line of Little and Chevrolet cars included closely-related L-head sixes, the Little Six and the Chevrolet Type L. There were also new fours derived from the Little roadster. Chevrolet was still the more costly, and became dominant as production of Littles was ended during 1915. The Little roadster left its mark on the design of the appealing Chevrolet Royal Mail, on the new Model H chassis for which Mason had designed an overhead-valve, four-cylinder engine in late 1913. This 2.8-litre four was the first of the three basic engines, each outstanding in its way, that have powered Chevrolets to marketing success.

In September 1915, Billy Durant pulled his mini-empire together by organizing the Chevrolet Motor Company of Delaware, which took over the stock of all his Chevrolet-related companies. By promoting the

Opposite page: brute force with elegance; the 1973 Corvette with the '74 model inset. Note how well the GM designers blended the mandatory 5 mph-accident-withstanding bumpers into the body-work of the '74 car

The lives of two great men of the motor industry were linked together by the birth of the Chevrolet Motor Company. One was the Flint, Michigan industrialist, William Crapo Durant, born in Boston in 1861. The other was Louis Chevrolet, who was born in Switzerland in 1878. Chevrolet was thirty years old, and recognized as a talented mechanic and an outstanding racing driver, when he and his brother Arthur were hired into the Buick company in 1908 by Durant, who was then assembling the ingredients of his greatest creation, General Motors.

At first the Chevrolets served Durant and his enterprise as chauffeurs and racing drivers for the successful Buick team but, in 1910, Durant pressed his expansion too far too fast and lost control of Buick and General Motors. This didn't stop the irrepressible Durant, however. In October 1910, he put Louis Chevrolet to work in a small garage on Detroit's Grand River Avenue. His assignment: to design and build a new car that would bear the name Chevrolet. Assisted by engineer Etienne Planche, Chevrolet prepared designs with engines of both four and six cylinders.

merits of this new firm, Durant encouraged holders of GM shares to exchange them for stock in Chevrolet. General Motors had not been paying dividends since 1910, so its shares had lost their appeal. In this remarkable way, Durant used Chevrolet to regain a controlling interest in General Motors. On 2 May 1918, Chevrolet was officially merged into the GM organization, the last of GM's five car divisions to be added.

In October 1915, Durant moved Chevrolet directly into strong competition with Ford by introducing the 490, so named because it was priced at $490 with an open body and without an electrical system. This placed it just above the Model T in price. Spurred by the success of the 490, Chevrolet factory sales leaped to 70,701 in 1916, then to 125,882 in 1917. They dropped, then bounced back to 150,226 in 1920, accounting for 39 per cent of GM's North American vehicle sales.

Chevrolet lost its most ardent advocate within General Motors late in 1920, when Billy Durant was forced out of the company for the second and final time. GM was rescued from financial collapse by the du Pont family, whose Pierre S. du Pont became President of GM and General Manager of Chevrolet. At this time a consulting firm was hired to survey the GM properties. Their verdict on Chevrolet was that it could never be made a competitor to Ford, and should be liquidated! Alfred P. Sloan Jr argued persuasively against this, and was in favour of keeping and building up Chevrolet. Shortly after that a policy was adopted to make Chevrolet the lowest-priced GM automobile. Expensive Chevrolet models, like the V8 introduced in 1917, were dropped from the range.

It was audacious to think that Chevrolet could ever challenge Ford. In 1921, Chevrolet, losing money at the rate of $5 million a year, had only 4% of the vehicle market, against Ford's 60%, but instead of trying to compete directly with the immortal Model T, Chevrolet aimed just above the Ford in both equipment and price. This policy provided a name for the successor to the 490 that was introduced in 1923: the Superior. In a boom car-sales year, it lifted the Chevrolet sales total for 1923 to 480,737 units, under the direction of a new General Manager, William S. Knudsen, who held that post until 1933.

Only 759 of those 1923 Chevrolets were of a

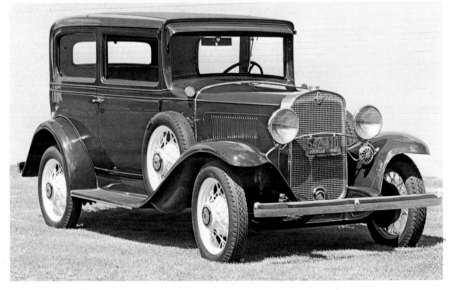

Above far left: 1915
Chevrolet Royal Mail H2

Above left, top to bottom:
1920 490 coupé
1923 Superior Sedan
1926 Superior Series V
1926 Station Wagon

Above far right: 1921
Chevrolet racing car

Above, top to bottom:
1929 Sports coupé
Series AC
1931 Independence
Series AE

revolutionary new design, the air-cooled or 'copper-cooled' model, and fewer than 100 of them had actually reached the hands of the public before they were all called back to the factory in June 1923. High hopes were voiced for this unique $725 model, which was to be built at the rate of 50,000 a month. Its fan-cooled engine was the latest product of Charles F. Kettering, but the 20-horsepower, 2.2-litre unit was not entirely satisfactory and the idea of a major changeover to air cooling was dropped. Instead, an improved Model K (an earlier car) was rushed into production for the 1925 model year.

Chevrolet started thinking about switching to a six-cylinder engine in 1925, after it had helped to design a new small six for the Oakland Division called Pontiac. Chevrolet's six had to suit the division's slogan, 'Valves in head, ahead in value', so engineer O. E. Hunt endowed it with pushrod-operated overhead valves, three main bearings and a capacity of 3.2 litres which produced 46 horsepower. The new six was introduced in December 1928 as the International model. This durable and easily-repaired engine became the second of the three great Chevrolet power units.

In 1927, Chevrolet won first place in US car sales when Ford shut down its lines early to convert to the Model A. That was also a milestone year for Chevrolet with its first annual output of more than a million vehicles, 1,001,880 to be exact. Ford took the sales lead

again in 1929 and 1930, and Chevrolet bounced back to first in the depression year of 1931. With the exceptions of 1935, 1957, 1959 and 1970, Chevrolet has been number one vehicle producer in the world ever since.

Harley Earl and his GM stylists first made major changes in the Chevrolet line in 1933, which also saw the division of the range into Master and Standard lines, the latter being a shorter, lighter version. At $455, the depression-era Standard was the lowest-priced Chevrolet ever made. In 1934, independent front suspension, known as 'knee action', was first fitted. It was the system developed in France by André Dubonnet. From 1935 until 1940, however, buyers could have a solid front axle if they wanted it. In 1939, a more conventional coil and wishbone front suspension was introduced.

It was 1935 that marked the end of a Chevrolet tradition, the open four-door touring car. In that year the last phaetons were built, only 1160 leaving the plants. Chevrolets were extensively redesigned in 1937, when a single wheelbase of 2855 mm replaced the previous differentiation between Master and Standard models. The 'Blue Flame' six-cylinder engine was totally re-designed too, with four main bearings and 3.55-litre engine producing 85 bhp. This engine went into production in a new plant, still important today, at Tonawanda, New York.

One of these engines, in a 1939 Master 85 coupé, played an important role in Chevrolet history. General Motors of Argentina helped a 29-year-old racing driver get a race-prepared car of that type in 1940. The driver, a certain Juan Manuel Fangio, became nationally famous in 1940 when he won the incredible 5900-mile road race from Buenos Aires to Lima, Peru and back again, he and his Chevrolet averaging 53.6 mph over some of the worst roads in the world. In the next two years, Fangio won four major races in a row with his solid-axled coupé. Fangio last raced a Chevrolet at the end of 1949, when his career as a Grand Prix driver was well under way.

What would be the shape of post-war Chevrolets? Remembering the business slump that followed World War I, GM executives felt at first that it would be a good idea to introduce a smaller, lower-priced car after World War II. A special design team created such a car and built several prototypes of it. A factory in Cleveland, Ohio, was set up to make it, but when it was

Above: the 1935 3.3-litre sports convertible

Near right: the 1936 Chevrolet Sport cabriolet

Far right: in the golden days of Hollywood it was fashionable for movie stars and starlets to be draped over late-model cars for publicity shots. This is Gloria Shea with her 1936 model Chevy

seen that car demand would remain strong, the decision was made to set aside the small car or 'light car', as it was known, and instead begin work on a completely restyled Chevrolet to be introduced in 1949.

As part of an overall changeover of GM's smaller 'A-bodies' in 1949, the new Chevrolets had flush front wings, a curved windscreen and a lower bonnet line.

With T. H. Keating as its new General Manager in 1939, Chevrolet set another all-time sales record at 1,550,669 cars and trucks. The 1950 Chevrolet became the first car in its class with a fully automatic transmission, the first Powerglide drive with a torque converter. That contributed to another record year, selling 2,108,273 units, some 300,000 of them equipped with Powerglide. Testing a 1951 Chevrolet, *Motor* magazine reported that it 'corners easily and steadily, under complete and precise control, at quite brisk speeds', and found themselves 'regarding the Chevrolet not simply as being good value, but also as being a good car'. If there has ever been a secret to the success of Chevrolet, that's exactly what it is.

In 1952 and '53 the Chevrolets, whether of good value or not, were dull cars compared with most others. Something was being done about this, however, because Edward N. Cole had been appointed Chevrolet chief engineer in 1952. Cole actively sup-

Above: the Master 85 Sport Sedan of 1940

Right: how Chevrolet styling changed over 6 years. The De Luxe Styleline of 1950 *(top)* got more window space and a tidier body and became the 1953 Bel Air, *centre.* The waistline then became lower still and the bodywork was 'squared up', becoming the Bel Air hardtop sport coupé of 1956

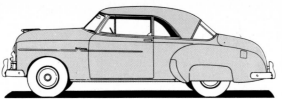

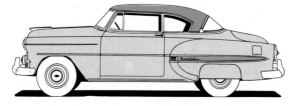

ported the idea, first proposed by Harley Earl, that Chevrolet should build a sports roadster. This was the Corvette, shown as an experimental car early in 1953 and put into production, with its revolutionary glass-fibre body, later that same year. Only a few years later, thanks to Cole and Zora Arkus-Duntov, the Corvette had become an extremely good sports car. It has since remained the only sports car in quantity production in the United States.

Ed Cole also set to work to transform the standard Chevrolet. The results of his labours were evident in the new 1955 model. It had a smooth new body with a wrap-around windscreen, Ferrari-like grille, anti-dive front suspension, 12-volt electrical system, and a new V8 engine that astounded the industry with its simplicity, cheapness and lightness. Starting out at 4.35 litres and 162 horsepower, this V8 became the third great engine in the history of Chevrolet. With fuel injection, in 1957 it became the first American pro-

duction car engine to develop one horsepower per cubic inch. Chevrolet sales reached a new peak in 1955 with 1,821,695 cars, and a total of 2,213,888 vehicles. In 1956, Ed Cole was made the General Manager.

Nineteen fifty-eight was another year of dramatic change, indeed the most complete in Chevrolet history. The cars were all new with an X-pattern frame, coil spring rear suspension, optional air spring-ing, a completely new 5.7-litre engine option, bodies that were strikingly lower and longer, and a new series designation, the Impala—destined for future fame. But America wasn't much interested in any of the 1958 cars and this was Chevrolet's poorest post-war sales year, only 1,543,992 cars and trucks leaving their factories. The even more flamboyant 1959 model moved still further away from the more rational cars that buyers were looking for then—and which Chevro-let hoped to provide.

Chevrolet's economy car made its bow in 1959; this was the controversial Corvair. The division's first production car with integral body/frame construction and a rear engine, it was deliberately planned to be different enough in design from the big Chevrolet to prevent it stealing sales from its own stablemates. Its clean lines were extremely successful, influencing the looks of many other cars around the world, but the air-cooled and independently sprung Corvair was a

costly car to produce and this, more than any other factor, led to Chevrolet's decision early in 1965 to phase it gradually out of production, just after the car had been restyled. The last Corvairs were made in 1970, so a troubled life came to an end.

The Corvair had some very good sales years, especially in its sporty Monza versions, which were even offered with turbocharged engines. But it started off very slowly, and Chevrolet started work at once on a much simpler economy car, the Chevy II,

which was introduced for the 1962 model year. It was the first production car to be fitted with single-leaf rear springs, and it was powered by all-new four and six-cylinder engines. The six was soon to become the basic Chevrolet engine and indeed the basic GM six, while the Chevy II was transformed into the Nova, in which V8 engines were also offered.

Yet another car was added to the growing Chevrolet family in 1963 under the general managership of Semon E. Knudsen, son of the Knudsen who had headed Chevrolet forty years earlier. It was the Chevelle, Chevrolet's entry in the move to a new size of car called the 'intermediate', being part-way between the full-size cars and the compacts. At first a rather bland car, the Chevelle later gained both style and power to become one of the best-selling car lines in the industry.

Chevrolet men at first considered Ford's Mustang to be a response to the Corvair Monza, but eventually they realized they had to have a Mustang of their own. This was the sporty four-seater Camaro, which did not appear until 1966. The Camaro gained great respect among real car enthusiasts with the introduction of the 5-litre Z28 option, a firmly-sprung car, with excellent handling and performance. This won two Trans-Am racing championships in the hands of Mark Donohue. A new Camaro appeared early in

were angled in two planes, away from each other, to combine good breathing with a compact combustion chamber. In 7-litre and, later, 7.4-litre form, this outstanding engine has powered many high-performance Chevrolet cars, especially the Corvette, Camaro and the Monte Carlos that have fared well in NASCAR stock car racing. Aluminium-block versions of the engine were the power behind the successes of McLaren cars in Can-Am racing during the years 1968 to 1971.

Varied models and high performance helped Chevrolet set another record in 1965 with the factory sales of 2,585,014 cars and 3,203,958 vehicles in all. In 1966, Elliott M. Estes took over as General Manager. He came from Pontiac, and was followed in 1969 by another ex-Pontiac engineer, John Z. DeLorean. It fell to DeLorean to introduce yet another new line of Chevrolets, the Vegas, which the division hoped would ward off the latest attacks by the smaller imported makes. It broke new ground with a cylinder block for its 2.3-litre four-cylinder engine that needed no liners for the high-silicon aluminium cylinder bores. Other Vega features were a belt-driven overhead camshaft and an integral body structure. Added to the popular Vega line for 1974 was a new model with a Cosworth-designed 16-valve aluminium cylinder head and electronic fuel injection. However, this model was dropped in 1976.

Expert in trucks as well as cars, Chevrolet moved in the late 1960s to hold its place as a builder of recreational vehicles. In 1969 it introduced the Blazer, a versatile four-wheel-drive vehicle, and in 1972 it began selling a small pickup truck called the LUV – for light utility vehicle. This set a new precedent for Chevrolet by being imported from Japan, although it was from the firm in which GM had a partial interest, Isuzu.

Yet another new line of cars was put under the Chevrolet dealer's roof in 1970 with the introduction of the Monte Carlo, a 'personal car' to compete in the Grand Prix/Thunderbird segment of the market. It helped Chevrolet become, in 1971 and 1972, a consistent seller of more than three million cars and trucks a year in the United States. The world looked forward to another innovation from Chevrolet, in the mid '70s, the first American passenger car powered by a Wankel rotary engine. This would have marked the end of the first phase of the experiments of General Motors and Chevrolet, sparked by Ed Cole. Although a prototype rotary-engined Corvette was shown in 1973, Wankel development was stopped in 1975 and when the European-style sub-compact Chevette appeared in the same year it was entirely conventional. In many ways

Top: the 1969 Impala Custom

Centre: the prototype two-rotor Wankel mid-engined Corvette

Bottom: the elegant Monte Carlo of 1979

1970 and was another exceptionally handsome car from the styling studios of Bill Mitchell.

Yet another great Chevrolet engine came along during the 1960s, one that may one day belong with those first three in historical importance. It started as a 7-litre racing engine for stock cars at Daytona in February 1963 and first appeared in production early in 1965 as a 6.5-litre V8. It was nicknamed the 'porcupine', for the way its pushrod-operated valves

the car was typical of the cosmopolitan approach of America's most enterprising and sporting manufacturer and it soon became America's largest selling sub-compact.

As the 1970s gave way to the 1980s, designation of car types by letter proliferated. The 1980 Chevy line-up included two full-size 'B-cars', the Impala and the Caprice Classic, the Monte Carlo and Malibu 'A-cars', Camaro 'F-cars', Monza 'H-car', the Chevette 'T-car' and the Corvette 'Y-car', plus the crucial, all new 'X-car', the Citation. Chevrolet introduced the front-wheel-drive, sub-compact Citation in April 1979 and the industry's 'first car of the 'eighties' was an immediate success. It set an industry record, with first-month sales of almost 38,000 which rose to 160,000 within six months. It was a perfect example of the American swing to European thinking, with a transverse, four-cylinder engine and manual gearbox as standard and a transverse V6 with auto as options. It was twenty inches shorter than the Nova, which it replaced, and could claim up to 38 mpg for highway driving—a far cry from a few years before.

The economy theme ran throughout the range. A new basic engine, a 3.8-litre V6, for the market-leading Caprice and Impala ranges and for the Malibu, Monte Carlo and Camaro lines, plus a weight saving of around 238 lb on the Corvette, helped Chevrolet exceed government fuel requirements. Turbocharging was introduced as an option on the V6 Monte Carlo, while V8s of up to 5.7 litres were also available.

1981 cars had computer-controlled fuel metering, further to improve engine efficiency, and Chevy introduced GM's first 'automatic overdrive' four-speed automatic transmission.

An even more dramatic change came when Chevrolet announced that 1982 would be 'the Year of the Diesel'. As many as 300,000 diesel-powered Chevys were projected for the 1982 model year, down to an Isuzu-built, 1.8-litre four, for the Chevette.

The American motor industry was in trouble now, as sales slumped disastrously, and even GM did not escape the problems. In May 1981, Chevrolet introduced the comprehensively equipped, front-wheel-drive Cavalier family—including a coupé, a hatchbach, a saloon and a station wagon. It was a direct challenge to the Japanese imports and a neat fit between the Chevette and Citation lines. Standard equipment was a 1.8-litre four with a four-speed manual overdrive transmission.

In looks, the new car was European; in offering so many features as standard it was very Japanese; in helping lead the ailing industry along the road to recovery it was *very* Chevrolet.

Chrysler

Although Chrysler is the smallest and youngest of the 'Big Three' American motor manufacturers, the company is an industrial giant

Top: the Chrysler Imperial Sedan of 1925 was the first of Chrysler's many successes

Above: another of the various Chrysler Six models, this being a 1925 phaeton version

ENGINEERING WAS WALTER P. CHRYSLER'S guiding passion and, fortunately for this farmer's boy from America's middle west, the town in which he spent his boyhood—Ellis, Kansas—was the site of a thriving locomotive workshop operated by the Union Pacific Railroad. Chrysler, born in 1875, started as an engine cleaner, but soon rose to be master mechanic on several middle-west railroads.

Soon after the turn of the century, however, internal combustion supplanted steam in his affections, and he decided to become a motor owner. Instead of starting with a second-hand vehicle, Chrysler set out to buy a brand-new luxury car—with just $700 in the bank. At the 1905 Chicago Automobile Show, he ordered a

$5000 Locomobile, borrowed the balance of the purchase money from a banker friend and then went home to tell his wife what he had done.

'She said nothing,' recalled Chrysler, 'but it seemed as though the kitchen door banged shut a little harder than usual!'

In his mid 30s Chrysler became plant manager of the American Locomotive Works, a railway engineering company which had a motor manufacturing subsidiary at Providence, Rhode Island, where carbon copies of the French Berliet car were built under the Alco trademark. Around this time Chrysler met James J. Storrow of Lee, Higginson & Company, who was heading the bankers' syndicate that had been organised to rescue Billy Durant's ailing General Motors Company—at that time encompassing Buick, Cadillac, Oldsmobile and Oakland (plus a few other concerns). Storrow must have been impressed by the young railroad engineer's capabilities, for he asked him to join the revitalised General Motors to supply the technical know-how that the syndicate's other nominee, Charles W. Nash (who had just been elected GM President in Durant's stead), was lacking. Even though it meant a drop in salary from $12,000 to $6000 a year, Chrysler accepted the offer, joining General Motors in 1912. Four years later, he had become President and General Manager of the Buick division, at an annual salary of $500,000, thanks to his immaculate record as a 'cost-conscious executive with a creative grasp of factory techniques', which included the installation of one of the industry's first moving production lines, only a couple of years after Ford.

By the end of World War I, Chrysler had established himself as one of America's top twelve industrialists.

In 1916 Billy Durant had used his success with Chevrolet as a lever to regain control of General Motors and while he had managed to persuade Chrysler to stay on by raising his salary, it was an association that was doomed to break up. Durant had an omnivorous appetite for company acquisitions, and while some of the firms General Motors took over proved to be a worthwhile investment—prime examples being Fisher Bodies and Frigidaire—many were lame ducks whose handicaps bordered on paraplegia.

Chrysler warned against a venture into the manufacture of farm machinery and tractors, but was overruled by Durant; it cost the group $30 million to find that Walter P. had been right and that William C. was wrong. Chrysler, described by a contemporary as 'a glittering personality with a rich railroadman's vocabulary, a short temper and a showman's pride', resigned in disgust.

Immediately he was offered the job of saving the ailing Willys-Overland company which, despite a $50 million investment by a group of bankers, was sinking fast. The salary was a cool $1 million annually, but Chrysler earned every penny by putting the company

Above: the 1928 Chrysler 72 was powered by a six-cylinder engine which produced 75 bhp at 3200 rpm. That year, a team of Chrysler tourers was entered at Le Mans and achieved a remarkable success by taking second and third places

Right: yet another of the numerous Chrysler Six variations, the 1926 roadster. By 1926, the annual sales of Chrysler cars were exceeding 200,000

back on a profitable basis; next he was asked to pull Maxwell out of trouble. After the war, Maxwell had united with Chalmers: both were popular marques, but a series of marketing mistakes caused sales to slump. Hugh Chalmers had formerly been an ace salesman with the National Cash Register Company, but knew nothing of production; Walter E. Flanders, president of Maxwell, was a production expert, but a poor engineer. His name had previously been associated with the EMF car, whose nicknames—'Every Mechanical Fault' and 'Every Morning Fix-it'—epitomised its reputation with motorists. The Maxwells built under his aegis had continued the doubtful tradition; the 1920 models had weak rear axles, which broke with crippling regularity. The result was a vast stock of unsold cars.

Walter Chrysler cleared the stocks by redesigning the rear axles, and the 'Good Maxwells' quickly regained the marque's lost reputation; by 1923 the losses had been converted into a profit of $2,678,000, and by 1924 the figure had risen to $4 million plus.

The revived company was an ideal basis for Chrysler's ultimate ambition—a firm bearing his own name. He had brought three gifted young engineers from Willys-Overland and the trio, Carl Breer, Fred M. Zeder and Owen R. Skelton, began work on a new car that would take advantage of wartime developments in high-compression engine design. Zeder had already made preliminary studies for a six-cylinder unit with a high-compression cylinder head that seemed to owe more than a little to the work of the British engineer Harry Ricardo; this 70-horsepower unit was used in a new model, the Chrysler Six, marketed under the Maxwell banner. To match its 70 mph performance, unique for a car in its price and capacity bracket, the new model was fitted with four-wheel

hydraulic brakes—an innovation of some magnitude for the ultra-conservative American market. The brakes were, however, of the slippery-when-wet external contracting type, which had long been obsolete in Europe.

Chrysler tried to exhibit an early prototype at the January 1924 New York Motor Show, but was refused because the car was not yet in commercial production, so he leased the lobby of the Hotel Commodore, which was close to the exhibition hall, and where the important members of the press and motor industry met.

The car was displayed to good effect, for the attention it aroused brought Walter Chrysler the offer of a

$5 million loan from a banking syndicate, which enabled production to get into full swing, and soon Chrysler Sixes were being shipped to agents all over the United States. At a basic price of $1565, the car sold rapidly, for its power and styling gave the owner the feeling that he was driving a far costlier vehicle. In the first twelve months nearly 32,000 Chryslers were sold, creating an industry sales record of $50 million worth of cars. It was the result Walter Chrysler had been waiting for.

In 1925 he bought Maxwell outright, killed off the Maxwell and Chalmers marques and formed the Chrysler Corporation; sales continued to rise, to the extent that, starting from 32nd place in the American industry in 1924, Chrysler had zoomed to fifth place by 1926, moving into fourth slot the following year, when sales reached nearly 200,000. Profits over the three-year period were around $46 million, which enabled Chrysler to finance an ambitious plan of factory modernisation and expansion.

The range now consisted of a four-cylinder model, the 58, introduced in 1925 to succeed the Maxwell, and the luxury Imperial Six, priced at $3095, in addition to the 70; by the spring of 1928, Chrysler was confidently planning the introduction of a new, lower-priced model, the De Soto, but the true mass-production market was still closed to him, for he lacked facilities for casting and forging iron and steel, which meant that the company had to buy in a great many components, and so could not maintain the necessary tight control over costs that would enable them to compete with Ford and Chevrolet.

To provide the necessary factory capacity would mean an investment of $75 million, an intolerable drain on capital reserves which could only result in the proposed low-priced model carrying an unwarranted price supplement, but if Chrysler delayed his expansion plans, he might lose his position in the industry. The only chance seemed to be a merger with another corporation; that was the opportunity presented to him in May 1928 by Clarence Dillon, representing the bankers in control of the Dodge Brothers Company.

For five days, Chrysler and Dillon argued the terms of a takeover, talking twelve hours a day in a suite in New York's Ritz-Carlton Hotel; finally Chrysler agreed to buy Dodge, although the terms of the deal meant that no cash would actually change hands at that time, for $70 million was paid in Chrysler stock, while the new owner agreed to meet the interest payments on Dodge bonds totalling $56 million. To Walter Chrysler, the takeover of Dodge was his greatest single business achievement; he put an able lieutenant, Kaufmann T. Keller, in charge of Dodge, whose factory, reorganised to suit Chrysler philosophies, soon proved a most valuable asset.

At Chrysler's new $1 million engineering laboratory

at Highland Park, Detroit, Zeder was working on the new popular car, which was based on the old Maxwell-inspired Chrysler 54. It was launched in July 1928 as the Plymouth, at a basic price of $670. 'Chrysler has gone into the low-priced field with the throttle wide open,' commented *Time*, and while Plymouth sales were initially hardly likely to set Lake Michigan afire, by May 1929 output was running at 1000 cars daily.

In 1928 Chrysler emphasised the performance and reliability of the six-cylinder models by entering a brace of tourers at Le Mans; although the battle for first place, between Bentley and Stutz, stole all the headlines, the achievement of the two Chryslers in

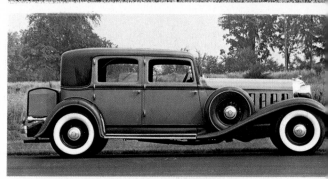

coming third and fourth was none the less remarkable.

By now, the marque had acquired a reputation for innovation, and the narrow-shell 'ribbon' radiators of the 1929 models were widely copied by European makers; internal-expanding hydraulic brakes were a further feature of the range.

For 1931, however, there was a new look: styling was obviously inspired by the long, low look of the L29 Cord, as was the gently-vee'd radiator shell. Two new straight-eights, the 40–125 hp Imperial 6.3-litre and the 29–80 bhp 3.9-litre, were introduced, in conjunction with the established 4.4-litre Model 70 and the economy 2.6-litre Light Six model. The three larger cars had four-speed 'silent-third' gearboxes.

Research and experiment had always been an important facet of the Chrysler Corporation's activities, but at the height of the Depression, Walter Chrysler proposed closing down the research department as an economy measure. However, an ex-Ford engineer, Harold Hicks, who joined Chrysler's research team in 1932, had been carrying out streamlining experiments which proved that altering the bodywork of a car to give a smoother airflow could raise top speed from 83 to 98 mph *and* cut fuel consumption.

Told of this, Chrysler is reported to have remarked: 'Well, if that's what research will do, we must always have research'.

It was research which was responsible for features such as the flexible 'Floating Power' engine mountings of the 1932 models, which also had automatic clutches and freewheels, while the announcement of synchromesh in 1933 was followed by automatic overdrive for 1934. Research also led to the introduction, in 1934, of the controversial Airflow range. Carl Breer had reportedly found, by wind-tunnel tests, that the average car of the early 1930s was more efficient, aerodynamically, going backwards—so he set out to design a 'back-to-front' car. The result was a technical success—and a commercial flop.

The Airflow had a wide, fully streamlined body whose steel-tube frame was welded to the chassis frame, while forward mounting of the engine reversed

CHRYSLER CORPORATION

Top: Chryslers have always been among the most popular of American cars. This is the Chrysler 300C of 1957. Like most American cars of that period it featured pointed tail fins

Centre: the 1966 Chrysler 300 hardtop used a 6.4-litre V8 engine producing 330 bhp at 4800 rpm

Bottom: Chrysler 300 V8 coupé hardtop of 1969

Opposite page, from top to bottom:

1934 Airflow Imperial coupé

1941 Windsor sedan

1938 Custom Imperial sedan

the traditional concept of weight distribution by putting 55 per cent of the car's weight on the front axle; long springs were intended to give a 'floating' ride.

However, the front-end styling proved to be too radical a step for the customers to take, although the Corporation's more conventional models, which shared the Airflow's full-width styling with spatted rear wheels from the scuttle back, apparently sold well!

So, for 1936, a dummy vee-bonnet was fitted to the Airflow range. The range was shelved after 1937, but technical progress continued under the skin of the other models with the adoption of independent front suspension in 1937, and of steering-column gearchange and optional fluid drive in 1939.

While the Airflow fiasco is so well remembered, it was no more than a mild ripple in the smooth progress of Chrysler's corporate success. Indeed, in 1933, the Chrysler group overtook Ford to move into second place behind Chevrolet in total sales, a position it was to hold until 1950.

With the company he had founded ten years before firmly established, and with the outstanding debts, incurred at the time of the Dodge takeover, fully paid, Walter P. Chrysler retired; he died in 1940. He was succeeded as president of the corporation by K. T. Keller, who held the post until 1950.

Chrysler styling had received a facelift in 1942, with

full-width wrap-round grilles, while a new model, the limited-production 'Town and Country', with external wood body framing, restored something of the marque's lost glamour.

Even the continuation of the Town and Country line after the war couldn't disguise the fact that Chrysler body styling was beginning to look a little dated by the end of the 1940s; in 1950 the corporation slipped back into third place.

Again, it was the marque's engineering that drew attention away from its styling shortcomings: in 1951 the company announced its first V8, a 331 cu in hemi-

Left: the 1973 Chrysler Newport Royal. The 6.6-litre V8 engine produced 185 bhp at 3600 rpm

Below: the 1979 model New Yorker Brougham used a V8 of 5.9 litres and was the most expensive of the year's Chrysler models

head with automatic transmission, which was, at the time of its announcement, America's most powerful production car.

Another V8, of 301 cu in, replaced the near-traditional L-head six in the sales catalogues in 1955; that year also saw the new 'Flight Sweep' styling that was to boost sales once more.

Experiments with gas-turbine propulsion, in 1954, led to a limited production run of 50 Plymouth jet cars in 1964 'for evaluation purposes'.

Technical progress continued with the introduction of unit body/chassis construction and alternators in 1960, while the V8 engines, which had become universal on the entire range, became increasingly powerful—and a favourite power unit for European luxury cars like Jensen, Bristol and Facel Vega.

But the real progress of the marque in the 1960s and 1970s was in the field of international expansion. There had been a small assembly operation in Britain since the 1920s, but now Chrysler began to look around for a more ambitious bridgehead.

They found it in the Rootes Group, which owned Humber, Hillman, Singer and Sunbeam; Rootes had embarked on an ambitious expansion programme, and welcomed the injection of a substantial amount of Chrysler capital and technical expertise. The initial agreement was concluded in August 1964; in January 1967 the Rootes board reported that in view of a continuing capital expenditure programme, running into millions of pounds, an even closer association with Chrysler would benefit both the economy and Rootes.

So proposals for Chrysler, which acquired its initial stake for £27 million, to invest a further £20 million were accepted; early in 1973 the group, which had become known as Chrysler United Kingdom Limited in 1970, became a wholly-owned subsidiary of the Chrysler Corporation.

Having been badly hit by economic and labour problems in the early 1970s, and by competition from Japanese imports, Chrysler operations in Europe, notably in Britain and in France (where Chrysler had acquired Simca) had been foundering for some time. The British government stepped in with financial aid for the British operation in 1975, but by 1978 Chrysler's domestic position was such that it had to sell the entire European operation to Peugeot, simply to fund vital investment at home. During 1978 and 1979 Chrysler was also forced to sell its South American and Australasian interests to raise capital. Unfortunately, the Corporation had not learned its lessons too well and when it invested its $450 million, it invested in more big cars. The energy crises which followed made the decision an unmitigated disaster; the investment was wasted and Chrysler was again struggling to survive.

New funding came largely from further bank borrowings (adding to a debt of already $4.4 billion) with government loan guarantees to the tune of $1½ billion. By the end of 1980, Chrysler was in debt for more than the value of the company and by early 1981, stuck with a range of largely unwanted big cars, it had run up losses of over $3 billion. It must have been with some small relief that in the second quarter of 1981 Chrysler showed an $11.6 million profit. Throughout this period, Chrysler was negotiating several possible ties with Peugeot, which might save the day.

As for the cars, the 1981 range comprised the Le Baron (based on the Dodge Aspen), the Cordoba (introduced in 1980), the lumbering Newport and New Yorker, and a revival of the Imperial name, a two-door saloon based on the Cordoba chassis and with up-market trimmings.

The latest forward thinking, now with former Ford man, Lee A. Iacocca at the Chrysler helm, was based around the do-or-die K-cars which would be Chrysler's, Plymouth's and Dodge's lifeline. Chrysler's version was a new Le Baron, a high efficiency, front-wheel-drive competitor for the contemporary Thunderbird and similar cars. It was a well-equipped, small 'big' car, and everything hinged on its success. The Cordoba would continue unchanged for 1982; the New Yorker was a new car based on the older Le Baron and no less than Frank Sinatra added his endorsement to the Signature series of the Imperial.

Chrysler had plans for a two-seater based on a shortened K-car and for a stretched K-car for the mid-1980s, as well as plans to offer a convertible version of the Le Baron in 1982—the first US convertible in more than a decade. There were plans for a 2+2, fastback K-car and for an image-boosting sports car, but all the plans hinged on whether Chrysler could ride out its current financial crisis. Whatever was to happen, Chrysler would not go down without a fight.

Above: the crucial 1982 range included the Le Baron convertible, the first US-built convertible in more than a decade

Right: the 1982 Imperial was based on the earlier Cordoba, continued Chrysler's 'big-car' line and included a Frank Sinatra Signature model

Cord

E. L. Cord founded the Auburn–Cord–Duesenberg empire. All three companies failed, but the Cord legend will live forever

HISTORY RECORDS that Errett Lobban Cord was both a restless character and a gambler who liked to play for high stakes. In his late twenties, he was running a successful car dealership in Chicago in 1924 when the ailing Auburn company offered him $36,000 a year to put the firm back on its feet. Cord demurred, and held out for 20 per cent of any profit he could generate, plus an option to purchase stock. Within a year, the youthful entrepreneur owned Auburn outright. Soon, his empire spread wider afield, to embrace Duesenberg cars, American Airlines, the Stinson aircraft company, the Lycoming engine plant, several coachbuilding companies and the New York Shipbuilding Corporation: a sizeable empire for such a young man.

However, it was not until 1929 that a model line bearing Cord's own name appeared. On paper, at least, the new Cord L-29 looked a worthy running mate for the super-luxury Duesenberg Model J introduced only a few months before. For one thing, it was the first American front-wheel-drive car to reach serious production status.

Moreover, the Cord had been designed by one of the few Americans to have experience of front-wheel-drive technology, Carl Van Ranst, who had worked with Harry Miller, builder of the fast fwd racing cars that had dominated the Indianapolis 500 since 1926. Not surprisingly, the new Cord followed the general layout of the Miller, with a de Dion-type front axle and inboard front brakes. There the resemblance ended, though, for the sleek Cord was a chassis built to carry the finest luxury coachwork and, as well as the more standard open and closed models, custom-built versions were produced by such coachbuilders as Murphy and Hayes.

The car used a similar straight-eight power unit to that of the Auburn 120, with a swept volume of 4934 cc. Instead of being turned round for the fwd installation, the power unit had its crankshaft extended at the front to take the flywheel, making the timing chain inaccessible.

The 125 bhp power unit was said to have the most efficient combustion chamber of its day, and Cord publicity underlined the promise of the overall specification: 'Docile and dignified in town, yet capable of unusual speed on the open road, the Cord commands your attention . . . the principles employed in its front-wheel-drive unit have withstood the rigorous test of racing, whilst its low, sweeping lines suggest amazing acceleration and power.'

The suggestiveness of the styling was not followed through in the vehicle's performance, however: an all-up weight of over 42 cwt, allied to inept ratios in the three-speed gearbox and final drive, limited the maximum speed to a fraction over 80 mph, which the cheaper, less sophisticated Auburn could exceed easily. Acceleration figures, apparently, were ten years behind the times.

Other features hardly likely to endear the L-29 to

the press-on motorists of 1929 were the low-geared steering—four turns from lock to lock—and the gear-lever, which protruded horizontally from the fascia. However, the inboard front brakes kept unsprung weight to a minimum, and handling was said to have been 'incredible', despite the restrictions of a 137½-inch wheelbase.

Price—around $3000—was high, though far from astronomical, and quite a few other specialist models, like Stutz, Marmon, Franklin, Lincoln and Packard, cost a great deal more. But the L-29 had been launched at the worst possible time, for within a few months came the Wall Street Crash, and the purchase of a new and untried luxury car of unorthodox specification was a venture that few well-off Americans were willing to make

The customers, it seems, looked, admired, and went away again. In three years, only 4400 L-29s were sold, and production ended in 1932. It can't have been the

Above: the Cord 812 was introduced in 1937. A supercharger boosted engine power to around 170 bhp. Although the 812 had a top speed of over 100 mph, it failed to revive the flagging fortunes of the Cord empire

Left: a man and his car: designer Gordon Buehrig with a magnificent example of his 1936 Cord 810

styling that let the Cord down, for the new 1930 Chrysler straight-eight copied several of its features, especially the design of the slightly-veed radiator shell. At least one owner, opera star Benjamino Gigli, was so fond of his L-29 that when the new Cord 810 appeared in 1935, he had his car rebodied in the striking style of the later model.

This second car to bear the Cord name was certainly unorthodox in appearance and so different was it from the other cars of 1935, that its designer, Gordon Miller Buehrig, took out a patent for 'a new, original and ornamental design for an automobile'.

Key features of the new Cord were its headlamps,

adapted from Stinson aircraft landing lights, which could be cranked down flush with the pontoon-style front wings, and the streamline nose, with wrap-around louvres replacing the conventional radiator grille. Its shape earned the car the unflattering nickname of 'Coffin-nose Cord'.

Other advanced features listed by Buehrig included the fact that the Cord was the first mass-produced American car to combine front-wheel-drive with independent front suspension (though, surprisingly, the rear suspension used a tubular axle with semi-elliptic springs), twin streamlined tail lights, no running boards, concealed door hinges, a petrol filler beneath a hinged flap, and a rear-hinged bonnet. It had, too, rheostat-controlled instrument lighting, variable speed windscreen wipers, complete sound insulation and a radio as standard. The box-section chassis formed a rigid unit with the all-metal body.

The power unit was once again a 125 bhp Lycoming engine, but this time it was a V8 with a swept volume of 4730 cc. The mechanical layout of the car, it was reported, was the work of August Duesenberg himself; indeed, the car was originally planned as a Duesenberg model, and was intended as the revolutionary shot in the arm that would save the by now ailing Auburn-Cord-Duesenberg empire from collapse. However, Erret Lobban Cord was seemingly so impressed by its sleek looks that he decreed that the car should bear his name.

But his blow-hot, blow-cold enthusiasm retarded development and, when the decision was made to launch the new car at the New York Motor Show in

November 1935, corners had to be cut to build the 100 cars that qualified a production model for entry in the exhibition.

To save time and money, only two dies were used for the doors on four-door models: right front and left rear and, because a big enough body press to turn out the roof as a single unit was not available, the panel had to be welded together from a number of mouldings. Interior handles were acquired cheaply at a bankruptcy sale, and fitted with showy, new round plastic knobs. Instruments were a job lot, too, but Buehrig devised an aircraft-style dashboard that showed them off to stunning effect.

Cosmetic jobs of this magnitude were not new to Gordon Buehrig, for he had created the 1935 Auburn speedster, largely round modified 1928 body dies.

All Buehrig's skills were nullified by annoying mechanical setbacks, and, although the 100 cars were ready externally for the 1935 New York Show, they lacked the complex front-wheel-drive unit, which was still undergoing development.

Unfortunately, as it turned out, the car was an immediate success, and many orders were taken at the show, with delivery promised for Christmas. After all, the initial production target was around 1000 cars a month, and surely the transmissions would be ready soon. They were not, however, and all the impatient customers got on 25 December was a tiny scale model Cord on a marble slab.

Although the advanced specification of the transmission—preselected gears controlled electrically by a tiny gearlever moving in a miniature gate on the

Top: the first of the production model Cords was the L-29. The car was powered by a straight-eight, 4934 cc engine which produced 125 bhp. The L-29 was greatly handicapped, however, by an overall weight of 42 cwt resulting in a top speed of only 80 mph

Above: in 1936 Cord presented this experimental 935 Limousine model with austere coachwork by Le Baron. It was, however, never put into mass-production

Detroit. The body dies for the revolutionary 810/812 Cord were acquired by another moribund motor company, Hupmobile, who adapted the shape to their rear-driven running gear in an attempt to stay in business. The poison was still in the system, though, and by 1940 Hupp, too, were at their last gasp. They had built the cars in the Graham factory and after Hupmobile expired, Graham tried the same trick, calling their 'Cord' the Hollywood. It, too, proved a failure. The reason, said Buehrig, was that the dies weren't designed for mass production.

The Cord dies were eventually thrown out as scrap, and found their way to Japan, but the Nissan company,

steering column, plus an overdrive fourth—promised great things, the unit turned out to be a lemon. Even when the system was properly set up, there was an annoying timelag between pressing down the clutch pedal and the automatic engagement of the selected ratio by a complex arrangement of electromagnets and vacuum-operated diaphragms. Moreover, early production models suffered from obscure transmission maladies and they were also prone to boiling-up, for the water passages in the cylinder heads were too small, and the aluminium heads tended to crack under stress.

In the first year of production, only 1174 Cords were sold—about a twelfth of the anticipated figure. It was the car's mechanical shortcomings that had caused the situation, rather than its unorthodox styling, which was widely admired.

By that time, however, Errett Lobban Cord was losing interest. In 1936, he had sold most of the major holdings in his empire for $4 million. Hardly surprisingly, sales continued to slide. Even the introduction of the 100 mph-plus 812 Cord in 1937 failed to save the situation, even though the new model, in which a supercharger boosted engine output to around 170 bhp, boasted huge external chrome-plated exhaust-pipes of which any enthusiast would have been proud.

By the end of 1937, the Cord saga was over. The marque's sponsor retired to Nevada to concentrate on his new loves, radio and television.

By 1938, the receiver had been called in, and the once-great Auburn-Cord-Duesenberg group was sold for what it would fetch to one Dallas E. Winslow of

who had bought them, hadn't the heart to put the hammer to them, so they remained, reverently crated, in the Nissan warehouse right through the war, and at least into the 1960s.

However, the Cord story didn't end in that Tokyo warehouse. Seven years later, what remained of the A-C-D empire (the names, designs and parts department) was purchased from Winslow by Glenn Pray, a teacher from Tulsa Oklahoma who, in 1954, announced the rebirth of the Cord as an 8/10th scale replica powered by a modified Chevrolet Corvette engine. Again, there were teething troubles, again the production figures weren't met, and again the receiver was called in. Between 1964 and 1967 only 85 cars had been produced. In 1967, aircraft manufacturer Harry L. Seale of Dallas headed a group which acquired the new Cord company's assets, and planned to get production under way again, but the price had risen to $6995 from the $4700 quoted by Pray, and the venture only lasted a year. In 1968, yet another new owner, SAMCO, came on the scene. However, the vehicle they offered was a Cord in name only, for both the front-wheel-drive and the retractable headlights were abandoned in favour of mechanical conventionality, though it must be admitted that the project outlived both Pray's and Seale's attempt to revive the marque, surviving into the 1970s.

Errett Lobban Cord died in January 1974, long after he had broken all his connections with the company which bore his name. However, it is unlikely that the companies which formed his empire, Auburn, Cord and Duesenberg, will ever be forgotten.

Above: the coffin-nosed Cord 810. Introduced in 1935, the Gordon Buehrig-designed 810 was powered by a 4739 cc Lycoming V8 engine. It was the first mass-produced American car to combine front-wheel drive with independent front suspension

Dodge

John and Horace Dodge liked nothing more than a stiff drink and a good fight. Yet, they were astute businessmen

THE SUPERINTENDENT OF THE engineering works at Windsor, Ontario glowered at the two young workmen. 'We've come for the job,' said the elder and more domineering of the two.

'We need only one man,' said the superintendent.

The retort was swift. 'We're brothers and we always work together. If you haven't room for two of us, then neither will start. That's that!' The Dodge brothers, John Francis and Horace Elsin, were like that. Though there was four years' difference in their ages—John was born in 1864, Horace in 1868—they were as inseparable as if they were twins. Both were red-

Above: the first Dodge built was this four-seater tourer, powered by a four-cylinder, 3½-litre engine

Right, top to bottom
1918 Dodge coupé

John and Horace Dodge pictured in Detroit in 1914

1918 Dodge hardtop

headed and both were quick tempered. They were, it was said, always ready to quarrel with anybody else or each other.

John was the natural leader, pushy and talkative; Horace was usually quiet, tolerant and slow-moving. They had left their birthplace, Niles, Michigan, in the early 1880s, determined to become engineers. They found work, and gained valuable experience, in machine shops in Detroit and Windsor; their idea of relaxation, once the week's work was over, was to spend Saturday night in a favourite saloon in the roughest part of downtown Detroit drinking themselves to a standstill.

One night, John ordered the bar owner to climb on to a table and dance. When the man refused, John pulled out a revolver and repeated his request. This time the man obeyed, while John hurled glasses at the mirror behind the bar. However, once he had sobered up, he happily paid for the damage.

In 1899, the brothers organised the Evans and

Dodge Bicycle Company in Windsor to produce a four-point-bearing bicycle of their own invention. When a Canadian group made a successful takeover bid, the brothers moved back to Detroit, where they established one of the best machine shops in the Middle West. Order, cleanliness and efficiency were its hallmarks and soon they were making components for the infant motor industry.

When, in February 1903, Henry Ford asked them to produce the chassis for his new venture, the Ford Motor Company, the Dodges were already considering substantial offers from the Oldsmobile and Great Northern companies, but there seemed to be far greater profits to be made from the new company so, on 28 February, the two brothers signed a formal agreement with Henry Ford to provide 650 chassis for Ford's first season of production.

The brothers undertook to deliver the chassis to Ford's assembly plant on Mack Avenue, Detroit, at a cost of $250 each—a total of $162,500. In return, they would receive the first payment of $5000 on 15 March, provided that they could show that they had invested that sum in equipment to service the Ford contract. If the investment was then doubled, they would get the next $5000 a month later, plus another $5000 when the first batch of chassis was delivered. This $15,000 was to pay for the first sixty engines delivered, the next forty would be paid for in cash as they were completed, and thereafter there would be a regular payment every fortnight.

It was an arrangement that suited both parties; the Dodges might not have had much formal education, but they were shrewd businessmen, and had known Ford for several years.

Within a short while, the Dodge works were engaged virtually one hundred per cent on building Ford chassis, employing a staff of 150. Deliveries started in early July, and soon Ford was assembling fifteen complete Model A cars a day. The Dodges employed their staff on piecework rates, which resulted in some slipshod workmanship, but, as the brothers had invested $10,000 in the Ford company, and as John had been made a director, they soon rectified this state of affairs, and sales forged ahead.

When Ford introduced the Model N in November 1905, it was announced that the mechanism for the new car would be made entirely within the new Ford factory on Piquette Avenue and that the Dodge brothers would make the chassis for the larger Ford cars only.

The brothers were now given 350 shares each in the Ford Motor Company, and John became Vice-President. However, as time went on, the independent Dodges became more and more dissatisfied with the prices they were receiving for the transmissions, rear axles, drive shafts and forgings that they were supplying to Ford. They were worried, too, that Ford might suddenly cancel their contract and leave them high and dry. By 1912, they were determined on a course of action: they would become independent of Ford, and build their own cars. In August 1913, John Dodge resigned from the board of the Ford Motor Company, though he maintained friendly relations with Henry Ford, and the brothers continued as shareholders. In fact, the 2000 shares that the brothers now held provided a large proportion of the backing for the new venture. They were receiving over a million dollars a year in dividends, and their properties were estimated to be worth $30–$40 million.

The Dodge car was unveiled on 14 October 1914; it was produced in the new Dodge factory at Hamtramck, Detroit, which had been built on a site acquired in 1910. The car was a conventionally designed four-cylinder model of $3\frac{1}{2}$ litres capacity, with a power output of 25 bhp. There were two distinctive features: the gear-change operated 'back-to-front', and the 12-volt electrical system incorporated a North-East dynastarter unit which automatically restarted the engine, should it stall with the ignition switched on.

Thanks to the company's long association with Ford, the Dodge name was already well-known throughout the American auto trade, and soon more than 22,000 dealers across the States were clamouring for agencies for the new car.

Below:
1924 15 cwt Dodge van

1930 Eight DC

1936 D2 coupé

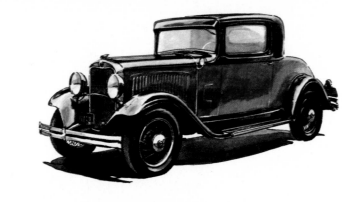

Right: the Dodge
Coronet D30 of 1949

Above: enough to turn anyone's head, the elaborately styled V8 Dodge of 1959

Right, top to bottom: The 1961 Dodge Polara model. Note the pillarless side-windows which were so popular during the early 1960s.

The 1963 version of the Polara showing the more sombre lines of the later model

Another styling feature that became popular with American motorists was the 'fastback', shown here to perfection on the 1966 Dodge Charger

The marque's rise was meteoric: by 1916, annual production was America's fourth biggest, with over 70,000 cars delivered. A big boost to Dodge sales came that year when General 'Black Jack' Pershing ordered 250 Dodge staff cars to help him in his campaign against the Mexican bandit, Pancho Villa. Villa subsequently returned the compliment by adopting the Dodge as his official car—but he was killed while riding in it in 1923.

John and Horace Dodge may have been illiterate, but they coined a word to describe the Dodge's performance that became an everyday term: dependability. In 1920, the Dependable Dodge was second only to the Model T in sales. By this time, the link with Ford had been finally severed: alarmed by Henry Ford's insistence, in 1916, that he would henceforth ignore dividends altogether, except for purely nominal payments, the Dodges brought a suit to protect their income. It ended in Ford buying them out—and all the other shareholders in the Ford Motor Company—for a total of $106 million, of which the Dodge Brothers' share was $25 million. However, although the case was hard fought, personal relationships between the Dodges and Henry Ford remained friendly and free of bitterness.

A major breakthrough came in 1916, when Budd all-steel tourer coachwork was adopted as a standard feature (a few all-steel saloons were also built). However, this was not the first time that this construction had been used on a production vehicle, for BSA and Stoneleigh in Britain had featured all-steel coachwork as early as 1911.

In life, John and Horace Dodge had been inseparable; in death, too, they were not parted, for in 1920 they died of pneumonia within a few months of each other. Ownership of the company passed to their widows, with Frederick J. Haynes, formerly Vice-President and General Manager, taking over the management of the firm, which was now making 1000 cars a day.

This situation continued until 1925, when the New York bankers Dillon, Read & Company took over Dodge for a reputed $146 million, of which $50 million represented goodwill, written down in the Dodge accounts as being worth $1!

The company's sole product was still the original 3½-litre four (now available either as a car or as a truck), although the basic design had been steadily

Left: the two-door Dodge Dart of 1960 featured heavy bumpers, tail-fins, pillarless side windows and a 4½-litre engine

Below: 1959 saw the tail-fin craze reach its climax. Typical of this styling trend was the Dodge Custom Royal of that year. This model also featured enormous tail lights and heavy chrome-plated bumpers

Opposite page, top right: a 1970 Dodge Challenger convertible. Various engine options were offered, ranging in power from 330 to 425 bhp

Opposite page, bottom right: the car which became a cult symbol in America, the Dodge Super Bee. It featured a V8, 430 bhp engine

Below: the 1974 Dodge Charger SE. Although still powered by the V8 engine, the car had become more refined than earlier models with the same name

refined over the years. The 1923 models, for example, had pioneered the stop lamp and the anti-theft lock—fitted, in this instance, on the gearbox, but four-wheel-brakes seem never to have been available on the Dodges imported into England, and were apparently only fitted for the last few months of the model's life in America during 1928. Although the company boasted of its 'sound financial standing, which permits uninterrupted development and adherence to the policy of constant improvement', its unadventurous marketing policy had brought it to the brink of financial disaster by 1927. Clarence Dillon of Dillon, Read & Company approached Walter Chrysler—and found him receptive to buying Dodge. After days of haggling, the two agreed on terms: Chrysler was to acquire Dodge for $70 million in stock plus the interest payments on Dodge bonds, worth $56 million. The merger, sneered one financier, was 'like a minnow swallowing a whale', but Chrysler always claimed: 'The greatest thing I ever did was to buy Dodge'.

He had acquired one of the world's largest and best-organised motor factories: the Hamtramck plant now covered 58 acres and employed 2000 people. It was a move essential to his continued expansion. Minutes after the contract giving Chrysler control was signed, his Chief Production Manager, Kaufmann T. Keller, had huge canvas signs reading 'Chrysler Corporation, Dodge Division' hung over the entrance gates, then marched in to take control—on 30 July 1928.

A new six-cylinder model, the Senior Six, had been introduced in 1927; its specification included four-wheel-hydraulic brakes and a seven-bearing crankshaft with pressure lubrication, and it was to this model that Walter Chrysler looked for the company's future expansion. The old four-cylinder model was rapidly pensioned off, and replaced by a new cheap six, the Victory, fitted with a short-stroke version of the Senior's power unit; in 1930, an even smaller six, the 19.8 hp 2.6-litre, appeared. At the extremely reasonable price in Britain of £297 for a saloon, it represented remarkable value for money.

At the same time, Dodge brought out a 26.4 hp straight-eight, with a power unit similar to that of the contemporary Chrysler; this model was only cata-

Right: the 1974 Dodge Dart Sport. By 1974, the styling of American cars had become much more sophisticated with smooth flowing lines. The Dart was the smallest of the 1974 Dodge models excluding, of course, the Japanese Mitsubishi Colt, later marketed in America as the Dodge Colt

Far right above: top of the 1974 model range was the Monaco Brougham powered by a bewildering variety of engine options

Far right centre: the 1977 Monaco intermediates were available in this two-door hardtop form, among several other variations

Far right below: the Aspen range saved Dodge from an uncertain future with its introduction in 1976. The 1977 range included the sporting R/T two-door coupé

logued until 1933. By that time, the Victory and Senior Six had acquired styling similar to that of the Model B Ford. These cars, claimed the Dodge copywriters, had 'every modern feature, not merely one'. The specification included automatic clutch, easy-change, silent gearbox, freewheeling, hydraulic brakes, non-burning, non-pitting valve seat inserts, self-oiling springs, Airwheel tyres, double drop X-type frame and a welded, monopiece steel body.

The virtues of the coachwork seemed a little ominous, however: the company said 'A Dodge steel body may be dented, it cannot be shattered—nor is there any wood to feed a sudden flame'.

Nevertheless, Dodge was once again the industry's fourth biggest manufacturer, with sales of 86,000 in 1933. Despite their close links with Chrysler, Dodge never adopted the controversial Airflow styling entirely, although their 1935 models followed the more orthodox vee-bonneted Airstream look.

For 1936, the Senior Six acquired, as standard, the new Chrysler automatic overdrive transmission, in which a centrifugal clutch brought in the overdrive top-gear when the car was cruising at speeds over 45 mph; rationalisation had by now proceeded to the

point where the Dodge had precious little of its former individuality remaining, and few changes other than new body styling and independent front suspension were made prior to World War II.

There was little to choose between the Chrysler Corporation marques in post-war days, either; indeed, some Plymouth models were sold as Dodges in export markets, and all shared a common bodyshell, introduced in 1949. The faithful old L-head six was still the Dodge's power unit, although in 1953 the option of the new Red Ram V8 was offered—and taken up by more than half the customers. What had been a relatively simple model range suddenly became highly complex: the 1954 line-up comprised eight basic series, two wheelbase lengths and two power units, all mixed according to choice.

Chrysler Corporation cars were dramatically restyled in 1955, although the same power-unit options continued. Larger engines and push-button automatic transmission made their appearance on the 1956 line, and a new four-door hardtop, the Lancer, made its debut. Powered normally by one of Dodge's V8 power plants, it could also be ordered with the side-valve six

Ride comfort was improved on 1957 models by the introduction of 'Torsion-Aire' torsion-bar front suspension plus oversize 14-inch tyres. The range now consisted of the Coronet, Royal, Suburban, Sierra and Kingsway, mostly with the Red Ram V8, although two six-cylinder models were still listed.

In 1958, the Chrysler Corporation produced its 25-millionth vehicle and, that year, Dodge cars underwent a fairly comprehensive facelift, gaining wrap-around, compound-curved windscreens and quadruple headlights in a restyled grille. Under the bonnet, a major innovation was the option of an electronically controlled fuel-injection system, which boosted the Red Ram's power output to 333 bhp. More than seventy per cent of the sales that year were of the Dodge Coronet range, and an astonishing 96.4 per cent of all cars produced were fitted with automatic transmission. Indicative of the driving priorities of the average American family motorist were two other statistics: 62.5 per cent of the cars produced had power-assisted steering, yet only 34 per cent could boast power braking.

By now, the side-valve six was definitely on the way out: only one 1959 model offered it, and that was the rock-bottom of the range, the Coronet MD1-L. Within a year, it disappeared completely.

Styling was at its nadir in 1959: tailfins had been growing in size throughout the decade and now, under the name of 'Swept-Wing Styling', they became positively overpowering. Twin radio aerials and juke-box-style rear lights completed the aesthetic mess. Top of the range was the Custom Royal four-door hardtop, which was available with 305, 320 or 345 bhp V8 power units, while the Sierra station wagon catered for the 'Quiverfulls' by offering six- or nine-passenger versions which were also available with various engine options.

In 1961, the Lancer name was revived for a new compact, this time based on the Plymouth Valiant, but the company's general trend during the 1960s was to build bigger. Its late-1960s 'compact', the Dart, boasted a 4½-litre engine. This model was backed up by the larger Coronets with six or eight-cylinder engines with overhead valves, plus the 6.3-litre Polara and 7.2-litre Monaco.

Mindful that it was missing out on the sub-compact market, the company concluded a deal in 1971 to import the Mitsubishi Colt sub-compact from Japan. This model became steadily more Dodge and less Japanese, until it was given a complete restyling in 1974.

1976 saw some Dodge engines equipped with a computer controlled spark timing device called 'Lean Burn' which cut pollution and fuel consumption.

Also in 1976 Dodge introduced their own compact car, the Aspen. It was available in a range of body styles, including a station wagon, and with a choice of straight-six or V8 engines. The new models were an instant success, giving Dodge a 15.1 per cent share of the domestic compact market. Following on the heels of the Aspen, in 1978, came the Dodge Omni sub-compact which was a badge-engineered version of the Chrysler Horizon. The engine was a miniscule, by American standards, transverse, four-cylinder, 1714 cc unit, and the car featured front-wheel drive. The Omni was yet another reminder that the European and American industries were moving ever closer.

In the short term the success of the new range of compacts rescued Dodge from an uncertain future in Chrysler's empire. In 1979 the rest of the Dodge line-up consisted of the four larger cars, the Diplomat, the St Regis, the Magnum, and of course, the Charger,

83

which was far removed from the sub-compacts with its 5.2 or 5.9-litre V8 engine.

For all the success of the Omni, the parent Chrysler organisation was in big trouble and the future of Dodge was all-important. In 1981 the much vaunted and desperately needed Chrysler K-car made its bow in the Dodge range, as the Dodge Aries. This sub-compact replacement for the Aspen had been a lengthy four years in the making. It was typically new-generation American: small, transverse-engined and front-wheel-drive, efficient with fuel and space and well equipped, in the image of the imports which it must conquer. The Aries was launched in three body styles, two- and four-door saloons and a five-door station wagon, each with a basic 2.2-litre, four-cylinder engine (Chrysler's first all-new engine in some twenty years) or an optional, Mitsubishi-built, 2.6-litre Silent Shaft engine. Four-speed manual transmission was paired with the 2.2 and three-speed auto with the Mitsubishi four. The car was well received by the motoring press, which must have allowed Chrysler a little relief, but then the motoring media always did like cars with a relatively lively performance. With a 96 mph top speed, 0–60 mph in $11\frac{1}{2}$ seconds and crisp handling the Aries *did* fit that bill.

It joined a range which, for 1981, comprised the Omni, the highly regarded Colt, a slightly updated Challenger, the long-in-the-tooth Diplomat mid-size, the Mirada and the Newport-lookalike, St Regis.

The St Regis survived only for another season, as fairly widespread changes were made for the approach of 1982. In 1981 Chrysler had been right at the forefront of the domestic industry's corporate average fuel economy (CAFE) regulations, with a creditable 26.4 mpg. For 1982, it was proposing to retain its lead, with a target of 27.5 mpg. Dodge, with its range of reasonably sized offerings, was helping the averages. The latest Colt came as a five-door hatchback and led the way in the fuel economy stakes, as well as being a very popular little car purely on the basis of being fun to drive. Its Mitsubishi-built brother, the Challenger, also gained a few more miles from a barrel thanks to a change in gearing. The Omni, another car which everyone seemed to love even if not everyone wanted to buy, was treated to some rather gaudy paint options as if to remind people that it really was a racy little number. It needed no other improvement to prove its point. A Dodge version of the K-car-based Chrysler Le Baron, the Dodge 400, also joined the range and the Diplomat finally re-emerged, a more svelte creation, as another Aspen reincarnation. Bringing up the end of the line was the ever more macho Mirada and the Aries, which celebrated the end of a reasonably successful first season by minor updating of the suspension and improvements in sound deadening.

The future of Dodge really depended on the ultimate survival of Chrysler, and, to a large extent, vice versa. The fighting spirit of the Dodge brothers was still around in the company but it remained to be seen whether it would be as successful in the 1980s as it had been in the 1880s.

Right: the Aries was all new for 1981. It was a fuel efficient, 2.2-litre, front-wheel-drive K-car, which offered the 2.6-litre Mitsubishi 'Silent Shaft' engine as an option and many extras as standard

Left: Chrysler's connections with the Japanese Mitsubishi company put the excellent Colt into the Dodge range. For 1982 a five-door version was available alongside the three-door shown here

Below: the Omni hatchback, sister to the long-running four-door Omni saloon which was in the vanguard of the domestic front-wheel-drive market

Duesenberg

In the beginning, the Duesenberg was hampered by its foreign-sounding name, which later became immortal

DUESENBERG—THE VERY NAME has an arrogant ring to it, totally befitting what is arguably the finest motor car to have been built in America. Yet, alongside the luxury cars for which they are now chiefly remembered, the Duesenberg brothers, Fred and August, produced some of the most successful racing cars of their day. However, although racing may have improved the breed, there is evidence that it did not much impress those rich enough to buy a Duesenberg.

The Duesenberg family originated in Lippe, Germany, and emigrated to America in the mid 1880s. As teenagers in Iowa in the 1890s, the two brothers started a bicycle business—they had received little formal education—and sometime around 1900 are reputed to have built a clip-on motor unit for one of their cycles. Fred was a natural engineer, and left the cycle shop to join the Thomas B. Jeffery Company at Kenosha, Wisconsin, where they were just switching over from Rambler bicycles to Rambler cars. In 1906, the brothers were in business together again, at Des Moines, Iowa, building a 24 hp, flat-twin car with an epicyclic gearbox and chain final-drive. Finance was provided by a lawyer named Mason, from whom the car took its name.

In 1910, Fred Duesenberg designed a racing-car engine whose horizontal valves were operated from the low-mounted camshaft by long rocker arms known as 'walking beams'. In that year, too, the company

Left: one of the last cars made before the collapse of the company in 1938 was this supercharged Le Baron Dual Cowl Phaeton of 1937

Below: showing how little the range changed in eight years, this Dual Cowl of 1929 is very similar to the later model; this car sold for $14,000

Above: actor Gary Cooper in his long wheelbase Derham 'Tourster' Phaeton, one of Gordon Buehrig's classic designs

Right: a Duesenberg Model J convertible tourer. Most Model Js came on the standard wheelbase lengths of 11 ft 10½ in (short) or 12 ft 9½ in (long), although one model was produced on an enormous 14 ft 10 in wheelbase

Right: Erret Lobban Cord could never be accused of soft-selling his products, as this example of Duesenberg advertising, liberally sprinkled with superlatives, shows

changed its name, being taken over by one Fred Maytag (later well known as a washing machine manufacturer), although the racing engines were known as Mason-Duesenbergs up to 1914, implying that Mr Mason (whose son George drove one of these cars at Indianapolis that year) was still backing the racing side of the business.

In 1914, though, the brothers cut loose from their sponsors, and set up in business at St Paul, Minneapolis, building racing cars which were largely similar to the Mason-Duesenbergs, except for a high exhaust pipe curling out of the top of the bonnet; breathing was improved on some 1916 engines by fitting four valves per cylinder instead of two. Many leading drivers raced Duesenbergs during this period—Eddie Rickenbacker, Ralph Mulford, Willie Haupt and Tommy Milton—and by 1916 the marque's reputation was such that the brothers were chosen to produce Bugatti sixteen-cylinder aero-engines for the US Government. They moved into a new factory at Elizabeth, New Jersey, but only 400 or so Bugatti engines were built in 1918–19, before the project was abandoned due to the power unit's unreliability.

The Duesenbergs sold their factory to John North Willys, and went back to building cars. At first, they worked in the garage of Fred's home in Elizabeth, then they rented a local workshop, where a new power unit, obviously inspired by their work on the Bugatti U-16 engine (in effect, two straight-eights side by side), was developed. This was a straight-eight of 4.26 litres, which was fitted into a modified racing-car chassis; Tommy Milton drove this car in the 1919 Indianapolis 500, retiring after 49 laps with a broken con-rod.

DUESENBERG

The old four-cylinder, walking-beam design was sold to Rochester Motors, who produced these power units for such assembled quality cars as the Roamer (which had a fake Rolls radiator), the ReVere and the Biddle, until 1923–24.

Duesenberg built a series of straight-eight racing cars for the 1920 season, then began work on two new

and exciting projects. The first was a sixteen-cylinder car with two 4.9-litre straight-eights mounted side-by-side; Tommy Milton set up an unofficial world land speed record of 156.05 mph with this car at Daytona in April 1920. More important, though, was the company's first passenger car, which had a 4.26-litre engine similar to the racing units (but with two valves per cylinder instead of three). This was completed in time to be displayed at the 1920 New York Salon.

This was the first production straight-eight on the American market, and also the first to feature four-wheel hydraulic braking. In the former respect, it was three years ahead of the rest of the market, while the brake layout was even more advanced. Valves were operated by a single overhead camshaft, and the engine design made extensive use of aluminium; it also pioneered alloy pistons in America, though cast-iron units were available for conservative buyers.

Only a handful of prototypes were built before Duesenberg moved into an impressive new factory, in Indianapolis, which could cope with all aspects of car production. Contrary to contemporary American practice, the Duesenberg brothers built their own engines and most other mechanical components; the three-bearing crankshaft was notably rigid, and carefully balanced to eliminate vibration.

At the time of the straight-eight's introduction, the racing models had already established 66 American records on the Sheepshead Bay Board Speedway, and the passenger version of the racer was naturally billed as 'The World's Champion Automobile—built to out-class, outrun and outlast any car on the road'. It followed that much testing of the production models was carried out on the Indianapolis Speedway, including stunts such as a three-week non-stop run (apart from halts to change tyres and drivers and to refuel) covering 18,032 miles, and a simulated high-speed dash across the United States without stopping (the car was refuelled on the move but, in fact, had to stop twice to change tyres). The 3155-mile run took just 50 hours 21 minutes, an average speed of 62.63 mph, and a remarkable achievement for a completely standard car with relatively weighty five-passenger touring coach-work on a normal chassis.

Even more impressive was the marque's victory in the 1921 French Grand Prix, a feat which has not so far been repeated by any other American manufacturer. Jimmy Murphy's car, aided by its four-wheel braking, beat the best cars and drivers that Europe had to offer on the Le Mans circuit: despite the poor road surface and flying stones, Murphy averaged 78.1 mph over the 322-mile race—10 mph faster than the quickest pre-war average and, indeed, faster than many French GPs over the following decade (for instance, Caracciola's Mercedes won the 1935 French GP at 77.42 mph over a similar distance on the far smoother Montlhéry circuit).

However, this victory, and other track achievements such as the Duesenberg first place at Indianapolis in 1924 (plus the marque's many other successes, which culminated in a second Indianapolis win and the AAA Championship in 1926), failed to have any great effect on passenger car sales. For one thing, the marque's Teutonic-sounding name counted against it in the years immediately following the Armistice; more importantly, while to European motorists a racing

Above: a fine specimen of the Model J, this being the convertible roadster version. The Model J had a top speed of 116 mph and its chassis price was 8500 dollars. The car was fitted with hydraulic brakes all round and much of the body was made of aluminium. On this chassis, many of America's finest coachbuilders constructed their greatest bodies and often the total price of a completed car was over 20,000 dollars

pedigree was indicative of high engineering standards and a good road performance, to the Americans rich enough to afford a Duesenberg, racing cars meant noise, smell and smoke, and though the Duesenberg Straight Eight was guilty of none of these vices, it was credited with them by association.

Sales, therefore, were not as good as they should have been; although poor body styling is a criticism sometimes levelled against the 1921–26 Duesenbergs, they were as good in this respect as most of their contemporaries, the plain fact of the matter being that American coachbuilders of the 1920s lacked the flair of their European counterparts, both in overall conception and in the treatment of details and accessories.

Also, Fred Duesenberg was an engineer first and a financier a long way after. He could, it is said, work out the dimensions of key components, like connecting rods, by eye, and arrive within one or two thousandths of an inch of the carefully stress-calculated computations of engineers with more formal training. What is more, he fully expected every member of his staff to work the same long hours as himself.

Small wonder, then, that the marque's *succès d'éstime* was not reflected in its bank balance, and that Straight Eight production totalled no more than 500–650 units in the model's six-year life. In 1926, the company was taken over by that up-and-coming entrepreneur, Erret Lobban Cord (he died at the beginning of 1974), who immediately instituted a programme of styling changes. Wisely, however, he left Fred and August in charge of engineering, and all he insisted on was that the brothers should produce a new car which, in terms of style, engineering and sheer panache, should rival the best the world had to offer. In December 1928, they revealed the result of their labours to the public—it was, they claimed, 'The World's Finest Car', the Model J Duesenberg. Its 6.9-litre power unit was built by another Cord subsidiary, Lycoming, well known as suppliers of proprietary engines; however, this was no off-the-shelf side-valve six, but a race-bred straight-eight with twin overhead camshafts operating four valves per cylinder. Claimed output was 265 bhp, twice that of any other American passenger car. The model J had a top speed in the region of 116 mph and its chassis price was $8,500.

The engine was rubber-mounted in a chassis of exceptional rigidity; frame side-members were $8\frac{1}{2}$ inches deep, and there were six cross-members plus diagonal bracing. Of course, much use was made of aluminium, and the car had hydraulic brakes all round (with variable servo assistance from 1929 on). Hardly in line with the best European practice were the long, willowy central gear lever and handbrake, but the standard instrumentation was obviously designed to impress the most gadget-conscious of owners. Across the somewhat spartan fascia were scattered 150 mph speedometer, altimeter, barometer, brake-pressure gauge, tachometer, ammeter, oil-pressure gauge, combination clock and stop-clock, and a complex set of lights operated by a train of timing wheels which drove a device known as the 'timing box' under the bonnet. Every 75 miles, the box automatically lubricated all the chassis greasing points; a red light glowed when it was working, a green one when its lubricant reservoir needed refilling. Every 700 miles, a third light exhorted the owner to have the engine oil changed while, at 1400 mile intervals, the fourth light acted as an *aide-memoire* to have the battery water level checked at the nearest service station.

On this chassis, the finest coachbuilders of America and Europe—Murphy, Derham, Bohmann & Schwartz, Hibbard & Darrin, Barker, Letourneur & Marchand,

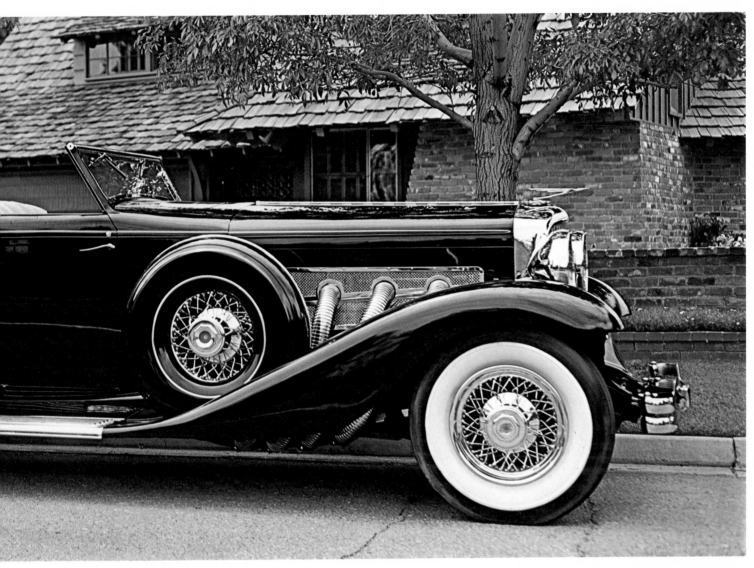

Graber, D'Ieteren Frères, Gurney Nutting and Weymann—constructed their finest bodies, bringing the total cost of the car, as the model name of one convertible phaeton version reminded the world, to 'Twenty Grand', give or take a few thousand dollars.

Most Model Js came on the standard wheelbase lengths of 11 ft 10½ in (short) or 12 ft 9½ in (long), though Father Divine, an evangelist, ordered his Duesenberg with a whopping 14 ft 10 in wheelbase, and graced it with the name *Throne Car*.

The old Straight Eight engine wasn't entirely abandoned after the Model J appeared: the introduction of the 'Junk Formula' for stock engines, at Indianapolis in 1930, saw the emergence of many Duesenberg-engined racers, although few, if any, raced under their marque name, preferring such patronymics as *Wonder Bread Special*.

The rise of the Model J Duesenberg is all the more remarkable when one considers that, at the time the model was on the market, there was a world depression, but the Duesenberg *clientèle* was made up of those who were above mere details like the collapse of the stock market; so it is perhaps not so curious that the company introduced an even more flamboyant model in 1932, when the American car market was virtually on its knees.

This was the SJ, which added a centrifugal supercharger spinning at five times crankshaft speed to boost the power output to a claimed 320 bhp and the top speed to almost 130 mph.

Above: in 1932, the American car market was on its knees and it was during this year that Duesenberg chose to introduce their SJ model. Against all the odds, the SJ survived and went on to become one of the world's great classic cars. Fitted with a supercharger, the engine produced 320 bhp and the car had a claimed top speed of almost 130 mph

Left: another version of Duesenberg's famous SJ model; this is a 1932 convertible tourer

The bulk of the blower installation made it impossible to accommodate the standard exhaust system under the bonnet, so Duesenberg brought the exhausts out through the bonnet sides in four chromed flexible downpipes. Outside exhausts were a relatively common styling trick in Europe (where the Duesenberg cost more than either Rolls-Royce or Hispano-Suiza), but came as a novelty on the American market. There were even owners of the 'unblown' J who had the external plumbing fitted to make their cars look more exotic. Rarest of all the Duesenbergs was the SSJ, built on the 'ultra-short' (10 ft 5 in) wheelbase; only two were made, one for Clark Gable and one for Gary Cooper, both famous actors.

Greta Garbo owned a Duesenberg, too; so did Marion Davies, Mae West, Joe E. Brown and William Randolph Hearst. Royal customers included King Alfonso XIII of Spain, King Victor Emmanuel of Italy, Queen Marie of Yugoslavia and Prince Nicholas of Romania, who raced one of his three Model Js at Le Mans, in 1933, 1934 and 1935, with an outstanding lack of success.

However, even all the top customers in the world could not save Duesenberg. Fate had already claimed Fred Duesenberg, killed in 1932 at the wheel of an early SJ, and now the break-up of the Cord empire would destroy the company he had headed. The first indication that the end was near had come in 1935 when the final shipment of 25 Duesenberg engines had been received from Lycoming; lack of a future sales programme precluded further production of power units in the Lycoming factory.

The company showed its 1937 models at New York and Chicago as though all was well, but then the Cord bubble burst, and the purchasers of the group's assets decided to curtail car production. The Duesenberg factory was bought by local truck builders Marmon-Herrington, one last chassis was assembled to the order of a rich German client by August Duesenberg and his devoted workmen in Chicago, and a new spares and service company was specially created in Auburn, Indiana, during 1938, for owners of Auburn, Cord and Duesenberg cars.

The Duesenberg name lived on, though. In 1947, Marshall Merkes of Chicago bought the company's remaining assets and employed August Duesenberg to design a new straight-eight. It was to have had fuel-injection and custom coachwork, but the realisation that the basic price would be at least $25,000 caused the project to be abandoned. August Duesen-

berg, founder of this legendary concern, died of a heart attack in 1955, aged 76.

In mid 1965, came news of another attempt to revive the marque, this time as a completely modern luxury car with contemporary Detroit styling, fronted by an updated version of the Duesenberg radiator grille. Styled by Ghia and over 24 feet long, the Chrysler-powered 1966 Duesenberg was America's biggest four-door sedan, but the price tag of around $20,000 was more than the customers were prepared to pay, and only one car was built. Then came the revival of the SSJ, by another firm, the Duesenberg Corporation of Gardena, California, that was still in production in early 1976. Based on a Dodge truck chassis, with commercial-vehicle suspension, but curiously with almost the same SSJ wheelbase, at 10 ft 8 in, it was powered by a supercharged Chrysler engine producing 500 bhp. The latter-day SSJ was an attempt to recapture the mystical aura of its earlier namesake (the car still had the mass of instruments and gauges), but, with the company announcing that the price was 'on application', the car could probably only be afforded by modern Gary Coopers.

Despite these latter-day failures, the Duesenberg name still carries the old magic—quite an achievement when you realise that total output of Straight-Eights, Js and SJs amounts to little more than a thousand cars in eighteen years. Nowadays, the large car manufacturers feel themselves unsuccessful if they turn out so few examples of their products in a day, the demand being so great.

Above: an eight-cylinder, 3-litre Duesenberg racing car pictured during tests at Monza in 1921. The car, driven by Jimmy Murphy, scored a great victory at the French Grand Prix that year, beating the best cars and drivers that Europe had to offer

Below: Derham 'Toursters' were certainly popular with actors—perhaps because they were the most expensive American car of their day. This is Joe E. Brown enjoying a 1932 model despite a rather restrictive speed limit at the Warner Brothers studio

Edsel

After much research and planning, the Edsel, launched amidst a blaze of publicity, proved to be one of the most famous company disasters ever

THE YEAR 1953 WAS A MOMENTOUS ONE for the Ford Motor Company, which celebrated its fiftieth birthday on 16 June. With the end of the Korean War, sales had taken an upswing, and the company could begin to think about implementing the expansionist policies which had been proposed by Henry Ford II a couple of years earlier.

Aiming at a range which would be fully competitive

with the General Motors line-up, Mr Ford had tentatively forecast that a suitable programme 'might require the introduction of another car name, a new dealer organisation and an additional car division', and had appointed John R. Davis (who had helped the late Edsel Ford create the company's Mercury Division in 1939) to head a committee to look into the viability of such a project.

'Yes,' the Davis Committee reported, 'there *is* a gap in our range. We need a model to compete with the higher-priced Buicks and Oldsmobiles. But there is no need for a new model name or dealer network—call it a Mercury or a Mercury-Monterey—for this would involve unnecessary marketing risks, as General Motors have found to their cost in the past.'

Their findings were backed up by R. J. Eggert, head of Ford's Consumer Research Department: 'As the general standard of living has increased, the consumer has tended to purchase a better car', he reported to the company's executive committee. 'To the average American our present car and its size represent an outward symbol of prestige and well-being.'

The successful launch of the Thunderbird 'personal car' in 1954 gave added strength to demands for a new up-market model and, on 18 May the same year, the

Lincoln-Mercury Division put *their* findings before the Executive Committee.

They thought that the new car should use a Lincoln body-shell on a Mercury chassis, and should sell in the price bracket immediately above the Mercury. For 'identification purposes', they referred to the model as 'the Edsel' (the name of Henry Ford II's father).

Everyone present, it seems, agreed, and the decision to proceed with the new model was taken, though no-one, apparently, gave Robert S. McNamara, newly appointed Assistant General Manager of the Ford Division, a clear answer when he queried: 'What is the new car intended to offer the car-buying public?'

In that heady sellers' market, with Ford missing the first place in US new car sales by only 9000 units in 1954, it seemed that the Lincoln-Mercury formula met every requirement. 'Today's average buyer,' commented *Automobile Topics*, 'clearly wants, and is willing to pay for, that "something extra" that will set his car apart'.

Ford sales figures supported this opinion. McNamara's immediate boss, Lewis Crusoe, had

Top: the first Edsel models were unveiled in 1957. There were two price levels for the new car, with a choice of two power units. Pictured above is the costlier 1959 Corsair model, which was fitted with a 410 cu in engine and was offered only with push-button automatic transmission

Above left: the unusual front-end styling of the Edsel

Above: offered with the 361 cu in V8 motor, this is the cheaper of the two models—the Ranger

found that the most basic Ford model, the Mainline, was practically non-saleable.

Enter now F. C. Reith, wearing in his buttonhole the ribbon of the *Legion d'Honneur* (awarded him by an admiring French government for his attempts to place the foundering Ford-France SA factory, at Poissy, on a profitable basis), freshly returned to Dearborn, and appointed to the Ford Product Planning Committee.

He had already proposed certain changes to the design of the 1957 Mercury range which the Committee had approved and now he was dealing with the projected E (for Edsel) Car. On 15 April 1955, he presented his findings for a better-balanced car range, with two E Cars—a low-priced model, and a high-priced model—bracketing the middle-range Mercury. The cheaper E Car was a rival for Dodge and Pontiac, while the more expensive one rivalled Buick, De Soto and Oldsmobile.

The board of directors was agreed: the E car was essential to the success of the company. R. E. Krafve, formerly Assistant General Manager of the Lincoln-Mercury Division, headed the Special Products

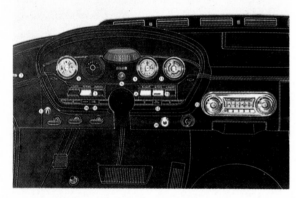

Division set up to develop the E Car.

Between conception and realisation of the new car, a time-lag had to be allowed for research, development and tooling; marketing policies, too, were firmly shaped. An added feature during the E Car's two-year gestation period was the search for an identity for the new model: Ford hired the poetess Marianne Moore to dream up possible names for the vehicle. However, the fair versifier's titles drew a blank, and the company returned to the original patronymic—'Edsel'.

A new dealer network was organised, and a publicity and advertising campaign set in motion. In September 1957, the new model was unveiled amid vast publicity. Its styling was, perhaps, over-fussy—certainly the front end, with its curious 'horse collar' radiator grille, heavy bumpers and quadruple headlamps, aroused a lot of discussion, and not a little sales resistance, while the wrap-round windscreen and heavily sculptured tail-fins were reflections of current styling trends.

Beneath the debatable attractions of its exterior, however, the Edsel offered a worthwhile package of engineering innovation—self-adjusting brakes, safety-rim wheels and a new luxury automatic transmission, controlled by push-buttons on the steering-wheel spokes—allied to such proven features as coil-and-

wishbone independent front suspension. There were, as Reith had proposed, two price levels for the new car, with a choice of two power units: both V8s, with swept volumes of 361 and 410 cu in respectively. The cheaper range, consisting of Ranger and Pacer series Edsels, was available with a choice of manual, overdrive or automatic transmissions, but the costlier Corsair and Citation models only had the automatic.

Something, however, had gone wrong, and the market gaps the two ranges were intended to fill no longer existed. In the few months since the project had been initiated, the entire picture of car-sale trends had changed, and the euphoric period of boom had

been succeeded by a mild depression, one in which the rapid growth of the post-Korean War years had given way to a more restrained expansion, and one in which the lower-priced automobile was once more playing a major role—at the expense of that carefully researched 'something extra' car.

In this restricted market, the Edsel collided head-on with the Mercury—and the older marque won. Only 35,000 Edsels were sold during the first six months and the bold sales campaign dwindled away.

Discouragement, it seems, set in too easily, perhaps as a result of the newness of the division controlling the fortunes of the Edsel. Had the campaign been redoubled, the marque might have established itself successfully. As it was, an attempt to widen the Edsel market with a low-cost, in-line, 223 cu in, straight-six engine came too late, and only weeks after the restyled 1960 models had been introduced in November 1959, the Edsel Division ceased operation.

It had been a costly demonstration of the fickleness of the car-buying public; estimates of the amount lost on the Edsel project vary between $250 million and $350 million, but it was a sum which the otherwise successful Ford Motor Company could take in its stride with hardly a falter. And, indeed, when that curious period, when the press claimed that 'Detroit is flying by the seat of its pants', had passed, the fundamental soundness of the new marketing policy was amply proven by the fact that the company was offering an eight-car line-up in 1963 that covered the market—and sold profitably.

The joker in the pack that trumped the Edsel had been the compact car, represented in the 1960 line-up by the new Falcon and Comet models; when the Edsel was planned, compacts represented only one-twenty-fifth of US car sales—four years later, they had a third of the market. Yet the models which filled that supposedly non-existent gap left by the Edsel also sold well. So was it the time or the car that was wrong? We shall never really be sure.

Above: the Edsel was launched with a great splash of publicity. This is an advertisement showing the front and rear-end styling of the Edsel

Left: also a feature of Edsel advertising was their claim that the model could be personalised to suit the owner. This is the 'dream interior' on offer to potential Edsel owners

Ford

From its fairly humble beginnings, Ford has become one of the most famous and respected organisations in the world

Left, upper inset:
Henry Ford I was born in 1863 and was the man responsible for founding the Ford Motor Company, which grew from extremely humble beginnings to be an industrial giant on a world-wide scale

Left, lower inset:
Henry Ford II, grandson of the Ford founder and the man behind the continuing growth of Ford

Left: the Model T, upon which the foundation of Ford was built

HENRY FORD I has a lot to answer for and if ever the anti-motoring lobby around the world decided to emblazon their T-shirts with their own public enemy number one, the face would be that of Henry Ford, the man who made the motor car not just an answer to the simple problem of personal transportation, but a mass mover for every man.

Post any question about mass production in industry and everyone will automatically recall the first Henry Ford and his spindly Model Ts. Talk about marketing excess and they will just as automatically recall the Edsel, a product of the reign of Henry's grandson, Henry Ford II. These two incidents, although important in their own way are just fragments in the massive jig-saw that is the Ford Motor Company today, one

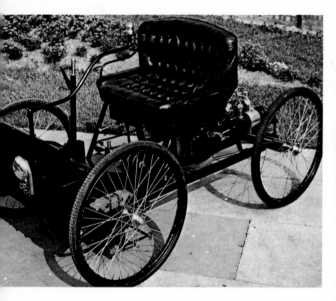

of the greatest success stories in the motor industry.

All great oaks in the industrial forest spring from acorns, and the footloose Henry Ford was a product of that pioneering spirit which infected most families in the period shortly after the American Civil War. The whole vast country lay before them and, with faith and work, a man could weave miracles. Henry Ford was born in 1863 and by the age of thirteen he had already shown his fascination for working with his hands by fashioning a screwdriver out of a nail and had even, it is said, repaired his uncle's watch.

The Fords were a farming family, but Henry wanted to be involved with machines and at an early age headed off for Detroit's satanic mills. He was gifted, and life looked good, but his father persuaded him to come back to the farm with the promise of land of his own. So engineering was put behind him as he married and settled down to work back on the farm.

Meanwhile, thousands of miles away, Dr Otto had long since patented his engine and the fledgling motor industry was emerging in Europe. Word reached America where the Duryea brothers, Frank and Charles, sat down and designed their own car, a single-cylinder Duryea which was to run for the first time on 22 September 1893 in Springfield, Massachusetts.

The Otto engine, however, had been noticed by Henry Ford, and he made a special trip to Detroit to see the stationary Otto engine on show in an exhibition. The light, quite literally, flashed in his mind, for he realised that he had to know more about electricity. He gave up the farm and set off for Detroit and a job with the Edison Illuminating Company; he was twenty-seven years old, a significant age in Ford

history. The motor car fascinated him. Three years later he made his own engine out of an old piece of gas piping. The story is told of Henry carrying his contraption into the kitchen on Christmas Eve 1893 and setting it up in the sink, making a primitive electric ignition by connecting a wire to the electric light and getting his wife Clara to trickle petrol into the pipe. And the engine fired.

It was to be three more years before he built his first car, the quadricycle, a primitive box-like vehicle devoid of such luxuries as brakes or any method of reversing save by pushing. In the true tradition of motoring genius, he had to take the door off the toolshed to get it out, but it worked and, what is more, he sold it for 200 dollars to a friend. From then on, Henry Ford's dream slowly became a reality. He built another car and this time he had perfected it to the extent that he gathered around him some friends who launched a company—the Detroit Automobile Company—to produce it. This persuaded Ford to leave his job with Edison and become a car builder. Alas, the idea was right but the public was not ready, and the Detroit Automobile Company died. Henry Ford was by now 38 years old with a wife and family and, in one of those twists that come only in a movie plot, he made the rather odd decision to go into motor racing. By today's standards he might be considered too old for motor racing, but Henry Ford had courage and ability. One of his partners was Childe Harold Wills, who was one of many people to prosper by helping Henry Ford on his

Top: still preserved in 1977, this is the original Ford factory in Detroit, which was built in 1903

Above left: the first vehicle built by Henry Ford I. It was a four-wheeler with tiller-steering and a two-cylinder engine which powered the car to a speed of 25 mph

Above: Henry Ford I, together with his friend Tom Cooper, built '999', one of the most famous Ford racers of all time

way. Wills was a gifted engineer and later in life he was to receive a percentage of the Ford profits.

The racing car Henry Ford built had two cylinders of massive dimensions and it lined up on 10 October 1901 at a dirt race track in Detroit for its first race. It was not much of a race, however, as the only other competitor was another fledgling motor manufacturer called Winton. Winton led for the opening laps, but Ford took over and won the race, confessing afterwards to having been scared to death throughout.

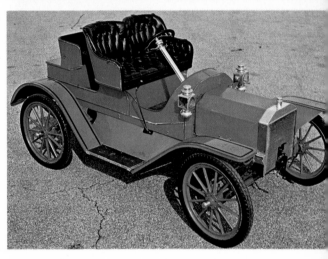

Above: a 1906 Model K. This model was powered by a six-cylinder, 6-litre engine and sold for $2500

Top right: the four-cylinder Ford Model F of 1905

Above right: now preserved at the Ford Motor Museum is this splendid example of the 1908 Model S

Right: the two-seater roadster version of the six-cylinder Model K of 1906

Oliver Barthel, one of Ford's engineers, claimed to have driven the car at over 72 mph when testing outside Detroit in July of that year. The land-speed record at that time was held officially by Jenatzy in the legendary *Jamais Contente* at 65.79 mph. Alas, there were no official observers of this but it was obvious that Ford had an engine of great potential and worthy of backing.

History is sketchy concerning the Henry Ford Company, which was in existence at that time and backed by various businessmen, but what is clear is that Henry Ford himself was not happy, eventually resigning from the company in 1902. The man who took over from him was Henry M. Leland who was another gifted engineer and, incidentally, the inventor of mechanical hair clippers. The same Henry Leland changed the name of the company to the Cadillac Motor Company and later the concern was taken over by General Motors. Leland remained for a time, but eventually left and founded the Lincoln Motor Car Company, which was purchased in 1922 by Henry Ford. It was a small world in those days.

Henry Ford left the Henry Ford Company with 900 dollars and the plans for two new racing cars. Along with his friend, a professional cycle racer called Tom Cooper, he set about building 999, the racing car for which he is most famous. It was named after the New York Central railway engine which had been timed at 112.5 mph. A second car, named the Arrow, was also built. At first neither car ran as well as planned, but after some more work had been carried out Ford and Cooper called in another cycle racer to drive the cars. This man had never driven a car in his life, but was to become one of America's legendary racing drivers. His name was Barney Oldfield.

The car was formidable and it was described as follows: 'Behind the giant, grease-spewing engine was a 230-pound flywheel, connected to the drive-shaft by means of a wooden-block clutch. At the other end of the shaft there was no differential, merely a Stone-Age crown wheel and pinion arrangement to send the power to the rear wheels; it was lubricated with grinding compound. There were no universal joints anywhere in the set up, all of it being bolted to the wooden frame, and to make things even more interesting there was no rear suspension. The driver's feet

Right: surely the most famous Ford of them all, the Model T. The T was introduced in 1908 and discontinued in 1927 after more than fifteen million cars had been produced

Above centre: a 1909 version of Ford's Model T

Below centre: a two-seater runabout version of the 1911 Model T

Bottom: now on display at the Ford Motor Museum in Detroit, this is the racing Ford 999 II of 1910

Opposite page Top: a 1913 Model T. This model can be seen in the Manx Motor Museum

Centre: a novel starting device at the end of the Model T production line of 1914

Bottom: testing Model Ts at the Ford Highland Park factory in 1914

were only a few inches from the exposed flywheel, and it was a rather grim proposition. It would seem the reason Oldfield went so fast right from the start was that he didn't know enough about the potential dangers to let them worry him'. The original 999 was never as fast as the Arrow but the whole matter is confused by the fact that, towards the end of that year and into the next (1903), Barney Oldfield drove the Arrow at various times under the name of Red Devil and even 999.

It was this kind of promotion which kept Ford's name in front of the public and paved the way for the foundation of the Ford Motor Company. So it was on 15 June 1903 that the Ford Motor Company was formed and, as one might expect, the shareholders were a motley collection of men each seeing in the company something slightly different. In time, this was to lead Ford into buying out all of his original backers. The key man, however, was Alexander Y. Malcolmson, who was involved in the coal industry, and he put up some money for Ford to design a car. James Couzens worked for Malcomson and became the man who dealt with the running of the company, whilst Ford was the designer and engineer. They decided to buy in their components, and this was where the Dodge brothers came in.

John and Horace Dodge were involved in the bicycle business and were good machinists. The company they formed was successful but was taken over by a Canadian firm, leaving the Dodge brothers to ponder their future. They moved to Detroit and opened up a machine shop making bits and pieces for the Olds Motor Works. Ford approached them and offered 100 shares in his company at a nominal value of 100 dollars a share in return for the Dodge Brothers' assurance that they would build the engines. Against the advice of friends they did so and prospered. So much so that, when they were bought out by Ford a few years later, they were able to found the Dodge Motor Company.

Henry Ford had proved to be a past master at raising money but this, his third venture, proved to be slightly more difficult. The Daisy Air Rifle Company was interested in a merger, but backed out when the stockholders got cold feet. However, the man who had brought Daisy and Ford together, Charles H. Bennett, the president of Daisy, maintained his faith and invested 5000 dollars. The major shareholder was one John S. Gray, who invested 10,500 dollars.

So it was that, with 28,000 dollars in cash, the Ford Motor Company was founded, and only one month later the bank balance showed just 223 dollars 65 cents. At about this time, they sold their very first car at the full price of 850 dollars. History does not record the name of the man who bought that first Ford car but he was not alone for, within a year, the directors shared nearly 100,000 dollars in dividends.

From those modest beginnings, the company grew to the giant it is today, with 67 assembly and manufacturing plants in the United States alone and manufacturing subsidiaries in Britain, Canada, Belgium, Germany, Australia, Argentina, Brazil and Mexico—not to mention sales and assembly plants in Europe, the Middle East, South America, Malaysia, Singapore, South Africa, New Zealand and the Philippines.

Apart from manufacturing cars, Ford owns the Philco-Ford Corporation, an electronics and radio company, Ford Motor Credit Company, the American Road Insurance Company and the Ford Leasing Development Company, apart from the massive Ford Foundation. Who, back in 1903, would have dared even to contemplate such an enormous success story?

The first Ford production model was the Model A—some years later Henry Ford was to re-introduce the name Model A, so leading to considerable confusion. The original Model A was a simple design, in line with most cars of the turn of the century. It had two cylinders producing 8 hp and was water cooled. Its maximum speed was just short of 30 mph and, at a time before thermostats had been developed, the original Model As were said to boil when nearing their maximum speed. This was, perhaps, just as well, as the car never had a great reputation for brakes. It also had the bad habit of recoiling on the starting handle if the ignition was not fully retarded, resulting in what became known as 'Ford elbow'.

For Henry Ford these were days of great fulfilment and he would spend his time devising ways of improving the car, getting down on the shop floor, giving encouragement and advice. Although the company was successful, there were internal divergences of opinion between the engineering faction, led by Henry Ford, and the business faction led by Malcomson. There is no doubt that Henry Ford foresaw, before almost everyone else, the impact of the motor car on the ordinary man in the street, and that he saw him as his ultimate customer, rather than the wealthy who could indulge in the pastime in those early days. To these ends he saw the need for a simple car which ·was inexpensive to make, and therefore could be sold in large numbers because of its low selling price. The businessmen in the company thought differently, however, and saw each individual motor car as an object of profit. They argued that the greater the profit per unit, the greater the profit at the end of the day, and they persuaded Henry Ford to make bigger cars. So it was that, before their first year was out, they were preparing to introduce the Model B Ford to sell in the 2000 dollar bracket; a lot of money in those days. In the midst of this preparation, however, there came the Selden Patent affair, something which was to dog Ford for many years before it was finally settled.

George Baldwin Selden was a patent attorney and Civil War veteran who had an inventive turn of mind. Although most of his engine designs remained stillborn, he did manage to produce an engine based on the

Brayton principle and applied for a patent in 1879. Selden was never able to do anything about his engine as he could not find anyone to provide him with money, but on the record book Patent No. 549160 'Road Machine' existed. Eventually, he managed to sell it on a royalty basis to W. C. Whitney.

Ford was taken to court by Whitney for infringement of patent as he refused to pay royalties on his engines. The problem was that when Selden had filed his original patent he had asked for a patent on the whole principle of the internal combustion engine rather than a specific design, so that every manufacturing company came into his line of fire. Alas for the industry as a whole, some of the manufacturers felt it was better to pay the royalty rather than fight the case and Packard and Cadillac, amongst others, organised their own association which duly collected $1\frac{1}{4}\%$ on the retail price of every car sold in the United States. Whereas other companies bowed to Selden's bidding, Henry Ford did not and came out with one of his celebrated quotations. When asked what he was

going to do about the affair, he replied: 'Selden can take his patent and go to hell with it'. So Selden sued.

There followed a chapter in the development of the Ford Motor Company where work went on in the shadow of legal wranglings over the Selden Patent. In 1909, the court ruled that Selden was right and Ford was wrong, but Ford refused to back down and appealed, carrying out an advertising campaign in opposition to a Pro-Selden campaign run by the Association of Licensed Automobile Manufacturers. It was a legal case which is still studied today because, on 11 January 1911 in the appeal court, the Electric Vehicle Company lost its case, on what now appears as a very simple matter of fact; namely that the patent was

held valid but that it had not been infringed as the motor manufacturers were using, not the principle of the internal combustion engine which Selden had modified from Brayton, but the German principle defined by Dr Otto.

Meanwhile, the Model B had proved to be relatively unimaginative, and to a publicity-conscious Henry Ford something had to be done to lift it up a little in the public mind. His earlier attempts at speed records came back to him and he resurrected the old Arrow car, aiming to set a new world land speed record and take the title away from the French. To do this he needed a straight stretch of roadway, as the Arrow was none too good around the corners, and eventually he

Top: a 1915 two-seater Model T 'Doctor's coupé'

Above: a 1922 Model T. This was the year in which the Ford Motor Company first produced a million cars in one year

decided to wait until winter and use the frozen Lake St Clair for the attempt. Ford went out for the magic 100 mph and made a run on which this speed was claimed, but there were no official timekeepers present.

Little is recalled today of the sheer bravery of the pioneer motorists and this particular attempt was one of the epic performances of all time. Picture the scene: a frozen lake on which a path had been scraped clear of

snow. There was a two-mile run-up to the measured mile and the ice was so rough Henry Ford took with him his loyal mechanic, Spider Huff, who agreed to operate the throttle—the reason being that on the rough surface Ford could not keep his foot steady on the throttle while steering. Contemporary photographs show the overcoated Huff draped over the top of the engine, half kneeling just behind the front wheel, and almost completely obscuring the driver's view of the track. The run itself was pure drama with the car sliding from side to side, occasionally hitting the snow banks and bucking in the air. Despite all this, it covered the mile in 39.3 seconds—an average speed of 91.37 mph. What made the whole trip even more exciting, however, was not the run itself but the fact that the course led straight into virgin snow and the car fishtailed at high speed through the snow heading for a schooner trapped in the ice. It eventually came to rest, and Huff had to be prized loose, such was the cold. After all this, the AAA officials then had a heated argument as to whether a record set on ice would qualify as a 'land' speed record.

Left: this is the 1923 version of the Model T. The concept of this model changed very little during its lifespan, as can be seen in the 1927 version pictured at the bottom of the page

Above: Model Ts were also put into commercial use. This example was used as an ice cream van as early as 1926

Closely following the Model B Ford came the Model K Ford, which went two cylinders better with six in line. It was this car of which Ford is quoted as saying, 'I've got no use for a motor car that has more spark plugs than a cow has teats'. He still tried to make something of the Model K engine and again used it for a race car, but on its first run it broke its crankshaft; nevertheless, by 1906, Ford had managed to persuade the engine to produce 100 bhp. At this time Fords were building six model Ks a day and the company was making money. This still did not satisfy Ford, however, as he dreamed about a car for the ordinary man. Indeed his dissatisfaction at some of his colleagues' lack of understanding led him into conversations with

Right: Ford's German subsidiary was founded in 1925. In 1926 they produced this Model T (*top*) while two years later they were building the Model A

Below left: successor to the Model T was the Model A of 1927

Below right: built by Ford's French subsidiary in 1934, this is the Asnières V8/40 model

Bottom: 1930 Model A roadster. The Model A was a conventional 3.3-litre four-cylinder machine with a three-speed gearbox

Billy Durant and what might have been one of the classic transactions in motoring history. Durant had taken over a company started by a Scot named Buick and, like Ford, he saw that the future was in the popular car; so he approached the finance houses of the day for the backing he needed. They were sceptical about Durant's plans for the renamed International Motors Company and Durant decided to finance his own project, changing the name of the company from International to General Motors. He too was successful and the story goes that he put out feelers about taking over Ford. Ford went to New York to discuss the deal, and it is said that he agreed to sell out to General Motors for eight million dollars. As it turned out, Durant could not find the money so the deal was off.

Finally, Ford won over most of the other directors and set out on the project which was to make his name famous: the Model T. The car was launched on 1 October 1908 after Malcomson and his friends, who had led the group in favour of bigger and more luxurious cars, had sold out to Ford and Couzens.

The Model T was introduced at around 850 dollars, and it not only gave the world transporation

over the roughest roads but added a new dimension to life, like such other American institutions as Coca-Cola and the hamburger. People sang songs about it, made jokes about it, wrote books about it, married, lived and died in it. Tagging on to the coat-tails of its success were the accessory manufacturers who had a field day offering everything to make it look or do things that normal Model Ts did not. They made wheels which allowed it to run on railway tracks and it powered all sorts of machinery. To say that the Model T became an institution would be no exaggeration and it is only a few short years since Ford Motor Company in Great Britain dropped Model T parts from their spares list, fifty years after the car was introduced.

Perhaps too much has been written about the car, although its effect on the company and the whole industry was enormous. On the same day the car was introduced, the directors voted themselves 100,000 dollars in dividends and repeated it a few months later. The money just rolled in. The dam had been breached. Motoring was here to stay. To put the success in context: Jim Couzens's sister reluctantly bought one share in the Ford Motor Company when it was founded

in 1903; by 1908, after a 20 to 1 share deal, her share had brought her 28,000 dollars in dividends.

It must be remembered that the Selden patent case still hung in the air and there had been heavy advertising advising the public against buying cars from non-registered companies, of which Ford was one. It did not matter, but it made Ford more determined to settle the Selden patent row.

The company had to grow to keep up with demand and Ford opened a factory at Highland Park. In 1910, 21,000 Model Ts rolled off the production line and, by 1912, nearly 200,000 were produced in the year. By this time, even with production line methods primitive by today's standards, the orders still ran well ahead of production. It was around this time that Ford, in despair, made his oft-quoted comment that people could have any colour of car so long as it was black. The fact was that there was no time to paint them any other colour, even though a Model T was now taking only a matter of minutes to manufacture on the line.

The year 1914 saw the start of World War I but, for Henry Ford, success and the ever-growing profits were beginning to become embarrassing. There seems

Below left: a 1931 Ford Model A. The four-cylinder, 3280 cc, side-valve engine produced 40 bhp at 2300 rpm

Below right: the 1932 Ford Type 18 V8 produced by Ford of Germany

Bottom: Ford began car production in Britain in 1911. In 1933, they were producing this Type Y 8 hp model, forerunner of the Popular

Right: in 1932, Ford again broke new ground by mass-producing a V8 engine. It was a 3.6-litre motor, producing 65 bhp at 3400 rpm, and was fitted to the Model B

Below: the 1938 convertible sedan V8. Two years previously, Ford had achieved another major triumph by selling one million of their V8s

little doubt that his early farming upbringing left him with the feeling that it was better to share wealth generally, rather than to restrict it to a small number of people. One day, when looking through a pile of orders for Model Ts, he decided to take 20% off the retail price of each car and he announced a plan which was, in a way, self-generating. He put it as follows: if more than 300,000 people bought Model T Fords that year he would return 50 dollars to every person who bought a car. As it transpired, this gesture cost him 15 million dollars, as 308,000 cars were built that year. This was not as disastrous as it might seem since, with greater volume, production costs were lowered.

By now, Ford employed 13,000 people and the company was still growing. In a typical gesture, Ford raised a storm when he decided that, instead of paying the work force at two dollars a day, he would raise this figure to five dollars a day. Needless to say, his fellow motor manufacturers and fellow industrialists in all walks of business life were horrified. There were predictions that Ford would ruin the country, and workers began to pour into Detroit; ten thousand arrived the next morning at the plant.

The effect of the five-dollars-a-day wage was considerable. It increased morale and it increased productivity. It also established a sociological department in Ford which has operated ever since, and Ford has an

enviable record in the area of caring for employees. Almost from this point, Henry Ford himself changed, and he became involved in many social causes during the twenties and thirties.

The Model T, in fact, changed everything. For one thing, it threw this relatively shy man into the limelight, for Henry Ford was not only a well known name in the United States but, with the Model T as his calling card, he was famous all over the world. Model Ts found themselves everywhere, on every continent, doing impossible things. Ford still lived modestly but by now he was the target of all who sought a few dollars here or a few dollars there. The begging letters came in by the sackload and it must have been a great blow to the man who saw, in the motor car, the great equaliser and the machine that would bring peace and happiness to the world.

Then there was the matter of the River Rouge plant which put Ford in conflict with his fellow stockholders as to financial policy. Ford foresaw continued expansion at a tremendous growth rate, and in 1919 bought a site near Dearborn on the Rouge River. However, the Dodge Brothers strongly disagreed with Ford over his expansion plans and led a band of stockholders who preferred to see dividends. Again Ford came out with an eminently quotable remark, 'Business is a service not a bonanza'. Ford lost the case and won the war. He was ordered to pay nearly twenty million dollars in dividends. As his own personal shareholding represented eleven million of this, the blow was not so bad, but he was so disgusted with the stockholders that he reacted in a typical Ford manner. After disappearing to consider his next move, he let it be known that he was going to form a new company to build a better and cheaper car. The net effect on the stockholders was disastrous and Ford, who had anticipated this, proceeded to buy everyone out at 12,500 dollars a share. It cost him 100 million dollars, but he was able to borrow the money, and the company, lock, stock and barrel, was owned by him and his family. In ten years, the company doubled in value; the gamble had paid.

In 1919, Ford had recovered well from the war and produced 750,000 cars, one third of the total of US production and, by 1921, they had over 50% of car sales in the United States. Edsel Bryant Ford, Henry Ford's son, was now president of the company, although the personality and character of Henry Ford still dominated the scene and appeared to keep Edsel Ford in the shadows. Where his father played hunches and was domineering, Edsel saw the importance of social changes and the pressures of the business world. It was he who suggested that the legendary Model T should be replaced by something more modern—and was snubbed for it. In 1922, Ford was looking into a possible air-cooled engine and, although development work continued through 1925, it was a conventional water-cooled, four-cylinder car which was eventually to supplant the Model T. This was the new Model A.

The car had a high body with a flat vertical windscreen, and it was attractive in its own way. It had taken some convincing to make Henry Ford drop his beloved Model T, but the Model A was something different. It was no longer a spindly automobile, it looked robust, strong and stylish and was just what the market wanted. Its engine produced enough power to make it a faster car than its rivals and it was a success from the start. Nearly 400,000 people put down deposits within two weeks of its announcement.

The last Model T to come off the line was produced in May 1927; no less than 15,007,033 had been built, a record for mass production of a single model only surpassed by Volkswagen with their Beetle. It took six months for the changeover to the Model A but it was worth the wait. During this period, the main production line was moved from Highland Park to the Rouge plant and, on 20 October 1927, the first Model A was ready—although the final transfer to the plant was not completed until eleven days later.

Amongst the items which created interest in the Model A was the use of a laminated safety-glass windscreen—the first to be produced as standard equipment in the motor industry. Where the Model T had established mass production, the Model A introduced proper assembly-line methods, with the careful weighing of piston and connecting-rod assemblies.

The Model A had a four-cylinder engine with a three-bearing crankshaft made of carbon manganese steel. The pistons were of aluminium and it used chrome-silicon alloy high-duty valves. There was a three-speed gearbox, worm and peg steering, Houdaille double-acting hydraulic dampers, cable-operated four-wheel brakes, welded wire wheels and a thief-proof Electrolock ignition. The car was offered with five different body styles.

In 1928, nearly 820,000 Model As were built and sent all over the world, and it looked as though Ford had hit the jackpot once again. At the same time, production of the Fordson tractor was closed down at the Rouge plant, where it had been made since World War I, and moved over to the Ford factory in Eire.

It is interesting that when Ford decided to build their plant in Ireland, they chose Eire rather than Ulster. Henry Ford felt that he wanted to help Eire and it is said he promised the City fathers of Cork that he would employ 2000 workers. Due to the post-war depression of the 1920s, only 1600 were employed and there was a threat from the authorities in Cork that they would cancel Ford's lease unless another 400 workers were engaged to honour Ford's promise. Ford's reaction to this was typical: he threatened to close the plant, stopped any further development, and

Above: a 1935 model 48 two-seater V8 roadster, seen driving down the Champs-Elysées during a rally in 1976 to celebrate the American Bicentennial

laid off 500 men. Around the same time, he built plants in Denmark, France, Spain, Italy, Argentina, Brazil and Mexico. By 1929, Ford employed 162,270 workers in the United States alone and the annual wage bill was 300 million dollars. On 4 February that year, the millionth Model A was produced, the second millionth on 24 July and on 1 December Ford raised his daily wage to seven dollars. In that year, there was a

town-car version of the Model A, complete with a chauffeur's roof and costing 1200 dollars, whilst at the other end of the scale was the Model A Tudor which sold for 500 dollars and came in grey, green or black.

These were heady days for Ford, the three millionth Model A in March and an all-time high in daily production of 9656 units. Before 1930 was out, four million Model As had been produced and there were

nine different models from which to choose. This following year, however, saw the first swing in the opposite direction and, although the five millionth Model A was produced in this year, the sales figures were slipping down and it was time to think of a new model again. What Henry Ford had up his sleeve was to cause a sensation. It was a V8-engined car at a very competitive price. It was not, of course, the first V8-engined car to be put on the market—the Hewitt company had produced a V8 as early as 1907—but it was the first one for the ordinary man in the street.

Ever since the failure of the Model K six-cylinder car in 1906, Henry Ford had distrusted the six-cylinder engine, so he ate his words and built the eight-cylinder. Just to hedge his bets, however, he introduced a Model B in April 1932. In the sales league, the V8, selling at a price not much more than a Model A, soon outstripped the model B and in 1932 the company sold 298,647 V8s, compared with 133,539 Model Bs. Contemporary commentators indicate that the Model B would have been a complete flop had it not been for the fact that the company could not tool up for the V8 fast enough to meet customer demand, and the dealers were switching buyers to Model Bs. The four-cylinder Model B cost 495 dollars and the V8 just ten dollars more. In 1933, production was speeded up and over half a million V8s were sold, but for 1934 the company were in top gear and were able to offer fourteen different models on

Far left: a 1958 Ford Fairlane and 1958 Ford Thunderbird stand alongside the 1957 Thunderbird. Note that the later model had a completely revised body including such features as twin headlights

Left: this 1959 Country Sedan shows that, when required, exaggerated tail fins could be combined with the station wagon style body!

Below: regarded as one of the first real sports cars produced in America, this is the Ford Thunderbird of 1955. Later versions, however, became more luxurious and eventually the sports-car image was dropped completely

the V8 chassis, with the Tudor the most popular.

On 19 June 1934, another milestone was reached with the millionth Ford V8 and a year later they made it two million. But this period was significant for, whilst Ford were rushing ahead with the V8, their other company, Lincoln, was going a step further and on 5 October, they introduced the twelve-cylinder Lincoln, produced at about double the price of a Ford V8.

Lincoln had been Edsel Ford's baby. He admired the beautifully made Lincolns and was determined to maintain this quality image even though his father tended to pooh-pooh the idea. The L series Lincoln of 1928 was the first of the Edsel Ford-inspired cars and it produced 90 bhp at 2800 rpm. The object of the L series was to give better reliability and it is said that

the gangsters of the 1920s preferred this car as they saw in it reliable and rugged transportation that would not let them down. At the same time, the police and law enforcement agencies also plumped for Lincolns.

Connoisseurs of Lincolns argue that, when Ford increased the bore of the Lincoln engine in 1928, it produced engine vibrations which were previously unheard of. These same experts, if given a choice, went for the Locke-bodied sport phaeton, a five or seven-passenger car with long, elegant lines and a comfortable cruising pace of 75 mph. The later L model Lincolns were fitted with built-in air compressors for inflating the tyres, inspection lights, leather upholstery and carpets and sold for 4200 dollars. If you wanted class, however, the choice was a Brunn-built cabriolet brougham at over 7000 dollars.

The new car was the V12 KB model. This used a 65 degree V12 engine which produced an effortless 150 bhp at 2400 rpm. This and the V8-engined KA model continued, with modifications to wheelbase and engine output, right into the 1940s. They nearly all featured special bodies by companies like Brunn, Judkin, Dietrich, Willoughby and the prestigious Le Baron. There was also the famous Lincoln Zephyr of 1935, which brought to the American public the concept of the streamlined car. Although its shape was to influence American car design right into the 1950s, the original Lincoln Zephyr never sold terribly well, partly due to poor performance.

Meanwhile, the V8 was selling well, the three millionth being built around the same time as the three millionth Ford truck. From this time, right up to World War II, Ford appeared to go from success to success, the Mercury range of cars being introduced in 1938. From the outside, Ford were riding on top of the world but behind the scenes the ageing Henry Ford

was seen to be losing his grip and Harry Bennett became the key man running the show. Bennett had a most unlikely background to be heading such a company. He was an ex-fighter and did not hesitate to display his craft. His nature contrasted greatly with the quiet and cultured Edsel Ford. Henry Ford insisted on making decisions helped by Bennett and, as Ford had a dislike of accountants, there began to appear cracks in the solid financial structure of the company. It was in this period that General Motors gained the edge on Ford. Soon after World War I, Ford had had 60% of the market, but by the end of World War II General Motors had 50% and Chrysler had 20%, which illustrates the drop in Ford fortunes during the 1930s and 40s. Some economists consider that, despite the sales of the V8, Ford made little or no real net profit in those years. The 1937 figures, for example, showed only a 1% profit on capital employed. On top of this Ford was anti trade union, which led to bitter clashes and a further erosion of confidence.

By 1941, things were serious. Henry Ford had suffered a stroke and was to suffer a second one. His son Edsel was also suffering from the despair of being president of a company but with little executive decision making, and two years later he died. The war was at its peak and Henry Ford returned to assume the presidency of the Ford Motor Company. A few months later, Henry Ford II was released from the Navy to return to the family business. During the war, Ford built many things, including bombers, but it was obvious that something had to be done to rescue the company. On 21 September 1945, Henry Ford resigned and Henry Ford II was named president of the board; he was 28 years of age, one year older than his grandfather had been when he started out.

Henry Ford II did not have to seek out any problems,

Top: a 1963 Thunderbird

Above: a 1967 Falcon

Top right: the 1963 Mustang prototype

Above right: a 1967 Fairlane GT

Below: a road-going version of the GT40 sports-racing coupé which won at Le Mans in 1968 and 1969

as the company was losing ten million dollars a month. Ford's aim was simple: lift morale and get Ford back into its competitive position. To do this, he displayed the drive and enthusiasm which had characterised his grandfather's early days, only this time it was channelled in the direction of business efficiency.

The Fords produced soon after the war were very similar to the models made in the 1940s before hostilities commenced. Edsel's last big car, the Mark 1 Lincoln Continental of 1940, was still being produced but there had been cosmetic changes to bring it into line with the demands of the public in 1948. The Mark 1 Lincoln Continental has become something of a classic car and was selected by the Museum of Modern Art as one of eight cars chosen for their 'excellence as

works of art'. In the original car, the power was too low to give the performance it deserved, yet over 5000 were built and sold up to 1948. However, when it was restyled that year, the car did not catch on with the public as the smooth wing shapes had given way to the heavy ornate chromework that was to characterise all American cars in the early 1950s.

Behind the workings of the company was the Ford Foundation, formed by Henry and Edsel Ford in 1936. This was set up to provide grants to charitable and educational institutions in the area around Dearborn, but in 1950 Henry Ford II was to make the Ford Foundation into an International organisation, its money coming from capital invested in various securities. It has become the world's largest philanthropic organisation, with much broader aims to advance human welfare. It has been used to promote better education and overcome social problems as well as for the developing of fine arts and by the late 1960s, the Ford Foundations had given more than three billion dollars to over 5600 institutions in the United States. Today, the Ford Foundation has programmes in education and research, national and international affairs, with the backing of Henry Ford II.

Ford's first big announcement after the war was the 1949 model, which was the first to show Henry Ford II's influence, and was the result of hiring the stylist George Walker to come up with a new look. This car, looked at today is hardly inspiring with its narrow side windows and dumpy body, but it caught on and the dealers began to clamour for it. That year, Ford made a profit and were well on their way. The Korean war was on the horizon but it was still detached from the American public and probably had less effect on the buying public than many people thought. Henry Ford II, despite his youth, was showing himself to be a superb organiser and he had more and more automation in mind. In 1951, there came the Victoria hardtop, while Lincoln produced a customised car called the Capri—a name which was to recur later in the history of Ford.

Just as Henry Ford I had had the Selden Patent case over his head in his early years, so Henry Ford II had the Ferguson patent to worry about. During the late 1930s, Ford had used some of the ideas of Harry Ferguson, the Irish inventor, in his Fordson tractor, and there was a gentlemen's agreement to produce and

Bottom: a 1973 Ford
Thunderbird. Originally
intended as a sports car,
the Thunderbird has
now become a high-
speed luxury tourer

distribute the Ford-Ferguson. It was decided that a new company be formed by Ford, called Dearborn Motors, to distribute the tractor and this was done in 1947. Ferguson, however, sued the company over his patents and, after a long case, Dearborn Motors were obliged to pay him over nine million dollars in settlement. Ford then bought out Dearborn Motors from the stockholders, so accepting the liabilities.

All the Ford companies were picking up after the war and launching new models.

This was the time when 'dream cars' began to appear at motor shows and in 1954 Ford produced the FX Atmos and the Lincoln Monterey XK800. This was also the year of the mergers, when Nash Kelvinator and Hudson got together to form the American Motors Corporation and Studebaker and Packard merged to form Studebaker-Packard.

In 1955, Ford and Chevrolet were running neck and neck with something short of 1½ million cars each and all the motor businesses in the United States were selling well. Wrap-round windscreens came in, tubeless tyres were being used as standard equipment and, as for colours, you could get a Ford in almost any colour so long as it was not black.

One of the results of a market survey which had been carried out on Henry Ford's instructions was the planning of what would be termed a sports car. Chevrolet had introduced the Corvette so Ford countered with the Ford Thunderbird. Both cars were introduced at a time when European and, in particular, British sports cars were infiltrating the United States and the idea was to produce a sports car with the features which appealed to the American buyer, namely a bit more power and the smooth power of a V8 engine. The Thunderbird perhaps offered more creature comforts than the dyed-in-the-wool enthusiast would want, such as automatic transmission, automatic windows and seat slides, power steering and power brakes, but it was introduced without the usual lathering of chromework which characterised many American cars of the time. It used a Mercury V8 engine of 4.2 litres and gave 160 bhp on an 8:1 compression ratio. Later, a 4.7-litre engine was introduced, boosting the power a little to give the car even more lively performance. Whereas Europe was sceptical about the Thunderbird, it sold in great numbers in the United States.

The car market was changing and Henry Ford II realised that there were now many different kinds of customer, from the man who wanted to buy the cheapest and most reliable, to the man who wanted the best. It was in the in-between markets that Ford needed more strength, and one of the results was the Ford Fairlane. Behind the scenes, though, other plans were being made, plans which were to cost a fortune. The ill-fated Ford Edsel was being developed.

By now, American car styling was absurdly extrovert: tail fins were in vogue and went to great lengths. Looking back on the cars of that period, cars like the Ford Fairlane Hardtop Convertible of 1957 and the even more outlandish Plymouth and De Soto models, one wonders what the attraction was. It has been said that this period marked the growth of marketing, but that it had taken a wrong turn. The industrial psychologists felt that the large tail fins emphasised virility and speed but (as was to be proved with the Edsel, introduced in that year) they could be wrong, very wrong.

Alas for Ford, the Edsel did not work. It arrived at a time when there was a recession and studies since have indicated that the marketing was wrong and that the public really did not want such a car. It is ironic therefore that an Edsel, in 1977, is probably worth more than it cost when it was introduced. It is a prized collector's piece. Just how much it cost Ford had never been revealed but it has been conservatively estimated at over 200 million dollars. This was a depressing moment for Ford Motor Company because, since 1956, it had become a public company, the Ford Foundation placing ten million dollars' worth of shares on the stock market. At the same time, the impact of the Volkswagen was beginning to be felt and European

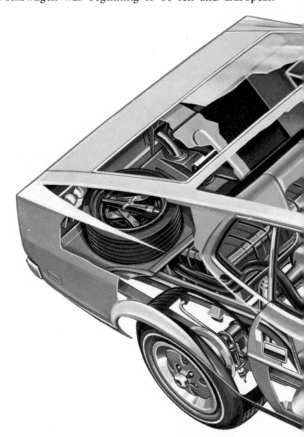

small cars were gaining a foothold in the market. With the launch of the Edsel, three Ford divisions were merged into the MEL division (Mercury, Edsel, Lincoln). With the demise of the Edsel, this reverted to the Lincoln-Mercury Division.

The company were still experimenting with various ideas, however. A unitary construction military vehicle was produced in 1957, along with a prototype gas-turbine truck. In 1958, they displayed a 3-foot model Glidecar which travelled on a thin cushion of air using the Hovercraft principle, but world events were exerting other influences. The Suez crisis in 1956, and the subsequent fuel shortages, brought about economy cars, and in 1959 Ford countered the Euro-

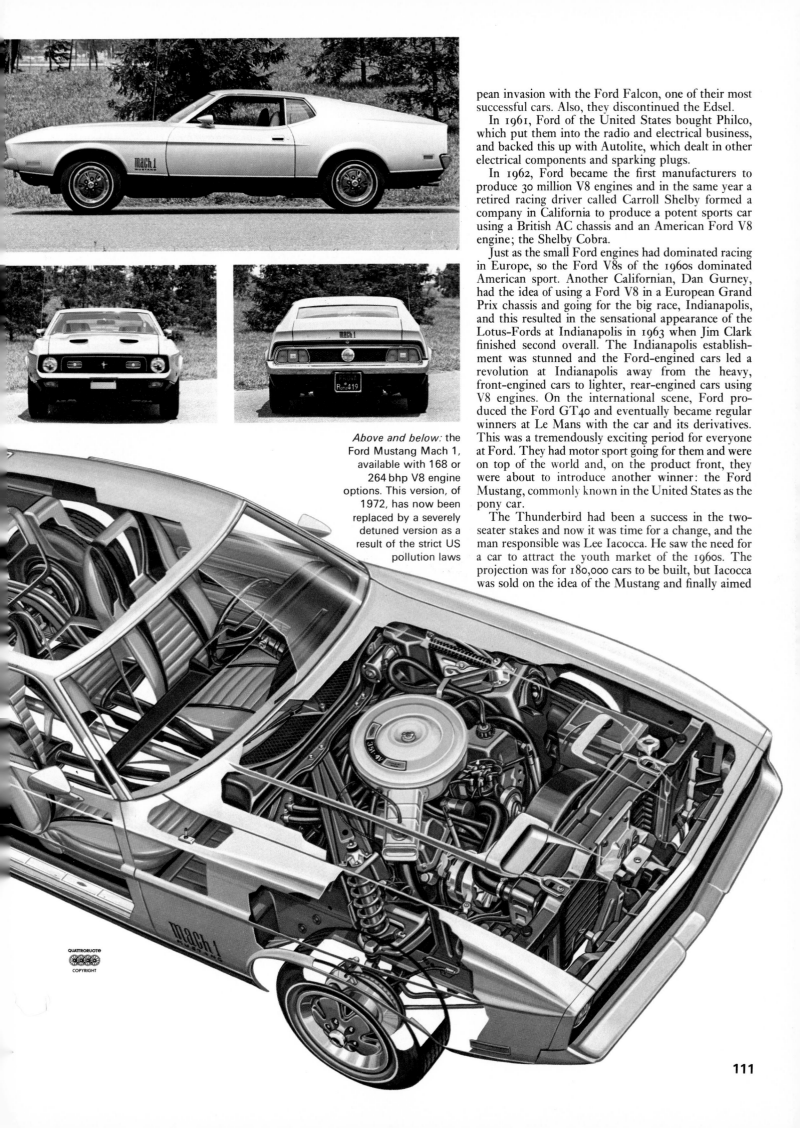

Above and below: the Ford Mustang Mach 1, available with 168 or 264 bhp V8 engine options. This version, of 1972, has now been replaced by a severely detuned version as a result of the strict US pollution laws

pean invasion with the Ford Falcon, one of their most successful cars. Also, they discontinued the Edsel.

In 1961, Ford of the United States bought Philco, which put them into the radio and electrical business, and backed this up with Autolite, which dealt in other electrical components and sparking plugs.

In 1962, Ford became the first manufacturers to produce 30 million V8 engines and in the same year a retired racing driver called Carroll Shelby formed a company in California to produce a potent sports car using a British AC chassis and an American Ford V8 engine; the Shelby Cobra.

Just as the small Ford engines had dominated racing in Europe, so the Ford V8s of the 1960s dominated American sport. Another Californian, Dan Gurney, had the idea of using a Ford V8 in a European Grand Prix chassis and going for the big race, Indianapolis, and this resulted in the sensational appearance of the Lotus-Fords at Indianapolis in 1963 when Jim Clark finished second overall. The Indianapolis establishment was stunned and the Ford-engined cars led a revolution at Indianapolis away from the heavy, front-engined cars to lighter, rear-engined cars using V8 engines. On the international scene, Ford produced the Ford GT40 and eventually became regular winners at Le Mans with the car and its derivatives. This was a tremendously exciting period for everyone at Ford. They had motor sport going for them and were on top of the world and, on the product front, they were about to introduce another winner: the Ford Mustang, commonly known in the United States as the pony car.

The Thunderbird had been a success in the two-seater stakes and now it was time for a change, and the man responsible was Lee Iacocca. He saw the need for a car to attract the youth market of the 1960s. The projection was for 180,000 cars to be built, but Iacocca was sold on the idea of the Mustang and finally aimed

Right: the 1971 Ford Pinto. This car is fitted with a four-cylinder engine with power options ranging from 70 to 100 bhp. The Pinto was one of the first genuine compact cars produced in America

Above: the elegant 1979 Ford Fairmont, available with four-cylinder, 2.3-litre, six-cylinder, 3.3-litre, or V8 5-litre engine. It is a good example of the 'downsizing' of American cars in the late 1970s, being 193.8 inches long and weighing 2627 lb, compared with the 219.5 in length and 4107 lb weight of the much loved, full size 1978 Ford LTD

for 360,000 units in the first year—a fantastic gamble, bearing in mind the Edsel's projected 200,000. Indeed, the story is told of the magazine reporter who asked Iacocca how many cars he would be happy with and he in turn asked the reporter what the world record first year's sale had been. On being told it was the Ford Falcon which sold 417,174 in the first year, Iacocca replied that he wanted to sell 417,175 Mustangs. Little did he realise that he was making an understatement.

The Mustang was a winner all the way. It was introduced as a convertible with hard top and two-plus-two models and a large number of options to follow. It could be bought with a 3.3-litre, six-cylinder engine, or with a 4.7-litre V8 giving over 200 bhp, and all sorts of bits and pieces to make it look good and stiffen the car up. For the men who wanted real performance, a later model was produced called the GT 350 with a 306 bhp V8 Cobra engine. In its first year, the Mustang broke all production records and started a legend.

To catalogue everything in the Ford story in recent years would be impossible as, along with other manufacturers, Ford have expanded greatly. In Europe, Ford Germany and Ford England have strong markets and enviable export records for their Taunus, Escort and Cortina models and in the 1970s there was a much greater degree of co-operation between the two plants with similar models being built to slightly different specifications. This rationalisation programme is likely to continue in the future. 1977 saw the British launch of a totally new car from Ford to give them a foothold in the lucrative small car market. The car was the Fiesta.

The sixties and seventies also saw Ford Australia developing fast and Ford USA is on to its second generation Mustangs and a wide range of family cars, like the Pinto, Granada and LTD. The full-size LTD in fact proved so popular that it was not discontinued in 1979, as had been planned at one stage, but retained in a smaller form. The Thunderbird was still available of course, but it was no longer a particularly sporty car. In 1977 the first of a new generation of smaller more economical Fords was introduced. This was the Fairmont.

Ford, however, like everyone else, was in deep trouble with its domestic operations. By late 1979 the company was trading in the red and leaning heavily on its European connections. Coincidentally, in October 1979 Henry Ford II stepped down as chief executive of the company, to be succeeded by former Vice Chairman Philip Caldwell. Ford did however remain Chairman of the Board. Early in 1980 Ford announced $2.5 billion cutbacks in its projected spending. As the company actively sought import restrictions and a billion dollar loan facility, its losses up to mid-1981 mounted to over $2 billion, including an industry-worst result of $595 million lost in the third quarter of 1980. During 1980 Ford was even talking of mergers with the Japanese company Toyota, which was looking for an American connection similar to that between AMC and Renault. In the second quarter of the year, however, things improved, to the extent of a $60 million profit—Ford's first for almost two years.

It was Ford's well-timed swing to smaller cars that

Left: Ford's 1982 US version of the 'world car' Escort. The front-wheel-drive sub-compact was developed in Europe and was an immediate best seller when adopted for the American market

Below left: the Fiesta was another European front-wheel-drive import, introduced for 1980 and linking Ford's worldwide operations ever more strongly

was saving the day. For 1980, the company had made sweeping changes. Over 40% of the year's cars and light trucks were all new. In pursuit of economy, Ford introduced the first US-built Automatic Overdrive Transmission, extended the use of the turbocharged 2.3-litre engine to the Fairmont and launched a new 4.2-litre V8. Four-cylinder engines outsold all other types for the first time in almost fifty years. With the new transmission and a 5.0-litre engine, the Thunderbird showed a remarkable 45% fuel economy improvement over the 1979 equivalent. The Thunderbird name had now sold almost $2\frac{1}{4}$ million cars in the twenty-five years since its introduction.

The home-grown cars of the period were no longer especially popular. In spite of sales indications, the Mustang was a pale shadow of its former self, the Fairmont (which had once been the most successful model ever introduced) was stagnating and the under-powered EXP, introduced in April 1981 as a two seater coupé, was unable to deliver the sporting promise of its looks. However, Ford knew where they were aiming; they knew that full-size cars would be all but dead by the mid-1980s, they knew that front-wheel-drive was being used in more and more applications and they knew that exciting cars would always sell. Ford's big step was the introduction of the German-built Fiesta, showing that even the long-running, sub-compact, 2.3-litre Pinto was not a small car by everyone's standards. The full 1980 range comprised the Thunderbird (16 in shorter for this year), the full-sized LTD, the Fairmont, Mustang, Pinto, Granada and the Americanised, front-

wheel-drive Fiesta (introduced in Europe in 1976).

For 1981, Ford introduced the front-wheel-drive Escort (already a big seller in Europe) to America, immediately rendering it the company's first 'world car'. First-day sales of the Escort were Ford's highest ever and in mid-1981, when sub-compacts accounted for more than 30% of sales, the Escort was the industry best seller. Its popularity was further enhanced by the introduction of a five-door hatchback model for 1982. Codenamed Topaz, a Fairmont replacement, featuring softer styling and based heavily on Escort mechanicals, was scheduled for a near future which Ford could again approach with some cautious optimism. Their philosophy now envisaged full-sized cars in the background, smaller, more economical and often sporty cars in the foreground, and 1983 as the year of the big turnaround.

Of all manufacturers in the world, Ford is perhaps the most difficult to assess, but it has always been a story of success linked to individuals and in particular to the drive and enthusiasm of members of the Ford family. Three Fords have ruled and two of them, both called Henry, have shown the kind of determination and organisational ability to withstand the pressures that occur in corporations which grow rich. Although the company has always been a leader in the rise of the automobile industry worldwide, it has had its ups and downs. One is left in wonder, however, at the remarkable ability not only of Henry Ford I, but also, later, of Henry Ford II, in steering the company from two false starts to the enormous institution that it has become today.

General Motors

General Motors is reputedly the largest company in the world

IT IS AN INTRIGUING THOUGHT that the biggest automotive company in the world might never have
happened had David Dunbar Buick stuck to making
bathtubs and U-bends for a living, instead of trying
to make money out of the horseless carriage. For, in less
than a year, the Buick company, founded in 1903, had
become an utter financial failure, and the worried
investors were seeking a miracle man who could pull
the seemingly doomed company back on to a profitable
basis. Their choice was a 44-year-old Michigan
carriage builder, who had little idea of how a car was
built and even less of what made it run; it was an
inspired decision.

The man they selected, William Crapo Durant, was
one of that select group of natural entrepreneurs who
were to transform America from an agricultural to an
industrial nation. Durant, who was born in 1860, came
from a family whose fortunes were large enough for
him to have lived a life of idleness had he so wished, but
young Billy had all the right 'go-getting' instincts and
started out to make his own career when he was
sixteen years old.

By the turn of the century, Billy Durant had
become the head of the biggest cart and carriage makers
in Flint, Michigan, America's carriage capital, in
partnership with one J. Dallas Dort. He was a natural
salesman, and proved it when he took over Buick by
selling $500,000 of company stock in a day.

Within three years, the Buick company had an
annual production of over 8000 cars in its new home in
Flint, and was one of the big four of the infant American motor industry. Durant, however, had bigger
ideas still. He felt that the individual motor company
offering a single model line was at the mercy of the
buying public and, if they failed to buy sufficient of its
products in a given year, that could spell disaster. He
reasoned that a consortium of major producers could
support each other in times of crisis, as well as organis-
ing their own parts-manufacturing companies to
ensure that they always had an adequate supply of the
right components in the right place at the right time,
and at the right price.

So Billy called a meeting of the four leading manufacturers—himself, Benjamin Briscoe of Maxwell-
Briscoe, Ransome Eli Olds of Reo, and Henry Ford. It
looked as though Durant's proposals for a merger
between the four companies was well on the way to
fruition when Henry Ford suddenly scuppered the
scheme by asking for the $3 million agreed value of the
Ford Motor Company in cash; this triggered Olds to
ask for payments in gold, too. Of course, Durant, who
had envisaged the merger as a gentlemanly exchange of
share certificates, could not raise $6 million in real
money, and the deal was off.

There was, apparently, a second attempt to buy
Ford in 1909 but, by then, the price had risen to $8
million cash, even further out of Durant's reach.

However, Billy had already decided that he could

Above: the massive
General Motors building
on Broadway, New York

Left: Thomas A. Murphy,
the Chairman of the
General Motors
Corporation in 1982

achieve his dream of dominating the American motor industry without the help of the other big four companies, and by 1908 he had floated the General Motors Corporation of New Jersey, which absorbed Buick by an exchange of stock. It was the first step in a breathtaking essay at empire-building.

Next, Durant took over the ailing Oldsmobile company, once the biggest of America's car makers, whose sales had plummeted from 6500 in 1905 to 1055 in 1908; then he acquired the Oakland Motor Company, founded less than two years previously. There followed, with bewildering rapidity, the take-over of a further twenty companies, including Elmore, Rainier, Rapid Cartercar, Welch, Reliance, Randolph, Welch-Detroit and Cadillac. That bearded patriarch, Walter Leland, of Cadillac had no intention of trading his company for a mass of share certificates and, like Ford, insisted on cash. The price was $3.5 million, and Durant was given ten days to raise it. When he returned, six months later, the price was up to $4,125,000; by the time the sale had gone through, Cadillac cost $4.5 million.

Durant's madcap spending spree, acquiring companies for their availability rather than their earning potential, could have only one end—it came in 1910. The gold-plated straw that broke the corporate camel's back was the Heany electric lamp company, acquired for $7,131,259 (although only $112,759 of this was in cash) on the basis that Heany owned the basic patent covering tungsten-filament lamps, which were

then being mooted as a replacement for oil and acetylene lighting. A costly law suit proved otherwise and, although General Motors as a whole had just made a net profit of $10 million, and produced one-fifth of all American cars, the Heany venture killed their chances of raising the much-needed capital. No bank would risk lending money to a man who had just squandered $7 million on a worthless patent, and General Motors needed $12 million to keep in business.

When Durant finally found a bankers' syndicate who would bail him out, the terms were crippling. The syndicate, headed by James J. Storrow, of Lee, Higginson & Company, was prepared to loan General Motors $15 million at six per cent. However, they took $2.5 million of this back as commission, as well as $6 million in General Motors stock. Durant, of course, was removed from control (although he remained on the board); in 1910, unable to stomach his loss in status, Durant resigned.

Having bailed out the General Motors Group, the bankers set about making it profitable. At first they thought of axing everything but the two most profitable companies, Buick and Cadillac, but Henry Leland persuaded them to keep the group alive. Even so, there were rationalisations—Rainier and Welch were amalgamated in 1911, to produce a car called the Marquette, which survived only a year, while Cartercar ceased production in 1916 (although its associate company, Pontiac, was revived later and has remained a key division of GM ever since).

Above: Billy Durant used Chevrolet to regain control of General Motors and Chevrolet has been a corner-stone of the corporation ever since. This is the 1982 Chevrolet Cavalier family

Left: another of GM's New York buildings. This one is situated on Fifth Avenue. General Motors is the biggest company in the world and markets many different items, ranging from refrigerators to luxury Cadillac cars

Below: one of the names synonymous with General Motors is that of Chevrolet; the car pictured is the 1974 Caprice Station Wagon

The Storrow syndicate put in its own nominees at the head of General Motors: Charles W. Nash became president in 1912, while Walter P. Chrysler became works manager. Both men were to make a major impact on the industry in later years as the heads of their own companies. Under their guidance, General Motors made a steady recovery, but they had not heard the last of the indefatigable Billy Durant, the 'Man with the midas touch'.

Durant had returned to Flint, and established the Little Motor Car Company on a capital outlay of $26,000, selling 3500 cars in the first year. Then he launched Chevrolet, which combined with Little in 1913; the success of the Chevrolet launch enabled Durant to seek capitalisation from the rich DuPont banking family. A new company, Chevrolet Motors of Delaware, was incorporated for $20 million—later raised to $80 million—to absorb the old Chevrolet company. Then Durant offered to exchange five shares in Chevrolet for one share of General Motors; the investors responded eagerly. In addition, Durant and DuPont bought up any shares in General Motors which came onto the market. Thus it was, that in 1915 Billy Durant could walk back into General Motors and say: 'Gentlemen, I control this company!'

Nash, who did not share Durant's ebullient vision of the future prospects of the motor industry, resigned; backed by Storrow, he founded the Nash Motor Company, aiming at the more conservative sector of the market.

At first, 'Durant's Second Empire' was based on the organisational nonsense that the part was greater than the whole, that Chevrolet, one of the manufacturing companies making up the General Motors organisation, actually owned the parent company. This situation, however, was remedied in 1918 when the General Motors Corporation was created to absorb General

1974

Motors Company and Chevrolet, as well as another of Durant's creations, a consortium of parts manufacturers called the United Motors Corporation, which linked such companies as Delco and the Hyatt Roller Bearing Company. It was a move which was to ensure the future growth of the General Motors Corporation, had Billy Durant realised it, for it brought into the company two men who were to play a vital part in shaping the organisation. They were Charles F. Kettering, of Delco, a brilliant research scientist who had perfected the electric starter (he was also a pioneer aviator who had helped the Wright brothers build their power unit) and, more importantly, Alfred P. Sloan, of Hyatt.

The Hyatt company had been founded by John Wesley Hyatt, who had invented celluloid as a substitute for ivory, so that billiard balls could be made more cheaply, and had then turned his attention to the design of tapered roller bearings. Sloan had joined Hyatt on graduating from the Massachusetts Institute of Technology, but Hyatt proved to be a far better inventor than businessman, and the company was soon in trouble.

Sloan's father stepped in with a loan of $5000, which saved the company, and his son took over from Hyatt as president. He acquired control at just the right time, for the motor industry was just beginning to expand, and there was an ever-growing demand for Hyatt roller bearings, which Sloan was ready to supply. In time, he had built up the Hyatt company to the point where he felt it had become too big to remain independent. Yet when Billy Durant suggested that Hyatt became part of United Motors, Sloan's initial reaction was one of reluctance. Then he reflected on the fact that he depended on orders from Ford and General Motors for the continued existence of his company: should they decide to make their own bearings, he would be out of business. It would be far better to throw in his lot with one of the two giants while he had the chance. So, Sloan joined United Motors and, when the General Motors Corporation was created in 1918, he became a GM vice-president.

As for Billy Durant, he was back in his element; almost immediately he set about a vast expansion programme. The Chevrolet, Buick and Oldsmobile factories were extended, a completely new Cadillac plant was built, while a new headquarters building rose 15 storeys high above Detroit, where General Motors also opened a new research laboratory. Inevitably, there were many more company acquisitions, as if to compensate for the closures under the James J. Storrow régime.

For $30 million, Durant acquired the Fisher Body Company which, for once, was an acquisition well worth what General Motors had paid for it; indeed, it has been said that if there had been no Fisher Body, there could have been no General Motors as it is known today.

The Fisher family had been engaged in the blacksmith and carriage-building industries for at least two generations when Fred Fisher came to Detroit in 1902, and found a job as a designer with a pioneer car-body manufacturer. Once he was established, he sent for his brother, Charles; then they asked William to join them. Eventually, the remaining four brothers— Edward, Lawrence, Alfred and Howard—were working in Detroit. Inevitably, they combined to form their own body-building company, in 1908. The Fisher Body Company was followed two years later by the Fisher Closed Body Company, and the two were then merged in 1916 to form the Fisher Body Corporation. All seven brothers stayed on after the 1918 takeover.

Left: all part of the GM family. These dummies, made of plastic skin over a skeleton of steel, aluminium and bronze, cost $20,000 each. They are used on an impact simulator

Another of Durant's acquisitions was an unsuccessful one-man operation, the Guardian Frigerator Company, run by Alfred Mellowes, who had built a refrigerator in Dayton, Ohio, in 1915, moved to Detroit to market his invention, and sold just 40 electric freezers in two years, losing $34,000 in the process. Durant bought the company for just $56,300, using his own cash for the purchase, and changed its name to Frigidaire; in 1919, he sold the company to General Motors for what it had cost him.

'What is an automobile manufacturing group doing manufacturing electric refrigerators?' queried his fellow directors.

'That is easy,' countered Billy. 'A refrigerator is really very similar to an automobile—they are both boxes with motors inside!'

GM broke into the finance field with the formation of the General Motors Acceptance Corporation, which provided hopeful customers with the necessary credit to finance the purchase of their new car.

However, the good wrought by such innovations was completely nullified by a mistake of typical Durant proportions. Inspired, no doubt, by the success of the Fordson tractor, Durant persuaded General Motors to build a range of tractors and farm equipment. Walter Chrysler, then heading Buick, warned against such a venture, but was overruled. Time was to prove him right for, in 1920, GM closed this agricultural side of their corporate business, having lost $30,000 in a very short space of time.

Had the post-war boom in car sales continued, Durant's wild spending might have paid off. As it was, the market suddenly collapsed in the mid-1920s, with disastrous results. Durant had tried to control the affairs of all the conglomerate companies of General Motors personally but, as he devoted most of his time to playing the stock market—he is reputed to have operated at least 70 different brokerage accounts—and either ignored his subordinates completely or else unnecessarily interfered with the way they were carrying out their work, the affairs of the GM corporation were slipping rapidly from his grasp.

Chrysler left in disgust over the tractor episode in mid-1920 while Sloan, equally frustrated, but not ready to resign, worked out a reorganisation plan which he presented to Durant. Billy approved the plan—but did not do anything about it.

Sloan realised that Durant was beyond help, and took a trip to Europe to consider what to do next. He decided to resign as soon as he got back to Detroit. But nemesis had already overtaken Durant, whose personal finances were heavily overcommitted, and who had been trying an impossible juggling trick to keep General Motors in business, for the corporation's stock had plunged from $400 to $12 a share. Durant pumped $90 million into the market in a desperate bid

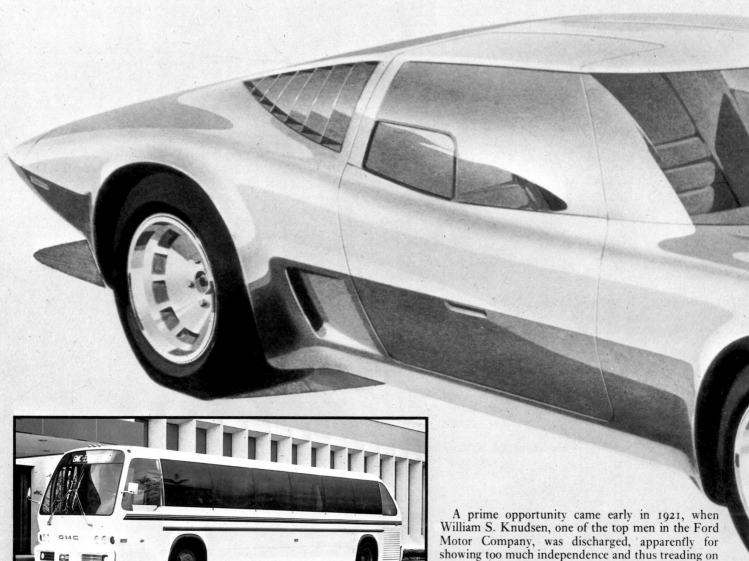

Above: an experimental GMC coach, scheduled for production in late 1975. Code-named the RTX (Rapid Transport Experimental), the coach had many novel features, including air-cooled front brakes, oil-cooled rear brakes, roof escape hatches, automatic transmission and a suspension system that enabled the bus to 'kneel' five inches lower so passengers could alight safely

to raise share prices, but without success. When Pierre S. DuPont heard that Durant was threatened with bankruptcy, he acted immediately and found that Billy's finances were so tangled that he just did not know where he stood. DuPont and the Morgan banking interests united to save General Motors, and bought out Durant, who held 2,500,000 shares in the corporation, on condition that he resigned.

DuPont, reluctantly, became president, but he was just a figurehead to inspire confidence in the corporation's renewed financial stability. The power now lay with Alfred P. Sloan, the new executive vice-president.

'General Motors had become too big to be a one-man show,' commented Sloan. 'It was already far too complicated. The future required more than an individual's genius.' 'Dictatorship,' he added, 'is the most effective way of administration, provided the dictators know the complete answer to all questions. But he never does—and never will.'

In place of Durant's erratic dictatorship, Sloan proposed that, while the corporation should follow a co-ordinated central policy, each of the component companies should operate as autonomous units within that framework. And he was ready to buy the finest talent available to ensure the new régime's success.

A prime opportunity came early in 1921, when William S. Knudsen, one of the top men in the Ford Motor Company, was discharged, apparently for showing too much independence and thus treading on the toes of his fellow-Dane, Charles Sorensen, Henry Ford's right-hand man. For a while, Knudsen managed a Detroit car accessory factory, and then he happened to meet Sloan. There was, in fact, no job available at General Motors for a man of Knudsen's qualifications, but Sloan at once offered him a place on the corporation's general staff. Within just a month, Knudsen had become vice-president in charge of the Chevrolet division.

In fact, Chevrolet sales had slumped so badly since World War I, that DuPont had considered abandoning it altogether: from 144,500 cars in 1920, Chevrolet sales had fallen to 75,700 the next year, and the result was a loss of $8.7 million. A group of consulting engineers reported that Chevrolet was no longer competitive, and should be liquidated, but Sloan thought that with lower prices and better salesmanship and engineering, the marque still stood a chance of breaking into the mass market, and he convinced DuPont to override the engineers' report.

Under Knudsen's inspired leadership, Chevrolet expanded rapidly; when he took over, in 1922, Ford was outselling Chevrolet 13 to 1. Only seven years later, Chevrolet became America's best-selling car.

Another ex-Ford man snapped up by GM was Norval A. Hawkins who, at a reputed salary of $150,000 a year, reorganised the various companies in the corporation so that their products should not compete with one another, reclassifying the marques

into their own distinctive price and style categories, and improving General Motors' financial efficiency.

Sloan and DuPont created a centralised budget for the corporation, instituted efficient control over the stock in-hand and co-ordinated retail demand with vehicle production. Most importantly though, Sloan set out to generate extra sales by encouraging people to trade in their cars when they went out of fashion, not when they had worn out. In short, Alfred P. Sloan created the annual model change policy, which hit at his principal rival, the Model T Ford, whose design was virtually immutable, and also countered the effect of second-hand deals on the new car market.

'I determined,' said Sloan, 'that my first job would be to concentrate all effort possible on making General Motors cars the very top in eye appeal, in engineering soundness, and in technological progress'.

Under Charles F. Kettering, the General Motors Research Laboratories kept the corporation ahead in the field of technological innovation, some of 'Boss Ket's' more spectacular developments being the reduction of engine knock by mixing tetraethyl lead with petrol and the first successful quick-drying paint finish for cars, conceived jointly with the DuPont chemical interests. This not only cut painting time

from hours to minutes, but made it feasible to offer a wide choice of colour schemes, a facility of which maximum use was made by GM's styling wizard, Harley J. Earl. Kettering also developed an efficient two-stroke diesel—and this led to General Motors moving into the manufacture of railway engines and rolling stock, with the acquisition of the Winton Engine Company and the Electro-Motive Corporation in 1930.

Meanwhile, on the car front, Sloan had built up an enviably efficient dealer network. He spent a great deal of time travelling to dealers' meetings and to individual dealerships, sometimes visiting five in a day, creating a close working relationship between the Corporation and its dealers. Helping to cement the bond was the fact that GM offered a 24 per cent discount against Ford's 17 per cent.

By 1927, Sloan's reorganisation had resulted in a doubling of General Motors' profits, and the corporation had become one of the ten American companies valued at over $2,000,000,000; it was the only one of the ten that was set up along the lines of the most modern principles of industrial management. Chevrolet, especially, was riding high, with a total production of 700,000 in the first six months of 1927, equalling the output of the previous twelve months. Ford dealers were switching to the Chevrolet franchise, discouraged by the flagging sales of the utilitarian Model T Ford.

Moreover, General Motors was now an international organisation: there were manufacturing plants in Britain and Germany, where GM had taken over Vauxhall and Opel to produce cars suited to the particular requirements of those markets, while sales outlets were operating in 125 countries. Chevrolets were assembled from Canadian-built components in Britain and Copenhagen, while Buicks had been built in Britain since before World War I.

The corporation had moved into a new element in the late 1920s by acquiring a number of aviation companies. Of these, the most successful was Allison, an Indianapolis-based firm which began building aero engines in the 1930s, and became a major producer in this field during World War II. GM also acquired the Fokker Aircraft Corporation and a 24 per cent interest in the Bendix Aviation Corporation. Fokker, later the General Aviation Corporation, was absorbed by North American Aviation in 1933, though GM retained their interest in this company and Bendix until 1948.

Above: the GM central technical studios at Warren, Michigan. The unusual steel dome is almost 4 inches thick. The building stands over sixty feet high and is one hundred and seventy feet wide

Like all the other American car manufacturers, General Motors suffered severely from the 1929 Depression, but this time there was no repetition of the financial scares of the 1920 slump. Under Sloan's guidance, the corporation rode out the storm, and made a convincing recovery. When he retired as president in 1937, to become chairman of the board, GM was building 40 per cent of all the cars made in America, and 35 per cent of world production. Chevrolet was topping the domestic market, and the company also offered the Cadillac, La Salle, Buick, Oldsmobile and Pontiac marques, as well as GMC and Chevrolet trucks. It was the greatest industrial empire in history.

Sloan was succeeded by Knudsen, who headed General Motors through the war, in which they produced $12,000,000,000 worth of munitions, two-thirds of it made up of items they had never built before. The effort wore Knudsen out, and he died in 1948. The next president, Charles E. Wilson, known as 'Engine Charlie' to distinguish from 'Electric Charlie' Wilson, who headed General Electric, later became President Eisenhower's Secretary of Defence.

By the 1950s, General Motors could boast that it had 50 per cent of the American market; when the Senate checked out Engine Charlie's credentials for

his post in the Eisenhower administration, he remarked with a straight face: 'What is good for the country is good for General Motors, and what is good for General Motors is good for the country'. In 1977 GM controlled 117 plants over 21 states and 73 cities of the United States. It had seven plants in Canada and could boast assembly, manufacturing or warehousing operations in 33 other countries. Indeed, the massive organisation that Sloan (who lived on well into his 90s) built, has far more money and resources at its disposal than many countries of the world. The corporation has diversified into several fields, including aero-engines, diesel locomotives, earthmovers, rockets, electronics and fridges.

Following Alfred Sloan's inspired marketing policy, however, their most important products are still 'cars for every purse and every purpose'. But at the end of the 1970s, and into the 1980s, the industry suffered another slump, brought on by energy worries and a general economic downturn. For a long time GM held up better than most of its competitors, posting record second quarter profits of $1.19 billion in 1979. However, production levels were beginning to reflect the market problems, and in September 1980 the company returned its first net loss for almost half a century. In 1979, prompted by the corporation's deteriorating financial position, Chairman Thomas A. Murphy and President Elliot M. Estes had taken pay cuts of around 3%, to $963,670 and $910,000 respectively! Fortunately, the company situation improved fairly quickly, until the second quarter of 1981 showed the corporation's highest earnings for over two years, at almost $515 million.

GM needed good results to fund its vital forward programmes. Various departments were shaping the future. Electric cars such as the Electrovette (built around a new, lightweight, high efficiency, nickel-zinc battery developed by the Delco division) were seen as serious production possibilities for the mid-1980s. A new 2.5-litre diesel with a strange, V5 configuration was planned for 1984's X- and J-cars and, at the far reaches of the economy scale, a three-cylinder, 1.5-litre engine (effectively half a 3.0-litre V6) was planned for the smallest of small cars. Nor was all this development plain sailing; between 1979 and 1981, GM had asked several times for waivers or extensions on their deadlines for meeting certain diesel engine emission requirements. In fact the EPA regulations were a millstone around the neck of the industry. Estes estimated that at the beginning of the 1980s emission equipment accounted for about $725 on each car.

As the domestic operations staggered back onto a more reasonable financial footing, GM was also pursuing its world interests—particularly with a view to pressing Ford's world market lead. In the USA GM was forecasting investment of the order of $40 billion before 1985 in new plant and production. That would include extending the use of robot assembly from around 425 units, which made GM the greatest user of robots in America in 1981, to around 5000 units by 1985. GM did at least have the advantage of building some of its robots itself. In addition to its home commitments, GM would spend some $3 billion on its Opel operation before 1982 and that included development of the front-wheel-drive Kadett, which was likely to form the world-car basis of forthcoming Chevettes. In late 1981 GM purchased 5.3% of Suzuki, opening up the possiblity of future engineering co-operation with the Japanese company, particularly in the field of very small cars.

Although GM had lost its 1979 position at the top of the US sales league (to the Exxon oil company), it still looked to be the motor industry's ultimate survivor.

Hudson

Named after a department store owner, Hudson was founded by some of the motor industry's finest brains

Right: 1909 Hudson Model 20. The roadster was an immediate success as the first public offering of the Hudson Motor Car Co, which was founded on 24 February 1909. The original price was 900 dollars and the original model was finished in maroon, trimmed in black

Below right: the 1910 Hudson Model 21, with four of the eight pioneers who founded the Hudson company. From left to right: R. B. Jackson, Frederick O. Bezner, Howard E. Coffin and Roy D. Chapin

IN A SENSE, the beginnings of the US motor industry had something in common with the Book of Genesis— the part where Adam and Eve start the ball rolling and all the subsequent begetting to get the show on the road. So it was in Europe, too, of course, with engineers dreaming up all sorts of ideas both weird and wonderful and then looking around for businessmen to provide the necessary finance. In Europe, there was much interchange of people as well as ideas across the national borders (for instance, Peugeot bought their first engines from Panhard, who made them in France under licence from Daimler in Germany) and involvement of families—fathers and sons, brothers and in-laws who worked together for a time before branching out independently.

In America, there was more money, and more businessmen were controlling it; and there was so much interbreeding in the begetting process, that the family tree of the motor world soon looked like a tropical jungle of intertwining branches under a dense foliage of thousand-dollar bills.

Top left: a meeting of two early motoring pioneers; on the left is a 1911 Hudson

Top right: the stark and sporting Hudson Roadster Mile-a-Minute model of 1912

Above: a 1922 Hudson Super Six. This was one of Hudson's most popular models. It was introduced in 1916 and remained almost unchanged until 1930

Who were the men behind the begetting of the Hudson Motor Car Company early in 1909? There was the president, Joseph L. Hudson, businessman, founder of a big Detroit department store, whose name was also used for the Motor Company presumably because his purse provided most of the initial capital; and there was Roy D. Chapin who had worked previously for Ransom E. Olds (who created the Oldsmobile and, later, the Reo) and gained personal fame some eight years before, in 1901, by driving a single-cylinder Curved Dash Runabout from Detroit to the New York Show as a reliability and endurance stunt. Between Olds and Hudson, he had helped to get the E. R. Thomas-Detroit Co off the ground, and its successor, the Chalmers-Detroit Co. However, the Hudson promotion was to monopolise his attentions until his death in 1936. Another begetter was Howard Earl Coffin from Ohio, who had built a gas engine in 1897, a steam car two years later, and joined

R. E. Olds in 1902. After becoming Chief Engineer there, he broke away to help Chapin launch the E. R. Thomas-Detroit and its Chalmers successor, and finally the Hudson. By 1910, when vice-president of Hudson, he was President of the Society of Automobile Engineers and, in that capacity, did much to establish the standardisation of items like material specifications, to the great benefit of the industry as a whole.

Hugh Chalmers, vice-president of the National Cash Register Co, came on the motoring scene in 1907 by joining E. R. Thomas-Detroit and, in next to no time, had bought half the stock—hence the Chalmers-Detroit. The begetting along this line later led to Maxwell and Chrysler. Looking forward to 1954, that was the year of amalgamation with Nash and the start of the American Motors Corporation, thereby linking Hudson retrospectively with other makes such as Rambler, Jeffery, Ajax and LaFayette.

In June 1909, the *Saturday Evening Post* carried the

first-ever advertisement for the new Hudson car and, on 3 July, the first example reached the end of the assembly line. It was called the Model 20, and conformed in every respect with the established US pattern for a low-to-medium-priced automobile in technical specification, appearance and body styles. Indeed, in retrospect, it may seem astonishing that so many engineers designed such similar products and yet were able to talk big business into backing them. However, history has proved time and again that the unorthodox is unlikely to sell well even if it works well, unless there is sufficient confidence and material support to keep it afloat until the buying public has been won over; the Volkswagen phenomenon exemplifies this. Slight variations around a familiar theme are generally a better bet for the 'Top Ten'.

Where the Hudson seems to have scored from the outset was in providing a healthy power output from a conventional engine and better than average performance through matching cylinder capacity to body style and weight. And, as we shall see, they tended more than most to stick to an established design, carrying forward outmoded features such as splash-lubricated big-end bearings and wet clutches long after these had been abandoned by other makers, but concealing them beneath visual ornament that changed to suit the times.

So, Howard Coffin's Model 20 had a 20 bhp, four-cylinder monobloc engine with side valves under an L-head. Bore and stroke was $3\frac{3}{4} \times 3\frac{1}{2}$ in, fired by an HT magneto, and it transmitted through a cone clutch and three-speed gearbox. It had half-elliptic springs at each end and rode on non-detachable wood-spoked wheels. The two-seat roadster, with the option of a single bucket-type rumble seat or an extra large oval petrol tank behind the front seats, was claimed to reach 50 mph with a 3.5 to 1 final drive, a 4 to 1 ratio being optional for the heavier bodies. Four thousand Model 20s were sold that first season and, by the end of 1910, Hudson were rated seventeenth in the league of American car makers.

For 1911, the 20 was succeeded by the more-powerful Model 33, for which there were three body styles—pony tonneau, roadster and touring four-seater, the latter having step-over sides for the front seat, and doors only for the rear tonneau. That year, sales reached 6486. 1912 witnessed the death of J. L. Hudson and the birth of the first six-cylinder Hudson, the Model Six-54, a big and handsome machine with 6 litres and 54 bhp to propel it. Advertisements

claimed a maximum speed of 65 mph for the car and the ability to reach 58 mph from rest in half a minute. Standard equipment for the Six and the four-cylinder Model 37 (now with a 4-inch cylinder bore) included electric lighting, 'self-cranking', and even a clock and speedometer. The larger car, with a 127 in wheelbase, was offered with a range of open and closed bodies to seat from two to seven, and the 118 in wheelbase four-cylinder had up to five seats. The sales line this year was that these cars were the work of no fewer than 48 design engineers, some coming from France, Italy, Germany, England, Belgium and Austria. They had worked in 97 factories and had a hand in building 200,000 cars. 'Experiment has been eliminated. The errors due to lack of experience and lack of knowledge have been left out of these cars.' A feature of the big Six was a four-speed transmission with geared-up or overdrive fourth, an arrangement that Rolls-Royce had tried with the first Silver Ghosts several years earlier, but soon abandoned because the plaintive whine of indirect gears in the normal cruising range was unacceptable.

By 1914, when the 4-cylinder had become the Model 40 (40 bhp) by virtue of having the crankshaft stretched

Top: a Hudson Super Six; to demonstrate the reliability of the car, the Super Six was driven from New York to San Francisco and back again, the first car ever to complete the journey. The outward journey took 5 days $3\frac{1}{2}$ hours while the return to New York took 5 days $17\frac{1}{2}$ hours—a remarkable feat by both men and machines in those days

Above: one of the many variations on the Super Six theme, this is the 1921 Landaulette, a model much favoured by President Hoover

with $5\frac{1}{4}$ in throws to bring it into line with the Six, Hudson considered themselves the world's largest manufacturer of six-cylinder cars, and total sales reached a record 10,261; by 1915, they were up again to close on 13,000, obviously unaffected by the war in Europe. The following year was even more successful, with production doubled (25,772) through the introduction of an instant winner, the Super-Six, and adoption of a one-model policy. Thereafter, there was never to be another four-cylinder engine behind the

famous red triangle badge, and the cylinder dimensions of the Super-Six were to remain unchanged right through to 1930, at $3\frac{1}{2} \times 5$ in (88.9×127 mm, 4739 cc). Right from its initiation, the Super-Six was marketed with either sedan, cabriolet, town car or limousine bodywork in addition to the touring versions, some having wire-spoked wheels. To demonstrate its staying power and performance over a long distance, a Super-Six became the first car to make the double crossing of the North American continent against the clock—outward from New York to San Francisco in 5 days $3\frac{1}{2}$ hours, and back again in 5 days $17\frac{1}{2}$ hours. A contemporary photograph shows a wire-wheeled touring car with four begoggled passengers looking (car and occupants) very travel-stained on a stony track in the Sierra Nevada. For a round trip of more than 7000 miles over every type of going—much of it unsurfaced and including mountain ranges and long tracts of desert—this was a very remarkable feat by both men and machine. Five years earlier the record for the single east-west journey, achieved by a Reo, had been only six hours less than the Super-Six's double crossing, but in the interim there had been a lot of road-building.

By 1917, the USA was embroiled directly in World War I and chief designer Howard Coffin's time was largely occupied with the US Board of Aeronautics, of which he was chairman. President Hoover had taken to a Super-Six landaulet and Hudson's output of almost 21,000 for the year included a large batch of military ambulances. Floyd Clymer's *Catalog of 1918 Cars* lists no fewer than ten body styles for the

Below: a 1922 Hudson Super Six Coach

Bottom: yet another of the Super Six range, this being the 1925 four-door sedan

Super-Six, each with identical specification apart from wheel and tyre dimensions, even the 125½ in wheelbase being common to all. In America, the elegant nomenclature of the Horse Age persisted in the motor industry and, indeed, to this day there are broughams and landaus to be had. Simplest and cheapest of the Hudson range was a Seven-Passenger Phaeton (open tourer) for $1950, and you could have bought two of those with a bit of change left over for the price of the Full Folding Landau ($4250). Between these extremes were the Four-Passenger Phaeton (more costly than the Seven-Passenger for some reason) at $2050, a Runabout Landau at $2350, a Four-Door Sedan at $2750, a Touring Limousine at $3150, a Limousine at $3400 and Limousine Landau for $3500, or Town Car for $3400, and a Limousine Landau or Town Car Landau for $3500. In those days, the House colour for Hudsons was blue, but there was a choice of blues—Coach-painter's, Hungarian or India; other finishes were also available. Limousine equipment included a heater for the rear compartment, footrests and pillows, a vanity case and courtesy lights. Wood-spoked artillery wheels with detachable rims were the standard wear, with the option of centre-lock wire wheels and, in each case, the back wheels only were braked by contracting and expanding shoes sharing common drums, and actuated by the pedal and hand lever respectively.

At the Detroit Show for 1919 models, Hudson introduced a cheaper line under another name, as other major US companies were to do. This was the Essex, destined to turn full circle again in later years via the Essex Terraplane, then simply Terraplane and finally Hudson Terraplane. In the years 1919–32, some 1,331,000 Essex cars greatly expanded Hudson business and, in fact, their sales in the peak years 1925–29 greatly exceeded those of the parent company. Through to the end of 1923, it had a 2.9-litre, four-cylinder engine with overhead inlet valves and side exhausts. One source credits it with 55 bhp, giving the car a top speed around 60 mph, but this seems scarcely likely when related to the Model A Ford of some years later, which drew only 40 bhp from 3.3 litres and could also reach 60 mph. However, in the USA, there have always been discrepancies between the brake-horse-powers developed in boardrooms and those actually provided for the customer to transmit to the road. Cylinder dimensions were 85.7 × 127 mm, or 3⅜ × 5 in, cooling was by thermo-syphon, the big-end bearings were lubricated by splash, and a three-speed gearbox was engaged through the customary Hudson multi-plate wet clutch. Initially, the Essex carried three body styles—four-door sedan, five-passenger phaeton and roadster with rumble seat. Advertisements extolled its light weight, durability, rich appointments, low cost and economy, and boasted it was a 'tremendous performer'. 'The Essex's motor would inspire a whole season's advertising campaign,' they wrote. 'A slogan might be written about its beauty.' Indeed it might, like: *'Even the right-angles are wrong angles'*. Not that it was any uglier than most US cars in that era of almost uniform sameness and drabness, before a brilliant nucleus of styling engineers, working first on their own account, had expanded their influence beyond the premises of the specialist coachbuilders. Even in its first year, however, the Essex outsold its costlier stablemate 21,879 to 18,175. In its second year, the Essex pioneered a very significant commodity, a two-door coach so inexpensive as to be within reach of humble buyers who hitherto had been denied closed coach-work. With its uncompromising boxy figure relieved only by a shapely posterior, it was not beautiful, but by

1925, 80% of Essex production was two-door coaches and other makers had had to follow suit. In 1920, a large fleet of Essex phaetons was ordered for rural deliveries of US mail and, to publicise this commercial jackpot, the company despatched four on transcontinental runs; one completed the classic San Francisco to New York marathon in 4 days 14 hours and 43 minutes. In that year, too, a specially equipped Essex phaeton was delivered to Edward, Prince of Wales. It quickly became a favourite in export markets and, in

Above: the Hudson Super Six, the model which formed the backbone of Hudson production for over thirty years. This is a 1929 model fitted with wire wheels and an elegant body coachbuilt by Grosvenor of London. The engine was a six-cylinder, 4739 cc unit

1922, a Japanese hotel proprietor in Tokyo acquired a batch of 42. It is not known how many of these survived the great earthquake and devastating fires there in 1923, but a record of vehicles registered in that city soon after the disaster reveals that Essex were second only to the Model T Ford.

In 1924 came the first six-cylinder Essex which very soon supplanted the Rapid Four, as it was called. It had a side-valve engine of only 2.1 litres capacity, increased by three stages (in 1925, 1927 and 1929) to 2.6 litres, which final form carried it through to the end of the marque's existence three years later. After several lean years of post-war depression, the Hudson-Essex fortunes rose rapidly from 1923's 89,000-odd to almost 134,000 customers in 1924 and over 300,000 in 1929, of which about a third were Hudsons; after that, of course, the bricks of Wall Street suddenly crumbled away and things were never the same again for the Hudson Motor Car Company. During this period, the Essex was given balloon tyres (1925) and front brakes (optional from 1927 and standardised the following season), a plated radiator shell in place of a painted one from 1926 and also, for 1927, this item was changed in form from pseudo-Rolls-Royce angular with horizontal shutters to the arched style of the Hudson. As a guide to its place in the industry, the cheapest US car in 1929 was the Ford 'A' roadster at a rock-bottom $385, and the cheapest sedan, on the same chassis, cost $495; next in succession came the Whippet coach at $535, Chevrolet and Durant at $595, Plymouth at $690 and Essex at $695. In England, one could buy an Essex for as little as £185 in 1932.

Reverting to the true Hudson, the Super-Six was in full swing in 1919, but we should look back two years earlier to this model's first competition success, when R. Mulford drove a stripped and tuned version to victory in a 150-mile race on a track at Omaha at an average of 101 mph; in 1919, another finished in ninth place in the Indianapolis 500 with Ira Vail at the wheel.

Then, in 1927, the famous cigar-smoking Barney Oldfield drove a two-door coach around the Culver City Speedway for a thousand miles at an overall average speed of 76 mph. It would have been powered by a new engine with the same cylinder dimensions ($3\frac{1}{2} \times 5$ in) but fitted with overhead inlet valves like the obsolete Essex Rapid Four. After a three-year run, the inlet-over-exhaust layout was again abandoned in favour of the simple L-head side-valve and, from that time on, no Hudson engines were made with valves in the head, although a few of the last cars to bear the name had ohv engines by Packard and American Motors.

In the peak year of 1929, Hudson-Essex combined rated third among America's best sellers, but this does not tell all the story because these cars were enjoying an exceptional popularity in overseas markets. For instance, more than 17% (about 40,000 cars) of the 1928 production went overseas, and this export prestige endured right through to the outbreak of war in 1939. The next landmark was in 1930 when a straight-eight engine was introduced to supplement the six-cylinder, but replaced it the following year as the sole Hudson power plant. This was a neat piece of rationalisation in that it shared the cylinder bore and crankshaft stroke of the six-cylinder Essex, so that certain parts were interchangeable. This five-bearing unit received an increase in cylinder bore to 76 mm in 1932, bringing the swept volume to 4168 cc, and in that form it remained in production, still with its splash-fed big-ends, through to 1953, with successive increases in power output from 95 bhp at 3500 rpm to 128 at 4200.

Although there was no aesthetic pleasure to be had within the engine room of a Hudson Eight or its derivatives, which frankly looked a mess by comparison with its European counterparts, this strictly conventional unit was undoubtedly one of the finest of its time. It gave a very good power output, with lively response and a healthy torque curve from very low revs. It was also silky smooth, easy to maintain and reliable over long periods. Moreover, the Hudson chassis was comparatively light so that the power/weight ratio was favourable. The proof of this is evident in the retention of the same engine for over twenty years within body shells that were changed many times, fundamentally or in details of decor, in the rat-race of the 1930s when Hudson were trying to recapture their earlier hold on the market now dominated by Ford, General Motors and Chrysler.

When the lighter Terraplane range had the option of the straight-eight from 1933, it inspired the first and most famous of a new breed of Anglo-American sporting concoctions which became quite a vogue in the 1930s. This was the Railton, which earned itself a reputation out of proportion to the small numbers sold—only 1460 including 81 with six-cylinder engines

—during the years 1933–39, plus a handful after the war. The Railton was sponsored by Sir Noel Macklin, who had previously been the driving force behind the all-British Invicta, and was assembled in the old Invicta works at Cobham in Surrey. He engaged the services of Reid Railton, renowned designer of land-speed-record and track-racing cars who, in later years, emigrated to the USA and became a consultant engineer to Hudson. Railton modified the Terraplane chassis to improve its handling characteristics and bring it closer to the European concept of a sporting platform; he dropped the frame to lower the build, fitted Hartford friction dampers and raised the steering box ratio. A handsome radiator shell strongly remininiscent of the Invicta was complemented by a long bonnet with the earlier car's characteristic raised rivet heads along the hinges. Considering the car's modest production output, the range of body styles offered was very ambitious. All were strictly British in appearance, emulating those of more expensive makes; for 1937, for instance, there were no fewer than three open tourers, three saloons, a coupé and convertible coupé on the shorter of alternative wheelbases, and a saloon, convertible and limousine on the long wheelbase. They were very lively performers with a maximum speed of around 90 mph, and a Light Sports Tourer with very spartan equipment, of which very few were made, was tested by a contemporary journal and recorded just over 100 mph, complemented by an acceleration time from zero to 60 mph of under 9 secs, which was sensational in those days. In 1938, one of these took the sports-car record at the famous Shelsley Walsh hill-climb.

For Hudson, the 1930s were a turbulent period of fluctuating fortunes, profits and losses, with annual production dropping from around 114,000 in 1930 to only 41,000 in 1933; thereafter, rising progressively to over 123,000 in 1936 and falling again to 51,000 in '38, in which year they suffered a trading loss of nearly

$4.7 million. While Europe was at war, the output was up once more to 87,000 in 1940, with a loss of $1.5 million but, the following year, they were in the black again with $3¾ million profit although fewer than 80,000 cars were sold.

In retrospect, the handsomest years from the styling viewpoint were perhaps 1930–33, before the arrival of valanced wings, ever more elaborate radiator shells and all the other gimmicky additives planned to date earlier models and attract new custom. In July 1932, the brave American aviatrix Amelia Earhart went to Detroit to christen the first-off Essex Terraplane in the presence of Orville Wright and, later that year, one of these cars broke the stock-car record for the classic Pike's Peak hill-climb in Colorado. Meanwhile, Hudson chief Roy D. Chapin was appointed Secretary of Commerce by President Hoover. Hudson fans also

remember 1932 as the year the company built the only really unconventional cars in its long history; these were six eight-wheeled specials commissioned by the Japanese Government and used in the Manchurian war. They had four wheels at the back, two steered front wheels and two idler wheels just behind these, raised clear of the ground by a few inches so that they only contacted the ground over very rough terrain. The bodies were typical staff-car open tourers.

In 1934, the Terraplane's 2.6-litre side-valve six, which developed about 75 bhp, was supplemented by a 3.5-litre six, which was later added to the Hudson range as an alternative to the eight. At about this time, there was a rather brief adoption of a curious form of independent front suspension named Axleflex. Each wheel was carried on a three-quarter length beam axle, giving it a swing-axle geometry, in conjunction with ordinary semi-elliptic springs. After a year or two, this was dropped in favour of a rigid beam axle located by radial torque arms, the springs being shackled at each end and relieved of all torque loads.

From 1934 to 1938, after the Essex name had been dropped, the Terraplane became almost indistinguishable from the top-line Hudson, sharing many of the body pressings as well as the 3½-litre, six-cylinder engine and, in 1939, the two 'makes' became one. For 1935, there was the option of an electric gear-shift—

Electric Hand—in conjunction with a conventional three-speed box having a constant-mesh middle gear, and vacuum operated clutch. This was the single-plate type with cork inserts and running in oil, which Hudson had adopted in 1929 and retained even through to the early 1950s for the 145 bhp 6-cylinder Hornet.

In February 1936, Roy D. Chapin died; his place was taken by A. E. Barit, who had been with the company since its inception and carried it through to the merger with Nash and formation of American Motors in 1954, whereupon he became a director of that combine. Bendix hydraulic brakes were adopted in 1936, replacing the Bendix self-wrapping mechanicals which were so effective when in good order with all the adjustments correctly set, but could be so fiendishly wayward and unpredictable if anything was amiss. The new hydraulics were supported by a mechanical system which took over whenever they sprang a fluid leak.

In the war years, from 1941, Hudson ran a plant, near Detroit, manufacturing anti-aircraft machine guns and sub-assemblies for aircraft, and stopped car production in February 1942 to devote all their resources to these and other military hardware—Helldiver folding wings, Airacobra cabins, engines for landing boats and many other items. The car assembly

Top: the Hudson six-cylinder business coupé of 1939

Above: a 1946 Commodore Eight Sedan. The post-war Hudsons were basically 1942 models with minor front-end styling alterations

lines started rolling again in August 1945 with 1942 models, the front-end styling being rehashed for the following year's products. A shortage of steel kept production below demand for a time but, in 1947, they were able to celebrate completion of the three-millionth Hudson made since 1909.

For the 1948 model year, Hudson took their first really bold step forward into hitherto untrodden territory by bringing out an entirely new line with unitary construction of body and chassis, the innovation being that the frame enclosed the rear wheels. They called it their Step-Down Design, since the floor was considerably lower than the structural sills forming the side-members, and only the lower part of the back wheels was exposed to view. Independent coil-spring front suspension was introduced for the new range. The old straight-eight 4168 cc engine, now

Below: Hudsons at the London Motor Show, Earl's Court in 1953. In the foreground, left, is the Italia, with coachwork by Touring; on the right is the Jet Liner; behind is the Hornet Special, one of the last Hudsons to be built in Detroit

and 3.8-litre, 112 bhp, six-cylinder engine. In the following year, the Hudson plant in Canada, set up in 1932, was again set in motion, and automatic transmission became optional for all the range.

However, once again, the company was in financial trouble: following a post-war peak in 1949–50, when production had comfortably exceeded 140,000, with the books showing over $10 million profit for 1949, there was a rapid decline to 93,000 in '51, 78,000 in '53 and a loss of over $10 million, and right down to 32,000 in '54. Unfortunately, the Hornet failed to retrieve the situation despite wide publicity for its virtual supremacy in stock-car racing, and extravagant styling with annual chromium-plated face-lifts to keep the fashions changing. The Hornet engine was just over 5 litres (96.8 × 114.3 mm) and gave 145 bhp at 3800 rpm, using a 7.2 compression ratio, and the

claimed top speed of the sedan was 98–103 mph.

Early in 1953, yet another major effort to keep the company afloat materialised in the form of a compact light car, the Jet, with 3.3-litre six giving 104 bhp and wheelbase of only 105 in. There were Jets, Jet Liners and Super Jets, but they never really caught the public fancy. Meantime, the Pacemaker had given place to the Wasp and Super Wasp, the Hornet engine was boosted to 160 bhp and the faithful straight-eight was finally abandoned. A special leather-trimmed coupé called the Hudson Italia, to be built in limited numbers with bodywork by Touring of Milan and powered by a 114 bhp Jet engine, appeared at the international motor shows; all to no avail, though, and after 1954, no more Hudsons left the Detroit factory.

Resulting from the merger with Nash-Kelvinator, concluded in May 1954, Hudson production was transferred to Kenosha, Wisconsin, and the 1955 Wasps and Hornets were Nash-bodied with Hudson stings, apart from the Rambler compact which could sail under Hudson colours, if you wished, simply by a change of badges. As mentioned earlier, the last of the Hornets were powered by first Packard and then AM V8 motors and, after 1957, they were at last allowed to fade away after being progressively stripped of all the individualistic character and respectability invested in them by Roy D. Chapin and his associates.

Above: the last ever Hudson to be built, model 35787-2, which was completed on 25 June 1957

developing 128 bhp at 4200 rpm on a 6.5 to 1 compression ratio, was still the mainstay for the top quality models, but was now supplemented by a slightly larger, 4.3-litre, side-valve six giving 121 bhp at 4000 rpm. Appropriately, this was named the Super-Six. To take the place of the pre-war Terraplane, a lower-priced series, the Pacemaker, was added in 1949, with the same step-down body construction

Lincoln

The Lincoln name is linked with that of Cadillac by a common founder and by sheer quality

'THE IDEAL LINCOLN OWNER is a man of means who enjoys the Lincoln's economies to the full . . . the Lincoln owner usually has both town and country homes, moving conveniently among them with his Lincoln . . . the Lincoln owner considers the world his playground and his base of business operations. His Lincoln car carries him far, swiftly and luxuriously . . . the ideal Lincoln owner has exceedingly high standards of taste. He enjoys the faultless upholstery, fittings, furnishings and finishing of his Lincoln car . . . an owner does not have to be an engineer to appreciate his Lincoln, although such authorities throughout the world proclaim the Lincoln "as fine a motor car as it is possible to produce".'

This litany of luxury appeared in 1930, at the height of the depression. Though the Lincoln had then been in production for only eight years, it enjoyed an immense prestige which was all the more remarkable for the fact that the company had been part of the Ford Motor Company since 1922, when the Model T was at its peak.

But the man who had founded the Lincoln company and headed it through its first years of production was a very different personality from Henry Ford. The name of Henry Martyn Leland, born in 1843, had become synonymous with the highest standards of precision manufacture long before the dawn of the motor age. Leland, the youngest of the seven children of a teamster from Danville, Vermont, had begun work in the Springfield, Massachusetts, armoury, then moved to the Colt gun works at Hartford, Connecticut, and subsequently to the Brown & Sharpe company at Providence, Rhode Island, claimed to be the world's finest producers of micrometers and machine tools. Here, Leland worked to tolerances as high as 1/270,000 inch, becoming so versed in the subject that he was appointed the company's 'super-salesman', capable of building, selling, and installing any of the firm's products and then instructing the customer in its proper use.

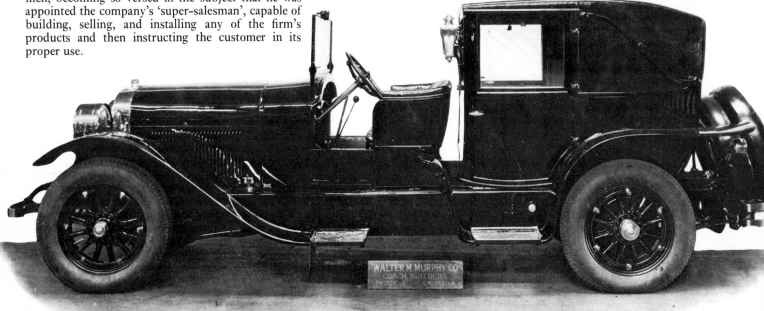

Left: the 5.8-litre, five-seat tourer of 1921, with a body by the American Body Co

Below: the Locke-bodied club roadster 151 of 1929; the number referred to the body type not to the car model

Bottom: a specially built Murphy-bodied Lincoln V8 of 1925

Next, Leland set up in business on his own, heading the Leland & Faulconer company, based in Detroit. Precision casting and gear-cutting was this company's forte, a field in which their supremacy was so marked that they could ask for—and get!—prices three times higher than those of their rivals. Among their successes was the development of the shaft-and-pinion transmission for the Columbia chainless bicycle.

After the Oldsmobile factory was destroyed by fire in 1901, Ransom E. Olds ordered engines from Leland & Faulcolner, who were also supplying him with gears. Thanks to the precision of their manufacture, the Leland & Faulconer engines were more than 25 per cent more powerful than the Olds-built units, which developed 3 bhp. Not content with this, Leland showed how the Olds engine could be tuned to give 10.25 bhp.

All this proved, apparently, too much for Mr Olds, who didn't fancy having to upgrade the rest of the engineering of his horseless buggy to match, but it was just what the Detroit Automobile Company, which had just been reformed, was looking for. Their chief engineer, Henry Ford, had just resigned to set up on his own account; he was replaced by Leland, and the result was the Cadillac Automobile Company. Leland brought new standards of precision to car manufacture —witness his Dewar Trophy-winning stunt in 1908, when three Cadillacs were dismantled, scrambled and reassembled from the mingled parts and components taken straight from storage.

A year later Cadillac became part of General Motors; and it was during the war, when Billy Durant refused permission for Cadillac to build the Liberty aero-engine that Henry Leland and his son, Wilfred (who had been Vice-President and General Manager of Cadillac for eight years), resigned and founded the Lincoln Motor Company for this purpose on 29 August 1917. Their sole assets were their technical skill plus a factory site; within two days they had signed a contract for 6000 engines, the first of which was running just seven months later. Within ten months, Lincoln was producing 50 engines a day, with a workforce of 6000.

Why Lincoln? He had been the elder Leland's boyhood hero, and the man for whom he had cast his first vote. And old Henry, like his namesake Mr Ford, was a firm believer in strong principles: he was president of the Detroit Citizens' League, had helped effect several electoral, educational and legal reforms and was convinced that tobacco and alcohol were evils. He had, at the time of the company's foundation, been President of the Society of Automotive Engineers for a year or so.

The end of the war came too early for Leland. Had the hostilities continued another six months, he would have produced sufficient engines to pay off the bank and government loans which had been necessary to put Lincoln into operation. Moreover, as his factory had been purpose-built for the manufacture of aero-

Above: the handsome 7.2-litre V12-powered KB roadster pf 1932, clothed by Dietrich; the leaping dog on the radiator is shown in detail

Above: a beautiful example of the KB— the first V12-engined Lincoln; this large, stately saloon was built in 1932 with Rollstone coachwork

engines, he couldn't convert it overnight to carry out his ambition of producing a luxury motor car. That was going to take both time and money.

On 26 January 1920, a new company, the Lincoln Motor Company of Delaware, was formed to produce the car, taking over the old firm's property, business and other assets (plus its indebtedness to the Government, some of which was, however, waived). Leland, with his insistence on absolute precision, had called for the very best machine tools available: and the company, which had attracted $6.5 million worth of investment when it had been launched, had spent it all before the first car was completed the following August. And this wasn't the entire story, for the Lincoln, despite its reputation as the product of Henry Leland's genius, incorporated a pretty high proportion of bought-in assemblies—axles, gears, brakes, chassis, bodies, lighting and ignition.

By September the company had had to borrow another $3.7 million, despite the fact that they already had orders for 1000 cars. There were, too, rumblings of dicontent about the way the company was being run. The bodies of the first cars were criticised as lacking style: they were, it seems, designed by Angus Wood-bridge, Leland's son-in-law, whose sole qualification as a stylist seems to have been that he was formerly a ladies' milliner. And, more damning still, Archer, the chief inspector, while he had a fine speaking voice and sang in the choir at Leland's church, was said to be incapable of telling a gauge from a washboard, according to Walter Wagner, who bought machinery and checked tools for the company.

Chief of the dissidents on the Lincoln board was Dr Fred T. Murphy, a nephew of William H. Murphy, who had been the main backer of the original Cadillac company, and while Leland boasted in September 1920 that 'We've turned the corner—from now on it's forward!', Murphy and his supporters took the opposite view. Certainly sales weren't up to the expected level, but then the US industry, which up to then had been at the euphoric crest of a sales boom, had suddenly collapsed into a unprecedented depression. But even if the styling of the new Lincoln car wasn't to everyone's liking, it was difficult to fault it mechanically. The power unit was a 5.8-litre V8, with the blocks at 68 deg to eliminate periodic vibration, and its cooling system was not only sealed to eliminate evaporation losses but also had thermostatically-controlled radiator shutters, the first significant use of this feature on an American car.

The Lelands, backed by Henry Nash, the company treasurer and G. Hermann Kinnicutt, whose firm, Kissell-Kinnicutt, had put the company stock on the market in 1920, argued that the company was basically sound, and needed only a modest cash injection to ensure profitable operation. But Murphy doggedly insisted that only a comprehensive refinancing programme could save the operation; and the failure of the Lelands, on 6 November 1921, to raise a large loan, gave him the ammunition he needed. In addition, two days later, the company received a larger bill from the Government, chiefly for alleged tax arrears. This, it later transpired, had been issued in error, but the damage had already been done. Despite the protests of the Lelands and Nash, evidence was produced that the

Right: the publicity literature for the Zephyr V12 of 1938; modifications for this year included a dashboard gearchange

Below: a 1932 seven-passenger KB saloon, one of the few to be fitted with an actual Lincoln body

Bottom: in 1934, the model K replaced both the KA and the KB, having an engine of 6.8 litres; this is the Brunn-bodied touring cabriolet of 1937

Top: the 1937 Lincoln Zephyr coupé; the unitary-construction Zephyr was so popular that it finally ousted the model K from the catalogues in 1940

Above: the Lincoln Sunshine Special built for President Roosevelt and based on the model K; although the K was withdrawn in 1940, this car was updated in 1942

company was running at a loss, due to poor sales, and a receivership was applied for.

According to Wilfred Leland, the Government claim had been issued at Murphy's instigation: apparently he wanted the company to fail so that he could acquire control at a bargain price, but the Lelands weren't willing to relinquish their company without a struggle. They announced that they were in opposition to the receivership, that they would attempt to buy and revitalise the company, and that creditors and stockholders would be reimbursed to the tune of $50 a share.

But to do this, they needed financial backing. They could either raise a loan to buy the company when it was offered for sale by the receiver and to keep it running until it was back on a profitable footing, or they could find a buyer who would acquire the company and then allow them complete autonomy to operate it as they chose, and to reimburse creditors and stockholders as the cash became available.

Although this was the less desirable choice from their point of view, the Lelands had already begun to make overtures in this direction before the Murphy faction had applied for the receivership.

The man they approached, Henry Ford, had himself suffered a major financial crisis only nine months earlier, but was now back in full production with the Model T and heading for mammoth production records: he, it seemed, commanded the necessary

resources, and had shown some interest in Lincoln.

When a meeting was arranged, Ford dragged his heels, and the Lelands left without a definite assurance; but after the door of Fair Lane, Ford's luxurious house, had closed behind them, Mrs Clara Ford, who had heard much of the discussion, is reported to have said 'Can't you do something to help them? It's a shame that all Detroit should stand by and see that company wrecked'.

Certainly Ford's 28-year-old son, Edsel, was interested. Ever since the age of ten, Edsel had been fascinated by car styling—a commodity conspicuously lacking in the utilitarian Model T—and longed for an outlet for his definite talents in this direction.

Around this time, during a round of golf with a friend, Edsel paused from his game to remark wistfully: 'Father makes the most popular car in the world; I should like to make the best car in the world'.

Now, it seems, he might have the opportunity . . . With his mother's backing, Edsel discussed the possibility of the Ford Motor Company acquiring Lincoln with the other members of the company top management, and told Henry that they would like to take over Lincoln. 'Tell the Lelands to come out and talk it over', Henry replied.

Although in later years the Lelands claimed that Ford had offered to buy their company so that they could run it without interference, and that they could easily have raised the necessary money elsewhere, it seems, on the evidence of Edsel Ford, that they were pretty desperate when they asked for Ford's help, and that they had received no other offers.

Whatever the truth of the matter, by December 1921 it was settled that the Fords would provide the money needed to save Lincoln. The Murphies—if it really was they who had engineered the company's downfall had faded from the scene, for when Henry Ford's representative bid $8,000,000 for Lincoln at the receivership sale on 4 February, his was the only offer.

There was a holiday atmosphere at the Lincoln plant: the Fords and the Lelands had attended the sale together, and when the offer was accepted, the watching crowd formed a line to shake hands with Henry Leland.

It looked indeed as though the Lelands had got what they wanted: 'The executive personnel of the two concerns', insisted Henry Ford, 'will be held separate and distinct, the management of the Lincoln company continuing with Henry M. and Wilfred C.

Leland'. The new Lincoln Motor Company, with Edsel Ford as second Vice-President along with Wilfred Leland, was indeed operated as a separate company, even though all its shares were now held by the Ford Motor Company.

And, with Edsel's influence, Lincoln became a viable proposition. The old body designs were phased out, and new, more attractive styles introduced. Prices were cut drastically, and orders worth $2 million poured in.

However, the Ford staff who now moved into the Lincoln plant to watch production methods and see what could be improved, what could be adapted to the Model T's manufacture, represented an intolerable interference to the Lelands, who resented any suggestions, however well meant or accurate, which would result in changing any of their methods or materials. Within a few months the situation had deteriorated to the point where reconciliation was impossible, and Wilfred Leland reportedly asked Henry Ford if he and his father could buy the company at the purchase price plus a reasonable rate of interest; no deal. 'Mr Leland,' said Ford, 'I wouldn't sell the Lincoln plant for five hundred million dollars.'

By mid June the Leland-Ford alliance was all over, and the two Lelands had been given their marching orders. Now that Edsel had sole command, the quality of the cars improved, certain production processes were rationalised, and limited conveyor-belt assembly introduced. The standard bodies were styled by Brunn, while custom coachwork was series-produced by LeBaron, Willoughby, Judkins, Dietrich and Locke. The cars were built to such accurate limits that they required, boasted T. J. Litle, the company's

chief engineer, no running in. Their acceleration made them a favourite with both police and gangsters. Indeed, special police models were available from 1924, with four-wheel brakes (the general public didn't get them until 1927), bullet-proof glass windscreens, twin spotlights, shotgun racks and, in some cases, special tuning to bring the maximum speed to more than 80 mph.

By 1924 the company was showing a profit, with 7875 cars produced in the 1923–24 season; and the President of the United States, Calvin Coolidge, had become the first such officer to own a Lincoln.

All cars were subjected to an intense test programme before leaving the factory, even those carrying coachwork by outside bodybuilders, and the standards of finish were comparable with those of any top quality car in the world. Yet the Lincoln incorporated many

Ford ideas, such as the interchangeability of parts between new and old models, so that the earlier cars could be brought up to date at modest cost. Exchange engines were available for a mere $100, and servicing was as efficient and as easily available as for the Model T.

The year 1928 saw an increase in engine size to 6.3 litres; the crankshaft was fitted with counterweights to retain the car's traditional smoothness of running. This Lincoln model was a very fine car indeed: some years ago the author drove a Lincoln limousine that had formerly belonged to a director of Ford of Britain. It had impeccable manners, going from a slow walking pace to its more than ample touring speed in top gear without hesitation, while the steering was exceptionally light—comparable in feel to the then-current Ford Corsair—for such a large and heavy (5190 lb) car.

The next major specification change came in 1931, with a chassis lengthened to give a 145 in wheelbase, and equipped with a freewheel. Eulogised N. W. Ayer & Son, Inc, who handled publicity for this model: 'Low-slung and rakish, this new open sport type is expected to be a familiar sight around country clubs and fashionable beach and mountain resorts during the coming summer'.

Typical of the standard equipment of the Lincoln range at this time was a cabinet inlaid with pewter, recessed into the back of the front seat. Access to it was provided by a door fitted on each side of a centre panel in which a cigar lighter, tonneau light and switch were fitted.

Further engineering innovation came in 1932, the year that the Ford Motor Company introduced the V8. Not to be outdone, Lincoln announced their new KB model—with a V12, hitherto the province of low-production, high-cost cars. It was one of only seven V12 models on the American market that year, the others being produced by Auburn, Cadillac, Franklin, Packard and Pierce-Arrow. It was, stated *The Autocar*, 'one of those exceptional cars which in both construction and performance rise much above the general practice of contemporaries . . . detail work is very well done, as would be expected, the whole car is beautifully finished, and the workmanship beneath the bonnet is reminiscent of the best European practice, than which there can be no higher praise'.

This was the last new Lincoln model to be introduced in the lifetime of the company's founder, for Henry M. Leland died a few months later, aged 89. Although the firm had been part of the Ford organisation for the past decade, there had been no let-up in the standards of accuracy to which the car was built. Indeed, many of the components of the Lincoln KB were machined to an accuracy of between 1/5000 and 1/10,000 inch.

But unfortunately sales of the new model and its slightly smaller stable mate, the KA, were disappointing—only 2112 in 1933—and for 1934 a new Model K was promoted, replacing both KA and KB, and having a swept volume of 414 cu in, which represented almost exactly the average between the cubic capacities of its two predecessors. A total of 21 different body types was available. Sales rose marginally, to 2170.

The opportunity to own a Lincoln was soon to be placed before a vastly increased sector of the public with the arrival of what Ford Sales Manager William C. Cowling called a 'sensational, completely new motor car'. This was the Lincoln Zephyr, which had a 110 cu in engine (V12 of course) in a 122 in-wheelbase body of semi-unitary construction and ultra-streamlined appearance. Price tag was only $1275, and the success of the new model was reflected dramatically

Above: the Lincoln Continental Mk II of 1956; this was powered by a 6-litre Ford V8 engine

'continental'). Several specials were built for Edsel's personal use on Ford chassis, but, despite Gregorie's pleadings, none was adapted for production.

The introduction of the Lincoln Zephyr gave Gregorie the opportunity he needed: he suggested that a distinctive car could be produced from the standard body components of the Lincoln Zephyr Convertible Coupé by a little judicious customising.

In November 1938 Gregorie had a 1/10 scale clay model of his proposed design ready to show to Edsel. He had achieved that long, low, 'continental' look that Edsel so prized by simply cutting a four-inch strip out of the doors and body sides.

Edsel's Continental was completed in March 1939, and shipped to his holiday retreat in Florida, where the sleek grey coupé created such a furore of excitement that he resolved to produce it as a 'limited edition'. And in October 1939 the first production Lincoln Continental came off the line. Though it was based on standard Lincoln Zephyr parts, each Continental was virtually hand-built. Architect Frank Lloyd Wright called the model the most beautiful car ever made, and three years after production ceased in 1948, the Metropolitan Museum of Art in New York chose it as one of only eight cars selected for their 'excellence as works of art'. Altogether 5322 of the original Lincoln Continentals were produced in the 1940–42/46–48 period, 3045 of them coupés and 2277 cabriolets, all with a close resemblance to Eugene Gregorie's original conception, the hallmark of which was the spare tyre vertically mounted at the rear of the car. This, though it had been a commonplace in the 1920s, had fallen out of fashion by the late 1930s. So it was inevitable that when it was revived for Edsel's dream car that this tyre placement should be for ever after christened 'Continental'.

As for the Lincoln Zephyr itself, having reached its sales peak in 1937, it went into a gentle decline; and it was quietly resolved that, when production ceased in 1942 so that the company could concentrate on its war work, the Zephyr would not reappear.

Meanwhile, Edsel Ford had died, in 1943, aged only 49. For some years his relationship with his father had been clouded by the hold that a strange semi-under-world figure, Harry Bennet, had over Henry. Retained originally to protect Henry Ford's grandchildren against kidnapping, Bennet had become Ford's head of security, often acting as a mouthpiece for the old man. A former prizefighter, Bennett kept tiger cubs in his office, where he also practised sharpshooting, knocking the points off pencils with an air pistol. Bennett had

in the sales figures: in 1936 a total of 18,994 Lincolns was sold, of which a staggering 17,715 were the new Zephyr model. And the following year was even better, despite a recession in the autumn, with total Lincoln Zephyr sales of 25,186. The Zephyr had, however, effectively stifled the more expensive Lincoln Model K, which was finally dropped in 1940, after only 120 cars had been sold in two seasons, including Franklin D. Roosevelt's famous 'Sunshine Special'.

Meanwhile, however, a new Lincoln model had made its appearance; this car, the Continental, was destined to become a legend in its own lifetime, and was the direct result of the setting up of a styling studio at Edsel Ford's instigation in the early 1930s. Heading the studio were John Crawford and Eugene Turenne Gregorie, and in 1932 Gregorie began work designing a sporting car of European type (which Edsel called

Left: the two-door Continental hardtop of 1966

Below: a Lincoln Continental Mk V, styled by Bill Blass

ambitions to become the head of Ford Motor Company, and was therefore opposed to Edsel.

Thanks to Bennett, Henry had become antagonistic towards his son and the situation was ruining Edsel's health. He had always been prone to stomach ulcers; now these had developed into cancer, and, in addition, he had contracted undulant fever from drinking unpasteurised milk from the Ford farm. On 26 May 1943, at 1.10 am, Edsel died. Deprived of the guiding influence of this man bursting with natural talent for styling, the first post-war Lincolns were little more than upmarket versions of the contemporary Ford range (excepting of course the Continental).

In 1948 Benson, Edsel Ford's second son, took control of the Lincoln-Mercury Division, which produced the first new post-war Ford models, the Lincoln and the Lincoln Cosmopolitan, which had independent front suspension. Then, in 1950, came news that the company was considering the reintroduction of a Continental model. On 1 July, 1952, a separate division of Lincoln-Mercury was formed to handle the new Continental, headed by William Clay Ford, youngest of the three Ford brothers, who had inherited his father's taste for styling. By June 1953, the first model of the new Continental was shown to Ford's executive committee, and in 1954 a special plant was inaugurated for its production.

The Mark II Continental made its debut late in 1954. Designed by John Reinart, it had little in common with its illustrious ancestor other than the spare wheel mounting. It was advertised as being a '$10,000 car', though the price tag was in reality lower than this. Just 3012 were built before production ceased in 1957: Lincoln Continentals were built to this design for another couple of years, designated Mks III and IV, but they had lost that traditional exclusivity, and no-one objected to the introduction of a new Lincoln Continental in 1961.

Squarecut and lowslung, the 1961 Continental was voted one of the world's seven best-made cars by *Road and Track* magazine: each car built—and production was restricted to less than 100 cars a day—underwent comprehensive testing, including a 12-mile road run. The range included what was claimed to be the world's only four-door convertible.

A complete restyling took place in 1970, with the cars acquiring a more pronounced kick-up over the rear wheels and squarer wheel arches, a line which was still in use in 1977, following Lincoln's policy of never making change simply for change's sake.

Standard equipment on the 1974 Lincoln Continental included automatic temperature control—'you

simply select the desired climate . . . it is then maintained constantly'—power windows, six-way power front seats, power front disc brakes, power steering, a Cartier clock, radio with four loudspeakers and lights for every compartment, even the ashtrays.

There is also the Lincoln Continental Mk IV, described as 'one of the most desirable and most wanted personal American luxury cars of this decade . . . a car whose classically beautiful simplicity will challenge the years'. Even more lavishly equipped than the standard Continentals, the Mk IV came in three incarnations, topped by the Continental Mk IV with 'Gold Luxury Option . . . the ultimate gesture in luxury . . . America's consummate luxury car'.

Exterior finish was, believe it or not, 'prized Unique Gold Diamond Fire', with a roof covered in 'Gold Flare Levant grain vinyl'. And there was the option of the Moonroof, a power-operated sunshine roof of gold-tinted one-way glass.

For 1975, there were new options, including disc-brakes all round and coachlamps.

Standard, of course, was the Continental spare wheel position, though the wheel now rode in burglar-proof luxury inside the cut-pile carpeted boot.

In 1977 the Mk V Continental was introduced, and the 1978 Diamond Jubilee Edition featured a 6.5-litre V8 producing 166 bhp, with disc brakes all round, electric windows and air-conditioning as standard and a limited-slip differential and sunshine roof as options.

Top of the 1979 range was the Collectors Series Continental Mark V and then, for 1980, Lincoln introduced its first all-new car for ten years. It was dubbed Lincoln Continental and its styling left no doubts as to its line of descent. The new car had the best year-to-year economy improvement of any car in Ford history, partly due to having lost a substantial 800 lb in

Facing page: The Lincoln Continental Mk III of 1968; this model had an added gimmick of headlamp covers

Inset top: the 1961 Continental was voted one of the seven best-made cars in the world by *Road and Track;* production was restricted to 100 cars per day

Inset bottom: a special Continental built for the White House; the foot rests at the front and back of the door sills are for Presidential security guards

its rebirth. Available in four models, with the 5.0-litre V8 as standard, plus electronic fuel injection, electronic engine function monitoring and Ford's new Automatic Overdrive Transmission, it offered a more than 40% fuel consumption improvement on its forerunner. The revamped Continental Mark, now dubbed Continental Mark VI, was similarly frugal and also 750 lb lighter. The Mark VI had electronic instruments as standard, while the Lincoln offered them as an option and a Keyless Entry System was a further option. The prestigious four-door Versailles came in a slightly smaller package and was no less luxurious than its big sisters but the real style came with the Designer Series of the two-door Mark VI; these were special editions whose paint and interior trim finishes were specified by the four designers, Pucci, Givenchy, Blass and Cartier.

The people at Lincoln had the happy knack of knowing when not to change a good thing (in sales terms) and for the 1981 model year the biggest change was the dropping of the Versailles from the model list. The only other changes were in names; the Lincoln Continental became the Town Car but otherwise stayed much the same as before except for the new trim options. The Continental Mark VI gained some more assorted electronic gadgetry and a few new colours.

The big change (by Lincoln standards) came at the end of 1981, for the 1982 model year, in the form of a new, and much smaller, Continental, derived from the highly successful (but recently renamed) Ford Fairmont, and intended as a replacement for the Versailles. It was only very *loosely* based on the Fairmont, of course, and inside it was all Lincoln, with the usual sumptuous trim, sybaritic comforts and options galore. It was a new Lincoln, certainly, but not new enough to frighten the customers; luxury was still the name of the game. Indeed, a Lincoln model catalogue could have been speaking of almost any car produced by the company in describing the Mk IV Continental: 'Rarely has so much personal luxury and comfort been combined in such a splendidly rewarding automobile.'

Henry Leland and Edsel Ford could not, one feels, have said it any better.

Left: the 1980 Versailles was the last of the series. It was an alternative to the larger Continental Mark VI and Lincoln Continental but was overshadowed by both

Below left: the 1981 Continental Mark VI was one of the most luxurious and best equipped cars in America. It also made extensive use of electronic equipment, including electronic instrumentation

Above: the 1981 Mark VI Designer Series two-door coupé

Right: the 1981 Lincoln Town Car four-door sedan featured the 5-litre V8 as standard. The previously available two-door model was dropped for 1982

Mercury

in the vanguard of the 'badge *engineering' trend*

As a division of Ford, Mercury were

Above: Mercury—the fleet-footed, winged-sandalled messenger of the gods, and the name given to the new car concern created by the Ford Motor Company in 1938

Left: a Mercury 3.9-litre sedan of 1940, the year in which Ford was dropped from the original Ford-Mercury name

MERCURY WAS AN IDEAL NAME for a motor car because Mercury was a Roman god with winged sandals who was the messenger of the gods. Several British and American companies used the name in the early days of motoring, but when the Ford Motor Company of the USA was looking for a new *marque* identification, the name of Mercury was available so they used it.

The first Mercury, which appeared on 4 November 1938, was in effect a Ford with a different body, becoming one of the fore-runners of today's much despised 'badge engineering' techniques where near-identical cars are sold under different *marque* names. In price the new Mercury fell between the existing Ford V8 and the Lincoln, so that Ford now had cars in over 90 per cent of American price categories. The Mercury 8 as it was called featured the Ford box-section, cruciform braced chassis with rigid axles front and rear, suspended on transverse leaf springs and double-acting hydraulic dampers. Four-wheel hydraulically operated drum brakes were fitted all round and power came from an enlarged version of the Ford V8

side-valve 3.9-litre engine, which gave 95 bhp at 3600 rpm. Power was taken via a three-speed gearbox through a torque tube drive to the rear axle. The four-door sedan body of the standard model was the first Ford product to be styled from a clay model within the company's own studios. The body was quite pleasant by 1938 standards. Its design conforming well with contemporary styling trends. As well as the sedan there was a two-door convertible with an electrically operated roof and leather upholstery.

Ford could do no wrong in 1939, as they were out-selling General Motors by 2 to 1 and the Mercury was enthusiastically received despite its similarity to the Ford line. Over 65,000 Mercury's were registered in 1939, although in the first model year the cars were actually known as Ford-Mercurys. The Ford name was dropped for 1940 when the only major change was a new four-door convertible version which was not very popular. A column gear change and sealed-beam headlamps were also introduced in 1940.

The Ford factories were still producing cars in 1942

Below: 1939 Mercury four-door sedan

Bottom: 1946 Mercury Sportsman

Top: 1949 Mercury club coupé

Above: Mercury Monterey Sun Valley

although the USA had entered the war in 1941. The Mercury models were restyled once again, the front end being drastically revised with a low, wide grille. The power output of the Ford 'flathead' was up to a claimed 100 bhp and for the first time a semi-automatic transmission was available.

Car production came to a halt in early 1942 and the factories switched to war production, building tanks, amphibious machines, jeeps and even B24 bombers.

Edsel Ford, who had played a large part in introducing the Lincoln and Mercury names to the Ford range died during the war and in September 1945 Henry Ford II became President of Ford. He immediately set in motion plans to divorce Lincoln and Mercury from Ford operations, setting up the Lincoln-Mercury Division of the Ford Motor Company. Work began on new factories in Los Angeles and Metuchen, New Jersey, and the St Louis factory was switched entirely to Lincoln and Mercury products.

The 1946 models were very similar to the cars that had been in production in 1942 with the exception of a new convertible called the Sportsman which had wood panelled bodywork like the station wagon. Yet another grille restyling job was carried out and nearly 90,000 Mercurys were sold in 1946. With demand running well ahead of production there was little need for change in the years that followed and the Mercury range was unchanged in 1947 and 1948.

The first really new Mercury since 1938 was announced in late 1948. The chassis remained much as before except that coil-spring independent front suspension was introduced and a hypoid rear axle fitted. The faithful V8 engine was increased in size to $4\frac{1}{4}$ litres and the power output was increased to 110 bhp. The three-speed gearbox was retained but an innovation was the availability of a Borg Warner overdrive, engaged by depressing the throttle pedal.

By 1950 the one-millionth Mercury had been built and it was now necessary to build a new factory at Wayne, Michigan to keep up with demand. A slightly modified Mercury Sport Coupé was added to the range in 1950.

By 1953 the range had swollen to eight different models and Mercury started to give models individual names; one new name was the Monterey, a model which stayed with the company until 1974, along with several other alliterative names.

In 1954 Ford's new V8 overhead-valve engine was introduced, this $4\frac{1}{4}$-litre engine giving 161 bhp in its Mercury form. The rest of the design changed little, the emphasis being on body styling to attract customers. One example of this was the Monterey Sun Valley, a coupé with the front half of the roof made from transparent plastic. It did not last long because buyers fried under the greenhouse roof. Mercury entered the dream-car field in 1954 with the XM800, which was simply a styling job in glassfibre on a standard chassis.

Mercury had offered little for the motor-racing enthusiast because their cars were just cheap, basic, unexciting transportation, but veteran mechanic Bill Stroppe had achieved some success in the Mobil Economy run and had persuaded Lincoln to give him cars for the Pan-American Road Race. His cars finished first, second, third and fourth in 1952 and 1953, earning Stroppe a contract with the Lincoln-Mercury Division. When Chevrolet began winning Stock-Car races in the early 1950s and promoting motor racing in a big way, both the Ford and Lincoln-Mercury Divisions retaliated with racing programmes. Stroppe ran the team for Lincoln-Mercury using Mercury cars, winning several races on the West Coast himself in 1955, but Ford were far more successful, largely because they put more finance into their effort.

The 1955 production Mercurys were considerably modified; the wheelbase was increased to 119 inches and two new versions of the ohv V8 were introduced, both of 5 litres capacity, one with a 7.5:1 compression ratio giving 188 bhp and the other with 8.5:1 compression ratio giving 198 bhp. Another restyling job was undertaken, with a big wrap-around windscreen, hooded headlamps and a full-width grille/bumper design. A new model was added to the range, the Montclair, to bring Mercury up to ten different models. In 1955 Mercury production was raised to its highest ever level of 434,911 cars.

Detroit's greatest styling excesses were perpetrated in the late 1950s, the Mercurys of the 1956 to 1959

Below: the Mercury Cougar, a car with a strong luxury/sports personality, added a new dimension to the American motoring scene in 1967. It was one of the new breed of compact cars very popular in the USA at that time. Outstanding performance was provided by powertrain combinations featuring either 289 cubic inch V8 engines, with two or four-choke carburation, or a 390 cubic inch V8, with four-choke carburation

model years, ranking as some of the ugliest ever made. Significantly, Mercury sales began to tail off at the start of this period with 1956 sales down to 327,943 cars. More new cars were announced for 1956 but they were largely adaptations of the 1955 models. The cheaper Medalist range was added to the Monterey and Montclair ranges and an optional 260 hp version of the V8 engine was available in 1956.

On the production side the 1957 cars showed the influence of the XM Turnpike Cruiser of 1956, for the cars were longer, lower and wider, the wheelbase now up to 122 inches and the standard engine being a 6-litre 290 bhp V8. Despite the new styling, sales slumped again to 263,245, little more than half of the

1955 production. However, the 3-millionth Mercury was eventually produced during the year 1957.

In 1958 Ford launched the new Edsel *marque* which was designed to fit between the Ford and Mercury price brackets. A new division, the Mercury-Edsel-Lincoln Division was formed and Mercury announced an additional range of cars, the Park Lane series which were built on a new 125 in wheelbase chassis. The horsepower race was still on with a vengeance, despite the so-called ban on advertising, giving a claimed 400 bhp. A new three-speed automatic transmission made its appearance, and was specified by most drivers.

Although the new Edsel was supposed to hit at General Motors' sales, it took a large bite out of Mercury sales which crashed to a modest 132,271 during the 1958 season.

The Edsel was a complete failure and was dropped in 1959, so the division was renamed the Lincoln-Mercury Division and great efforts were made to improve the Mercury range. The Monterey and Montclair models used a 126 in wheelbase while the Park Lane used a 128 in wheelbase chassis. Overall styling remained largely unchanged, but dual-headlamp systems were now almost universal. The range was now huge, with many permutations available on the basic chassis, while engines ranged from the 5-litre 210 bhp V8 of the Medalist to the 7.2-litre 345 bhp V8s of the Park Lane. Sales in 1959 improved to 161,237.

The American motor industry was beginning to panic in the late 1950s at the inroads made into the US market by imported cars, most notably the Volkswagen. Prior to this, the US manufacturers had felt that imports were little more than a pinprick, but suddenly the imports were heading for a 10 per cent market share and 10 per cent of 5 million cars was a little more than Detroit could bear. So the big three makers hurriedly designed and built their so-called Compact cars, which, although fairly small by US

standards, were still big compared with the European cars which were invading the market. Ford brought out the Falcon and Mercury produced an almost identical car called the Comet. This was a very conventional car on a 114 in wheelbase powered by a 2.3-litre straight-six cylinder engine giving 114 bhp. The Comet was an immediate success with 100,000 sold within six months of its announcement, helping to push Mercury sales back up to a healthy 317,055 for

1960, firmly establishing the 'Compact' concept.

For 1961 Mercury decided to capitalise on the Comet successes by offering another economy range, the Meteor 600 and 800 series powered by 3.6-litre 135 bhp straight-six engines developed from the Comet unit. However, the Comet still took the lion's share of sales in 1961, racking up 197,263 sales against the 120,088 of all other Mercury models put together.

The 1962 range followed the clean cut, uncluttered style of the previous year's cars and more sporty models were being produced with four-speed manual gearboxes, separate bucket seats, and a variety of optional engines. Sales improved slightly to 321,817.

Ford had decided in the early 1960s that a return to factory racing participation would be advantageous and they gradually began to build up their involvement in practically every branch of the sport, especially in Europe with rally cars, saloon-car racing and even single-seater racing with especial emphasis on Indianapolis. Mercury were not left out although their task was to concentrate on stock-car racing through Bill Stroppe once again.

By mid-1963 the Mercury Marauder had been announced; this was a high performance car fitted with a 7-litre V8 giving options of 415 or 425 bhp. This car formed the basis of Parnelli Jones' successful racers.

In 1964 Ford invented the 'pony car' with their Mustang, a medium-sized, sporty looking car with performance potential which took America's youth market by storm. Rival manufacturers quickly reacted by bringing out their own 'pony cars' but it was some while later before Mercury brought out their Cougar,

Above left: the Mercury Cougar XR7 two-door hardtop of 1969

Top: the convertible version of the 1969 Mercury Cougar

Above: another 1969 model, this is the Cyclone CJ two-door fastback

143

a somewhat up-market version of the Mustang with a rather different body, although it, too, was a two-door hardtop. The Mustang went on to achieve success in the Trans-Am series for medium-sized saloons of up to 5 litres in capacity but Mercury did not enter their similar Cougar.

By 1967 the Comet was still in production but the accent had swung away from economy and the wheelbase had increased by 2 in to 116 in. Not too many owners specified the straight-six engine as most buyers wanted good acceleration. A whole new range of models had come in including such models as the Capri (a two-door coupé having no connections with Ford of Britain's Capri), the Caliente, the Cyclone GT, the Villager station wagon, the S55 convertible, the Monterey, the Montclair, the Park Lane, the Brougham, the Marquis and the Colony Park. By careful manipulation between Ford and Mercury it was possible to offer a seemingly endless series of cars, although very often there was little to choose between them in specification.

By 1970 Detroit was again worried about the threat of foreign imports and Ford announced the Maverick, a sub-compact, 2-door coupé powered by a straight-six 2.7-litre engine giving 105 bhp in standard trim. Mercury did not follow suit immediately but eventually the Comet range was completely revised to follow the Maverick lines, but was available as a two-door coupé and a four-door saloon as well. The same engine was used, although in standard trim it gave only 82 bhp, and the cheapest version, the 2-door coupé, cost 2193 dollars in 1972.

Mercury also attracted some attention in the performance-car market with the Cyclone GT and Spoiler, the latter model having an aerofoil mounted on the boot lid. The standard engine for the Spoiler was a 370 bhp version of the 7-litre V8 which gave the car a top speed of around 120 mph. An optional engine was a 375 bhp version of the same unit.

By 1972 the US motor industry was in a state of panic over the safety and pollution laws which were promising to be more stringent than anticipated. Most manufacturers found it difficult to make their big V8s comply with the pollution tests, so gradually the

bigger engines began to fade from catalogues and power outputs dropped drastically as engines were 'de-toxed' to cope with the regulations. The necessity to cope with crash tests on all models caused manufacturers to trim their model ranges considerably, while all convertible models were soon abandoned as the US manufacturers felt they could not be made to comply with the regulations. However, the 1972/3 Mercury range was still quite extensive for they had the Comet, the Montego, the Cougar, the Monterey, the Marquis and the Colony Park station wagon. But the Marauder, Cyclone and Brougham ranges had been dropped as had all the convertible models except the Cougar.

In 1973 the fuel crisis arrived and with it yet more demands for smaller cars. The Mercury Comet sold well during late 1973 and through much of 1974 while the bigger cars would hardly sell at all. To cash in on the new boom in smaller cars, Ford instigated a crash programme to bring out new small cars. The Ford Mustang 11 was a much smaller car than its predecessor and in late 1974 Ford announced their Ford Granada and the equivalent Mercury Monarch. Both these models were fairly unsophisticated semi-compact cars weighing around 1½ tons and available with either the straight-six or V8 engines.

With the arrival of the Monarch, Mercury decided to drop one of their biggest cars, the Monterey, a name which had been with Mercury for many years. However, the loss of the Monterey was just another sign that Detroit felt the day of the 2½-ton car had ended. Indeed, the company launched its first sub-compact car, the Bobcat in 1975. This was powered by the 2.3-litre, four-cylinder Pinto engine and it heralded a new era for Mercury.

The Bobcat was still around as Mercury went, a little unsteadily, into the 1980s. Sporty styling and reasonably good economy had given the Pinto lookalike steady sales, but it was no longer fresh and different alongside its newer rivals. Nowadays it relied heavily on a long list of standard accessories and a competitive price. Fortunately, Mercury had added another racy package to its line-up in 1979, the Capri. The Capri was distinctly European in character (not surprisingly, since

Above: the 1982 Mercury LN7 was another Ford clone, this time sister to the much maligned Ford EXP 'bubbleback sports coupé'. The performance of the sporty two-seater did not match its looks.

that is where, like several contemporaries, it had originated). In 1980 it came with a choice of straight-four, turbocharged four, V6 or V8 power. The turbo-four was the popular 2.3-litre engine and the V8 was Ford's new lightweight 4.2. Also in the 1980 range were the latest Monarch, the Marquis (with Ford's new Automatic Overdrive Transmission), the completely re-engineered, mid-sized Cougar XR-7 (now 15 in smaller and 700 lb lighter) and the compact Zephyr, with the 2.3 turbo. The 1980 range also continued the Ford corporate trend towards eliminating or simplifying many maintenance requirements.

In spite of mounting financial losses, Mercury managed a few changes for 1981. The Monarch was finally deposed, the Marquis continued, with the 4.2-litre V8 in place of the old 5.0-litre, the Cougar line was extended to include two- and four-door saloons (which were in reality sisters of the new Ford Granada and replaced the Monarch) and the Zephyr, which was largely unchanged. Overshadowing all the rest was the new Lynx, Mercury's rendering of the front-wheel-drive, European-engineered, Ford Escort 'world car'. It was a vital car for the future of the Mercury Division, the much needed economy model to satisfy the dealers.

A year later, it seemed the Escort formula had worked. Around 400,000 were sold during 1981, bearing one badge or the other (mostly Ford, of course) and it eased the pain of poor sales of other lines. There was better to come, too. For 1982, the car became

available in four-door-plus-hatchback format and was treated to much engineering improvement, especially in terms of upgraded engines, transmission and suspension—with a still more powerful motor promised for mid-1982. The Lynx/Escort became what it was supposed to be in the first place, a lively and refined, four-passenger car on a shoestring. The more-power theory was also carried over to (and much needed on) the LN7, which had also been introduced in 1981. It was dubbed a 'bubbleback' sportcoupe and was sister to the much maligned, two-seater Ford EXP. With a 1.6-litre engine it was bigger on economy than on performance and, like the Lynx, it was destined to receive more horses and a more suitable set of gear ratios early in 1982. The Capri, particularly with the optional 5.0-litre V8, needed no such treatment and was already giving the frustrated hot-rodder all the zip he could wish for. The more sedentary Mercury buyers were still catered for by the Zephyr (due for a front-wheel-drive replacement in the autumn of 1982), the Cougar XR-7 and the long running Marquis.

Previously, Mercury has avoided any advanced engineering features in its products, preferring to stick to uncomplicated, well proven designs, with annual styling changes. As a subsidiary of Ford, the company has never really established its own identity, largely for financial reasons, and still labours under the stigma of being a Ford with a different badge. Yet if Mercury has never made an exciting car, neither has it built a really bad one.

IF THERE WAS EVER an example of the proverbial All-American rags to riches success story in the motor industry, it was that of Charles W. Nash who was born in 1864. Orphaned at a very early age, he was bound out to an Illinois farmer when he was six; he hated the life so much that he ran away six years later, when he reckoned he was old enough to fend for himself. But his adolescence was spent in grinding poverty, wandering from farm to farm as an itinerant labourer; before he was 27 Nash never made more than $300 a year.

He eventually found himself a job as a trimmer in the carriage works run by Billy Durant and J. Dallas Dort in 'America's carriage capital', Flint, Michigan. By sheer hard work, Nash rose to be general manager of the company; meanwhile, Billy Durant had taken over Buick and founded General Motors, and was merrily running up huge debts. Only a year or so after General Motors had been incorporated in September 1908, Durant owed the Durant-Dort carriage company several million dollars for car bodies; not unnaturally, Charles Nash asked to be allowed to sort things out, and was promptly made president of Buick.

Shortly after that, General Motors ran out of cash and credit, was saved by a bankers' syndicate, and was put under new management. Durant, ousted from control, recommended Nash to James J. Storrow, who headed the syndicate, with the result that in 1912 the former farm labourer became president of General Motors. His technical assistant, Walter Chrysler, took over Buick.

However, when Durant leapfrogged back into control of General Motors via his hugely successful new Chevrolet company, Nash resigned. His policies were diametrically opposed to those of the ebullient Billy; even so, Durant offered him an astronomical salary to stay on—'It was more than any man's worth,' commented Nash.

Nash
From poverty, Charles W. Nash managed to reach the top

In any case, Nash had a long-standing ambition to build a car under his own name, and the easiest way of doing this was to take over an existing company. He acquired the Thomas B. Jeffery Company, of Kenosha, Wisconsin, founded by an English-born bicycle manufacturer—'the inventor of the clincher tyre and railroad velocipede'—who had built his first experimental car in 1897 before going into production with his first Rambler in 1902. Jeffery died in 1910, and four years later the company changed its product name to 'Jeffery' in his honour; model names of some cars, like the 1915 Chesterfield, were chosen by Ned Jordan, whose purple pen was later to give the advertising world the immortal 'Somewhere West of Laramie' copy which extolled his Jordan Playboy model. Jeffery were tending to concentrate on truck production, having entered this field in 1913, and in 1914 had introduced their four-wheel-driven Jeffery Quad, which was bought by the thousand for war use by the British and French governments. In 1914 the Jeffery Company built 10,417 cars and 3096 trucks; a year later the position was reversed, with truck output up to 7600, car output down to 3100, while in the year

Below: a 1918 six-cylinder Nash tourer; the first Nash car had appeared in the autumn of the previous year. This first Nash was unusual in that its engine had pushrod-operated overhead valves, a feature not widely used during that period

of the takeover, pasenger car production rose again, to 4608, with trucks down to 2117.

A few weeks after his acquisition of the Jeffery company in July 1916, Charles Nash called the dealers and the 3000 employees together for a pep talk: 'We shall build up to a standard, not down to a price,' he told them.

During 1917, the Jeffery name was phased out in readiness for the new Nash car which was being prepared for production; meanwhile, truck output was stepped up again, reaching 11,490 in 1918, making Nash Motors, it was claimed, 'the world's largest manufacturer of trucks', a position they would not bother to maintain as peacetime demand for private cars overtook the market for commercials.

Below: a 1926 two-seater Nash runabout; during this year Nash reached a record sales level with an output of 135,520 cars

Bottom: a convertible Nash tourer of 1927; at that time, Nash were offering 26 different models to the motoring public

The first Nash car appeared in the autumn of 1917; a 4-litre six-cylinder model, it had the unusual feature for the period of pushrod-operated overhead valves, an obvious legacy from Nash's period with Buick, which had never built anything but ohv engines since its inception in 1903. The model line-up included five and seven-seat touring cars, a 'chummy', a coupé and a sedan. Sales were moderately encouraging at 10,283 for the 1918 season.

The following year, roadster and sport models were added to the range, while sales more than doubled, reaching 27,081. Meanwhile, truck output had fallen to 4090, and would be phased out at the end of the decade, as a result.

Expansion was in the air in 1919: 'All companies are increasing production as rapidly as possible and expect more business than they can possibly deliver this year,' exulted *Automobile Topics*, and Nash were well in the forefront of the industry's expansion plans, opening a new assembly plant at Milwaukee in June 1920. But already there were rumours of slump in the air, and in the autumn of 1920, the bottom fell out of the worldwide car market. Nash was among the first manufacturers to be hit by the recession, and on 22 November 1920, the Kenosha plant was temporarily closed down, 'to allow an inventory and completion of plans for readjustment of labour conditions.'

It was only a brief cessation in the company's affairs: by the end of 1921, Nash was not only back in full production, but had also introduced a new model, an ohv 2½-litre four of similar design to the six. There were nine distinct body styles in the range, in contrast to the six models in the six-cylinder lineup. The following season saw another innovation, the use of rubber engine mountings to reduce vibration. Nash

claimed this as an industry first, but in fact Mors had done it a quarter of a century before.

Nash were now well established as manufacturers of cars in the middle-price bracket, their models costing from just over $1000 to just over $2000. Now they decided to break into the luxury market; again, Charles Nash followed his original tactic of buying an established company. In 1922 he became president of LaFayette Motors of Mars Hill, Indiana, who were building a luxurious V8 designed by D. McCall White, an Englishman who had formerly worked with Napier and who had been responsible for the original V8 Cadillac engine of 1914. The LaFayette was a well-equipped, beautifully engineered 5.6-litre car, which pioneered such fittings as thermostatically controlled radiator shutters and fitted luggage which could cost anything up to $7500 in standard guise; Nash transferred LaFayette production to Milwaukee in 1924, but the marque failed to flower in new soil, and was soon discontinued by its owners.

Nash were now boasting of their self-sufficiency, claiming: 'To the best of our knowledge, there is no other manufacturer of motor cars who builds so large a proportion of his products as does Nash', a rash boast which must have afforded Henry Ford, who made everything but the tyres for the Model T, some quiet amusement at the time.

The company was in expansive mood, anyway, for on 2 April 1924, they purchased the Mitchell Motor Company, of Racine, Wisconsin. Mitchell, a couple of years earlier, had produced a model in which the radiator shell was raked backwards. 'Harmonious' was how *The Autocar* described it; 'The Drunken Mitchell' was what the public called it, and the company gently ran out of steam.

Below: pictured is a four-door, six-cylinder Nash sedan of 1932. During this year Nash was one of only two American motor manufacturers to make a profit, the other being General Motors

In any case, Nash had not bought the Racine plant to revive the Mitchell. They needed the extra production capacity for a new line of cars, which would be marketed under the name Ajax. A separate company was formed to market the Ajax, a 3-litre side-valve six-cylinder, priced at $925 for the tourer and $995 for the sedan. Standard colour was Mallard Green.

The new cars were announced to Nash dealers and distributors at a gala reception in the baseball ground at Racine on 6 May 1925. Although Nash sales were enjoying a steady upward trend, the Ajax failed to benefit by association and after a year the Ajax name was dropped altogether and the Racine-built model became known as the Light Six.

Though the Ajax had proved a failure, in the year of its demise the parent company reached a sales record, with an output of 135,520, the first time that Nash production had exceeded 100,000. The range now consisted of the Special Six and Advanced Six, available in 24 different models, nine of which were sedans and six were tourers.

The following year saw a slight fall in sales, output from Kenosha, Milawaukee and Racine totalling 122,606, made up of 26 different models. It seems that the Kenosha plant employed a fair number of ex-patriate Scandinavians, who subscribed to buy a Nash Ambassador Six which they presented to Prince William of Sweden on 14 October 1927.

In 1928, sales were up again, reaching a record 138,137, a figure that would not be beaten until 1949. This achievement gained 3.67 per cent of the American market. That year, the model 328 Nash, with 'French-type roof panels' and dummy landau irons, sold at $1085, which its makers claimed, qualified it as 'the lowest priced 7-bearing six' on the American market.

The 1929 season cars were announced as early as July 1928; heading the lineup was the 400 Series of 'twin-ignition' models, available on 116 inch and 130 inch wheelbases.

Rumours of mergers were in the air again, for on 27 January 1929, the *Kenosha News* reported that a merger between Nash Motors and Packard was being arranged, though these reports subsequently proved to be unfounded. Output in that first year of the Depression reached 116,622; truck production, which had been in steady decline since the end of the war, was finally wound up.

There was a new model for 1930, the Twin-Ignition Eight, which, like the Six, had twin coil ignition systems; swept volume was 3920 cc. This brought the range of Nash variants up to 32, based on the Single Six and Twin-Ignition Six (both of 3378 cc) and the new Eight. The technical specification of the cars aroused *Autocar*'s admiration: 'The principal feature is not only that the crankshaft is exceptionally large and stiff in days when most crankshafts are nearly as big as they can be, but that seven wide main bearings are provided. In addition, the makers have maintained their opinion that the advantages of the aluminium piston outweigh its disadvantages considerably. Moreover, this is one of the few American cars in which oil is forced not only to the main engine bearings, but also through drilled passages up the connecting rods direct to the gudgeon pins and cylinder walls, this fully forced system being well calculated to promote long bearing life and ensure freedom from trouble.'

Another feature of the Eight was its starter, which was brought into action when the clutch pedal was depressed, which, said the car's makers, removed the danger of 'in-gear' starts.

In 1930, too, Charles Nash, the man they called 'the modest millionaire', became chairman of the board of Nash Motors; he was succeeded as president by E. H. McCarty. An unassuming man, Nash placed his private life high in his list of priorities, and used to boast that the longest he had ever been separated from his wife was ten days—and that had happened only

Top: a 1932 Nash convertible; during this year Nash embarked on an ambitious expansion programme designed to combat the loss of production due to the Depression

Above: this is a 1933 Nash model known as the Advanced 8.

twice in their long marriage!

As the Depression deepened, Nash cut back their model range—only 24 variants were available for 1931, and production fell to 38,616 cars. Nevertheless, the company managed to maintain earnings of $4,808,000, representing a return of more than 20 per cent on investment. By comparison, the same year Ford sales were down by nearly 50 per cent, representing income of $46 million and a net loss of $37,181,000.

For 1932, Nash Motors embarked on an ambitious expansion of their model range in order to boost sales. They announced the 'First Series', available in 25 separate body styles, and the 'Second Series', with 28. Six different wheelbase lengths were listed—114 in, 116 in, 121 in, 128 in, 133 in and 142 in—and a new Big

Six series was announced in mid-season, bringing engine options up to two sixes and two eights. The new cars had fashionably veed radiator shells and parking lights on the front wings rather than the scuttle cowl; a choice of wood, wire or steel disc wheels was available, and the gearboxes were fitted with synchromesh.

To emphasise the wide appeal of the Nash range, the company issued a press release showing a diminutive 78-year-old, Mrs Carrie Mueller of Minneapolis, who had just taken delivery of a new Twin-Ignition Eight. Another 1932 customer was Anton J. Cermak, Mayor of Chicago, who took delivery of a snow-white Model 994 sedan which was to be used as an official guest car for the city. Alas, poor Anton! Only a few months later, in Florida, he was assassinated by a lunatic in mistake for the incoming President of the USA, Franklin Delano Roosevelt!

Nash Motors were still showing a profit, one of only two American car manufacturers still registering their accounts in the black; the other was General Motors. Though sales had slumped to only 17,696 cars, sound management policies enabled Nash to register a profit of $1,029,552 compared with GM's $164,979 for the same period.

But the fall in sales was too great to be contained by even the most skilled board of directors: in 1933, production reached an all-time low of 14,973, with each car bringing in the company an average of only $600. The total value of sales was $8,983,974, and the com-

Below: in 1936 Nash produced this unusually shaped convertible coupé. It was fitted with a six-cylinder engine. This design feature, known as 'aeroform', was also used on several other Nash models of the period

millionth car, an average of 62,500 a year since the inception of Nash Motors.

Sales were up again in 1935: 44,637 Nash and LaFayette cars were built, bringing in $27,811,719 (an average of $623 per car), but the company was still operating at a loss, though it was reduced to $610,227.

Rationalisation was the theme of the 1935 model range, with the number of options sharply reduced. Now there were only two six-cylinder body styles and four eight-cylinder styles. With its pontoon wings and streamlined tail, the Advanced Six Victoria echoed current European fashion as exemplified by contemporary Talbot and Bentley models. Nash christened the new sleek look 'Aeroform design'.

The swept-tail styling was continued for 1936, though customers were still offered the choice of conventionally styled models with a luggage boot. This carried the extra advantage that the rear seat and boot area could quickly be converted into a double bed. Nash were now using all-steel unit construction for their bodywork, with the floor integral with the body sides. Another advance was the adoption of overdrive, 'which enables a more silent and economical cruising speed to be maintained'.

The range now consisted of two side-valve sixes, of 3779 cc and 3037 cc, which were fitted in the cheapest model of the range, the 400, to choice (and, in Britain at any rate, at no extra cost for the larger power unit). Next in the range was the Ambassador Six, which had

pany lost $1,188,863.

Nor would the situation immediately rectify itself. The 1934 models featured revised styling, with spatted wings, raked tails and rear-mounted spare wheels, plus a new radiator shell. There was a new, low-priced line, too, which bore the proud old LaFayette name. Built on a standard 113 in wheelbase, the new models retailed from $585 to $745 (£117–£149) and had a side-valve six-cylinder engine developing 75 bhp.

Sales revived to 28,664, and the company received an average of $687 on each car, making net sales $19,679,777—but the company still reported a loss, which amounted to $1,625,078.

Amid all this gloom, Nash Motors still found time for celebration in 1934, for the company produced its

overhead valves and a marginally longer wheelbase; roomy, well appointed and considerably neater in detail finish than the 400, it had the same engine dimensions as the cheaper model.

Largest of the 1936 Nashes was the Ambassador Eight, which had a 4231 cc ohv engine, and a wheelbase of 10 ft 5 in, and was 'particularly smooth and easy riding', according to *The Motor*.

The LaFayette line was continued under the slogan 'the big car in the low price field'; it was possible to obtain a three-passenger coupé for as little as $595.

A total of 53,038 cars was built during 1936, with a sales value of $30,965,894, to bring the company's operations back into the black with a profit of $1,020,708. But the big news of the year was the announcement of a merger between Nash Motors and the Kelvinator Corporation, which would come into effect on 4 January 1937. Like General Motors, the Nash-Kelvinator Corporation would combine the manufacture of cars and refrigerators. Charles Nash was elected chairman of the board; president was George W. Mason, a gifted engineer and administrator, who had headed production at Chrysler in that company's formative years, and who had subsequently turned Kelvinator into one of the leading suppliers of household appliances.

It seemed as though the combined fortunes of the two companies were on an upward trend, for car sales rose to 85,949, contributing to a corporate profit of $3,640,747. Variety was still the keynote of the range, though model availability was austere compared with the early 1930s; there were now eight versions of the LaFayette and twelve of the Nash.

In 1938, however, there was a general recession in car sales, and this, combined with the development costs of a new model scheduled for the 1941 season, caused a group loss of $7,655,138; car output fell to 32,017, made up from 18 different Nash and LaFayette models. The company continued with its policy of building cars that were technically more interesting than their rivals, fitting vacuum-operated gearboxes, actuated by a dashboard lever, to all Nash models; this was the first year, too, of the famous 'Weather Eye' conditioned air heating and ventilation system.

Sales were up again in 1939, a total of 65,662 cars leaving the company's works, though Nash-Kelvinator still managed to report a loss of $1,573,524. Styling was different, with a tall, narrow radiator slit in the high prow, an arrangement of chrome strips like a boot-scraper across the front and massive triple overriders. Wings were much squarer and the headlamps were faired in to increase the streamline effect, though the 'sweptback or trunkback' option still applied.

All Nash models were known as Ambassadors, with sixes built on a 121 in wheelbase and eights on a 125 in wheelbase.

Styling was, if anything, even more exaggerated the following year, with the tall radiator grille curving inwards at its foot. The flashy lines of the new Nashes seemed made for Hollywood, and, indeed, there was some sort of tie-up with Universal Pictures, who used Ambassadors in several of their movies that year. And when Universal production manager Martin Murphy celebrated 25 years with the company during 1940, his associates presented him with a new Ambassador Eight Coupé, the news photographers being conveniently to hand.

Topping the 1940 model range was the $1195 Model 4088 four-door Ambassador Eight Sedan; and though car production was slightly down at 63,617, the Nash-Kelvinator Corporation could still report annual sales of $73,489,574, representing a $1,505,151 profit. Perhaps the highlight of the season was the production of a limited run of about fifty Nash specials, a sporty convertible variant of a standard Nash model created by the top Californian stylist Count Alexis de Sahknovsky; among its distinguishing features were elbow cutaways in the door and a vee-screen.

But the year that Nash really hit the headlines was 1941, for they announced that new model that had so drained their finances three years earlier. 'In automotive history, the year 1941 will probably be noted for the introduction of a new kind of automobile body construction', proclaimed their advanced publicity, conveniently failing to notice that several European manufacturers had preceded Nash with this 'new kind' of bodywork, with its integral welded

Top: a good example of a 1933 Nash straight-eight drophead coupé, which featured a 4.9-litre, overhead valve, pushrod engine

Above: the 1956 Ambassador sedan, with its unusual lines, was one of the last Nashes to be marketed. At the end of the following year, the Nash name was withdrawn from the motoring scene and thereafter all AMC products were known as Ramblers

body/chassis unit.

The press was equally chauvinistic: 'The only completely new car in 1941' was what *Time* called the new Nash 600, which, with a 2.8-litre six-cylinder engine in a vehicle weighing around 2615 lb, promised a fuel consumption of 30 miles per gallon. The '600' model name, indeed, was derived from the claim that this car could cover 600 miles on one 20-gallon tankful of petrol.

Suspension was by coil springs all round, independent at the front, beam axle at the back, a combination which promised all the ride comfort of a well-worn double bed. Like its bigger sisters, the 600 had steering-column gearchange, twin-tone paintwork, air-conditioning, overdrive, and sweptback or trunkback bodywork as part of its specification.

The Ambassador was still available in six or eight-cylinder guise, though the LaFayette had been discontinued in favour of the 600 range. Annual output totalled 80,408 cars, and profits of Nash-Kelvinator during the 1941 financial year reached $4,617,052.

There was a shadow of the future in the group's new involvement in the rearmament programme: during 1941 they built 44,628 military cargo trailers in the Racine plant, and took over the old Reo truck factory at Lansing, Michigan, to produce aircraft propellers.

It was a happy accident that the 600 had arrived so soon before the introduction of petrol rationing; just before Pearl Harbour, a 600 sedan carrying a placard reading 'I'm using one-third less gasoline' carried out a nation-wide publicity tour. It was, however, a little too late to be of much use to sales. During 1941, the company had started build-up of the 1942 line; but with America's entry into the war, output was halted in January, and the Nash-Kelvinator factories turned entirely to war work. During the period 1942–46, the group's plants at Detroit, Grand Rapids, Kenosha, Lansing and Milwaukee produced over $600,000,000-worth of aeroengines, propellers, helicopters, bomb fuses, flying-boat sub-assemblies, cargo trailers and binocular cases.

And when they resumed car production in late 1945, their president, George W. Mason, told the Press: 'Our car is the forerunner of cars to come' though cynics might have noticed that the juke-box front-end styling and general specification were just as they had been back in 1942! Only six-cylinder models were now available.

A total of 6148 cars were built in 1945, and 98,769 in 1946, despite post-war steel shortages. Preparing for the future, the company built a 204-acre proving ground near Burlington, Wisconsin. Recalling the past, chairman Charles W. Nash was one of the 12 automotive pioneers honoured in the celebrations of the Golden Jubilee of the American motor industry during 1946.

Two new factories were acquired in 1946, at El Segundo, California and Toronto, to assist West Coast and Canadian distribution.

That some degree of expansion was justified was proved by the 1947 sales figures, which at 113,315 represented the first time Nash output had passed 100,000 since the onset of the depression; and a new Nash assembly plant was opened near Mexico City on 18 June 1947. The Burlington test track was obviously being well used, for the company built a one-off 12-passenger eight-door Ambassador Limousine to transport engineers between Kenosha and Burlington.

Nash were still achieving publicity results: a canary-yellow Ambassador sedan was the official pace car at the Indianapolis 500, driven by George Mason, who managed to persuade screen star Clark Gable to sit in the car for photographers.

Then, in 1948, the famous stock-car driver Cannon Ball Baker set up a new speed record for the ascent of Mount Washington at the wheel of a Nash 600.

Production continued to expand: the El Segundo plant got under way in October 1948, and Nash returned to commercial vehicle manufacture with a limited run of trucks built for the export market. Limited, too, was the first postwar batch of Nash convertibles, of which only 1000 or so were built. But the year's increased output – 118,621 cars – represented a success overshadowed by the death on 6 June of Charles W. Nash at the age of 84; he was succeeded as president by George W. Mason.

A completely redesigned Nash range was introduced for 1949, featuring 'Airflyte' styling, with all four wheels enclosed by the bodywork, unitary construction and one-piece wraparound windscreens on all 600s and Ambassadors and a 'uniscope' instrument panel.

The company's advertising waxed lyrical about the benefits of the new styling: 'Here is roadability undreamt of in yesterday's cars . . . the hushed, rattle-free quiet . . . the solid strength and safety only Airflyte construction makes possible. This Nash Airflyte splits the air with 20.7 per cent less windage than the average car of current design.' And sales reached a new record level at 142,592.

The 600 must have been acquiring postwar avoir-dupois, for the company could no longer guarantee 30 mpg, so for 1950, they changed its name to 'States-man' ('with the thrill of new Super-Power engines'). The Airflyte carried a new load of superlatives, too.

'You never saw this before! It's a Sky-Lounge in the 1950 Nash Airflyte. Your airliner reclining seat

Top: this drawing is of the Nash Ambassador Slipstream Sedan. It was available with engine options of either six or eight cylinders

Above: a cutaway drawing of the 1951 Nash Rambler Country Club convertible

(optional extra in all divided-seat models) has five positions. The seats can become twin beds. Note the wide, curved, undivided windshield in all models. Note the glove locker that pulls out, instead of spills out. All driving dials are in the Uniscope.'

It was, however, a year that justified superlatives. On 18 April, the two-millionth Nash was produced at Kenosha, while annual production reached an all-time record of 191,865. Making a major contribution to that sales record was an intriguing new model, 'America's first compact car'. Bearing the revived model name of 'Rambler', this compact was a relatively large car by European standards: just under 15 ft long, it had a 2.8-litre side-valve engine and scaled 2576 lb, a combination which promised 25–30 mpg economy. Initially available as a convertible (with unitary construction), the Rambler was soon being built as a station wagon as well.

But this was not the sum of Nash's 'small-car' thinking: in January 1950 over a quarter-of-a-million people were invited to 'surviews' held all over the USA to see a prototype of a tiny two-passenger model, the NXI (Nash Experimental International). Then they were asked whether Nash should put the model into production. It would be four years before their verdict bore fruit.

Meanwhile, a slightly larger two-seater *had* made production status: this was the Nash-Healey, with sports bodywork built in Warwick, England, by the Donald Healey Motor Company, and 3.8-litre ohv engine and other mechanicals by Nash. Built for the American market, this model nevertheless succeeded in taking fourth place at the Le Mans 24-hour race in its natal year, 1951.

Rambler sales were still making a significant contri-

Top: a collection of the unusual Nash Metropolitans as used by an American traffic control department

Above: the Pininfarina-designed Nash Palm Beach of 1956. It was never put into production

bution to group profits: of the 161,140 cars produced during 1951, 57,555 were Ramblers. A third Rambler model was introduced during the season in the shape of the Country Club hardtop convertible, announced in July. Success had come early to the Rambler project, for the station wagon already held 22 per cent of the American estate-car market.

Also available during the year was the Rambler 'Super Suburban'.

In 1952 Nash celebrated its—or rather, Rambler's—50th anniversary with new Ambassador and Statesman models featuring bland new contours designed by Pininfarina. Among the plus-points of the Golden Anniversary Nash range were 'eye-level vision' (though where else Nash expected vision to come from seems obscure), improved steering, more engine power and what was euphemistically referred to as 'striking new color combinations and interior designs'. Rear seats on Ambassador and Statesman were now 12½ in wider, while tinted Solex glass was an optional extra. Ramblers could be specified with a rear-mounted 'Continental' spare tyre.

Annual production was 152,141, of which 53,055 were Ramblers and hardly any were Nash-Healeys. This limited production model now had an English chassis, an Italian body (by Farina) and American engine and transmission. It was available from December 1950 to August 1954, output finally totalling just 506.

The Toronto plant made a significant contribution to an upswing in sales in 1953, which totalled 153,753; Ramblers acquired new front-end styling and Continental spare-tyre mounting as standard, while the Ambassador became available with a 'Le Mans Dual Jetfire' power unit, producing 140 bhp. There were now four different Ramblers, including a new, cheap sedan, five Statesmen and five Ambassadors. Hydra-Matic engine transmission was offered on the Rambler in conjunction with a larger engine—it had been available on other Nashes since 1951.

Meanwhile, rumours that another independent car company, Hudson, was heading for a merger after turning in a $10,411,060 loss for 1953 began to look more than idle gossip: on 1 May 1954 Nash-Kelvinator

Corporation and the Hudson Motor Car Company were merged to form the American Motors Corporation with George Mason as President and George Romney, whose concept the 'compact' had been, as executive vice-president. When Mason died after only a few months in control, Romney took over the presidency; born in 1907, he had distinguished himself as managing director of the Automotive Council for War Production and would later become Governor of Michigan.

Just before the merger, Nash had unveiled a 'sub-compact' descended from that little NXI of 1950; built in England by Austin and Fisher & Ludlow, the new Metropolitan had, initially, an ohv 1200 cc engine, later a 1500 cc unit, in a flashily styled, typically Nash bodyshell that had all the *élan* of a wheeled bathtub allied to garish colour schemes, among them a particularly nauseating green-and-white duotone.

Ten thousand Metropolitans were produced during the first year of the model's currency, and marketed in the USA and Canada by Nash, in England by BMC.

As a result of the formation of American Motors, the old Hudson factory in Detroit was closed down, and Hudson production transferred to Kenosha, where the new Hudsons were discovered to be Nashes with a restyled radiator grille and a host of extras.

Nash production for 1954 looked disappointing, having plunged to 67,192; but it was only a temporary set-back.

Once production of the Hudson was under way at Kenosha, the figures rose sharply: in 1955, American Motors produced 194,175 cars, of which 57,635 were Nashes, 52,688 were Hudsons and 83,852 were Ramblers, which were now available either as Nash or Hudson Ramblers, the only difference between the two being in the nameplates.

Now, however, the Nash developed an eccentric new personality. The Rambler was showing signs of independence—and would, indeed, soon become a separate marque—but the Nash Statesman and Ambassador were given an odd-looking grille with inboard headlamps and the option of a weirdly applied two-tone paint scheme which made the car look like a refugee from a 1930s science-fiction movie. AMC purchased V8 powerplants and Ultramatic transmissions from the ailing Packard company for the top-line Ambassadors, but it was only a token rejuvenation.

Romney, committed to the compact, was concentrating on the Rambler, a policy which brought four lean years in which AMC's losses totalled a staggering $40 million plus before the market really swung his way and the public began buying compacts in ever-increasing numbers.

The day of the Nash was past as far as AMC were concerned, and in 1956 only one Statesman model, the four-door sedan, was available. And production of this and the new Nash Ambassador Special, powered by a Kenosha-built 190 hp V8 engine, totalled a meagre 2435 for the year.

In 1957, it had become quite obvious that the Nash and Hudson marques were on the skids, for out of a total of 118,990 AMC cars, 114,084 were Ramblers. In mid-season the Statesman was axed, leaving just the Ambassador Eight, and at the end of the model year, it was announced that henceforth all the products of the American Motors Corporation would be known as Ramblers. And that compact cuckoo-in-the-nest quietly did away with Nash and Hudson and waited confidently for the profits that would start to roll in the following year.

Oldsmobile

Ransom Olds was determined to build an alternative to the horse, whose smell he could not abide

Above: in 1899, Ransom Eli Olds and S. L. Smith founded the Olds Motor Works. Their first product was a car that has become famous in the history of American motor manufacturing, the 'curved dash' Oldsmobile; it was powered by a single-cylinder engine of 1563 cc and weighed 700 lb. The car sold for $650

Above right: one of Olds' earlier attempts at producing an automobile, the 1897 Olds motor wagon

YOUNG RANSOM ELI OLDS did not like the smell of horses on the farm, so he decided to invent an automobile. That was in the early 1880s, when Ransom was in his early 20s. Born in 1864, he was the son of Pliny Fisk Olds, a village mechanic in Geneva, north Ohio, not far from Cleveland. Cleveland was already a major engineering centre, with iron and steel manufacture, farm implement production, oil-refining and ship-building industries firmly established; and it was here that Ransom went to school.

His father encouraged him to tinker with machinery almost as soon as the boy was big enough to grasp a spanner, and Ransom soon became a proficient mechanic.

Pliny Olds eventually moved to Lansing, state capital of Michigan, where he established an engineering shop on River Street. Young Ransom's role in the household economy was to get up at five o'clock, light the two household fires, and then walk down to the workshop and fire up the boiler in the adjoining lean-to which provided the power for the steam engine. Then he went home for breakfast, attended school, and at four o'clock was back working in the machine shop. He spent all day Saturday, and all his holidays, in the shop, for two years quite unpaid, and thereafter for fifty cents a day.

The result of this hard training was that by the time Ransom had finished high school, he had become an expert machinist, and was proficient in pattern-making and moulding. When he started to build engines in the little lean-to beside the Olds barn, the neighbours began to prophesy that no good would come of it. 'That kid of yours will blow his head off one day, Pliny,' they forecast; but Ransom survived unscathed. Indeed he was abetted in his experiments by his father, and together they began to develop a crude internal combustion engine based on the Otto stationary unit.

Ransom was now 21, and had bought himself a half-share in the family business, paying his father his $300 savings and a promissory note for $800 at 8 per cent interest.

'At the time I went in with him,' Ransom Olds recalled 40 years later, 'Father's work consisted mainly of repairing, but I wanted to manufacture, and it seemed to me that we could create a demand for small steam engines. We gradually worked out plans for a small engine or boiler of one or two horsepower, which could be operated by an ordinary stove burner. But there was so much deposit in the river water that the small boilers filled up with mud and were not very satisfactory. Next I invented a gasoline motor which was the first manufactured in the United States to use gasoline directly in the cylinder. We made this up as high as twelve to eighteen horsepower.'

Like most American pioneers, Olds was apt to pre-date his early experiments, so his claim to have built an internal-combustion car in 1886 must be regarded with more than a modicum of suspicion. According to B. C. Forbes, who interviewed Olds in 1925, the vehicle 'was crude, built as it was from the various parts he had been able to pay for out of his careful savings. The body was made of whitewood, the frame was substantially built of oak, and this somewhat ungainly structure rested on three, steel-tyred buggy wheels of conventional size.'

'What troubled him most,' said Forbes, 'was the transmission, for its construction was crude indeed.

The rear axle had a ratchet on each side, and it was steered by an iron lever. The main drive wheel was an iron wheel with half-inch pointed pins screwed into the face to make a sprocket. The driving chain, made of strap iron, with rollers on pins to hold the links together, was operated through a set of lathe gears—the transmission! Unfortunately, there was no transmission case, and when the car was run the wood supports for the gears magnified the noise like a sounding board.

'When young Olds ran his motor vehicle out on the street in the early morning, the terrific noise of the gears shattered the peaceful silence and aroused the entire neighbourhood. Within five minutes, his progress had caused so much excitement that he decided a few hundred feet was sufficient for the first exhilerating tryout. . . .'

But one wonders how Ransom Olds had any spare time at all for experimenting with horseless carriages in 1886, for the family machine shop was in trouble. They had put up a small factory in the hope of increased sales of their gas engines, but in doing so had exhausted their finances—and attracted some customers who were incapable of paying for the goods

Top left: another example of the 'curved dash' Oldsmobile; this is a 1903 model and is on display in the Egeskov Veteran Museum in Denmark

Top right: the 'curved dash' Oldsmobile in action

Above: superbly restored, this 1902 'curved dash' runabout can be seen in the Lucerna Transport Museum

Left: the 1901 'curved dash', regarded as the world's first mass-production car, and, *above left*, its interesting front suspension

they had ordered. The Olds had to borrow as much as they were able, in an effort to rebuild the business.

'But in all that time I never lost faith in my idea of gasoline locomotion,' claimed Ransom Olds. 'All through those months I spent every spare minute tinkering with engines and experimenting with different forms of combustion. That little gasoline engine I had invented sold so well that it finally pulled us out of the hole and it convinced me more than ever that mechanical power as applied to all our regular functions was the coming solution of big business.'

Possibly much of that bold statement was romanticised hindsight, for it took three years to get the company back on its feet; and by then it was obvious that Pliny Olds was on the way out. Perhaps young Ransom's expansionist ideas frightened him; whatever the reason, when the Olds Gasoline Engine Works Incorporated was launched in 1890 with a capital of $30,000, Ransom Olds was made president and general manager. Within two years, he had entirely bought out his father's share in the business. Already engines were being shipped from coast to coast, and quite an export trade was built up with Great Britain.

By then Ransom Olds had built and run his first authentic motor vehicle. This was a three-wheeled steam car with a flash boiler, which attracted sufficient attention for the august *Scientific American* to despatch a correspondent to Lansing to write a feature on the vehicle. Olds told the reporter: 'It never kicks or bites, never tires on long runs, and never sweats in hot weather. It does not require care in the stable and only eats while on the road.' This article eventually found its way to India, whence Olds received an offer for his vehicle, and it was duly shipped overseas, the first-ever export by the American motor industry.

Around 1895, Olds began work on a gasoline buggy, with high wheels running on $1\frac{1}{2}$ in rubber tyres; the engine was mounted on the reach bars which linked the front and rear axles into one unsprung unit. In typical American buggy fashion, the dog-cart body wavered around above the axles on its own full-elliptic springs.

It probably made its first test runs in December 1895, for Olds recalled that the car was not ready at the

time of the *Chicago Times-Herald* race on November 28 that year.

By 1896 the car was a regular feature on the streets of Lansing, where it attracted the attention of a local capitalist named E. W. Sparrow, who persuaded two friends living in Detroit, S. L. Smith and Henry Russel, to join him in backing Olds to produce horseless carriages. Between them, they subscribed $50,000, and the Olds Motor Vehicle Company was founded; it was decided to locate the factory in Detroit, as Lancing was then a town of under 2000 inhabitants, with unpaved streets, while Detroit was an expanding industrial centre, with a rate of growth second only to Chicago, and a population of 205,876, which made it America's 14th largest city.

Notwithstanding its title, the company made very few motor vehicles in its new home on East Jefferson Avenue; its specialities were stationary gas and petrol engines, with marine power units a profitable sideline. Car manufacture was not seriously considered until 1899, when S. L. Smith, who had made his fortune in copper and lumber, decided to take over the company so that his two sons could have a lucrative hobby.

So he put up $199,600 and took 95 per cent of the stock: Ransom Olds chipped in $400 for the remaining 5 per cent, and was appointed president and general manager, though the former title was obviously only a courtesy one.

The Olds Motor Works was launched with grandiose schemes to build a $1250 luxury car with such advanced features as pneumatic clutch, cushion tyres, and electric push-button starter, but at that stage of the game the car-buying public regarded innovations of this kind—with complete justification—as the prime ingredients of mechanical failure, and the car failed to sell to such an extent that 1900 saw the Olds company running at a loss of $80,000.

At this point, Ransom Olds had the proverbial blinding flash of inspiration: 'After a long, sleepless

night, I decided to discard all my former plans and build a little one-cylinder runabout, for I was convinced that if success came it must be through a more simple machine. The plans which had formulated in my mind were very clear. It was my idea to build a machine which would weigh around 500 pounds and would sell for around $500. The result was the curved-dash 'Oldsmobile', weighing 700 pounds and selling at $650. My whole idea in building it was to have the operation so simple that anyone could run it and the construction such that it could be repaired at any local shop.'

In 1901, the prototype was ready, and the blueprints had all been drawn up ready for production: Olds had been working day and night to develop the new model, a little buggy whose toboggan-like body was perched on two long springs which served the dual function of locating the front and rear axles and acting as auxiliary chassis sidemembers. The single-cylinder engine displaced 1563 cc and drove the back axle through a

Top: the fabulous Limited model Oldsmobile of 1910 had an 11 ft 6 in wheelbase and was powered by a six-cylinder, 11,569 cc motor. One of these cars raced the 20th Century Limited railway express from New York to Albany and won— hence the name Limited. The model photographed can be seen in the Harrah Museum in America

Above: the six-cylinder model 53 of 1913

chain via a two-speed epicyclic transmission unit.

Then came instant disaster! A workman pulled his forge fire too close to a rubber gasbag which was being used to fuel one of the factory's engines, and the inevitable terrific explosion resulted. The factory, which was almost certainly principally built of clapboard, burst into flames, and the upstairs staff barely had time to save themselves, let alone bother about looking for blueprints. Within an hour, there was nothing left but scorched ruins—and the prototype runabout, which had been saved by a young timekeeper at the factory named James J. Brady who, hearing the explosion, had rushed to the section of the factory where the model was stored, and persuaded the staff to help him push the car out into the open.

tion as quickly as possible, and the Detroit automobile component industry was born.

They ordered engines and transmissions from the Dodge brothers, John and Horace, and further engines were supplied by Leland & Faulconer (though these were built to more precise standards than the Dodge units and showed up the engineering deficiencies of the Oldsmobile chassis).

The little Oldsmobile was an instant success. Pre-production models were used to test market reaction, and proved so popular that the decision was made to stake everything on this car: and the gamble proved an outstanding success. Some 600 Oldsmobiles were sold in 1901, and Olds then staggered the industry by announcing that he planned to build 4000 cars the

With supreme resilience, they started again from scratch. The car was taken apart, new blueprints were drawn from the parts, and work began on duplicates. At that time Olds was ill in hospital; within a month, the first 'duplicate' Oldsmobile was driven up to his ward window to assure him that all was well.

At that time the Olds company was a considerable reservoir of talent: among its staff were Charles Brady King, who had built Detroit's first car in 1896, Jonathan D. Maxwell, formerly with the Apperson brothers, Robert C. Hupp (who would later found Hupmobile) and two young University of Michigan graduates, Roy D. Chapin and Howard E. Coffin, who would go on to launch the Hudson car in 1909.

These varied skills were interwoven to make the Oldsmobile America's first successful mass-production petrol car—though like many other American mass-producers, Oldsmobile didn't manufacture all the components themselves. Indeed, it was essential for them to sub-contract in order to get into produc-

Above: an advert for the 1927 Oldsmobile 'Six' coach sedan showing the car in a very English setting. Note the size of the car in relation to the passengers who are dressed in typical American 'Jazz Age' clothes

following year. In fact, output for 1902 was 2500, but that was more than enough to silence those who had thought that there would not be sufficient demand for cars to support such outputs.

One reason for the popularity of the little car was a well-publicised 820-miles-in-seven-days endurance run from Detroit to the New York Automobile Show by Roy Chapin (though by all accounts the breakdown-fraught journey proved the driver's endurance rather than the car's); Olds talked one major New York firm, A. G. Spalding & Company, into ordering 100 cars and taking an agency, but they soon cancelled the order after a directors' meeting had agreed that there was no chance of selling as many as 100 cars in New York City.

Then, however, the Cleveland agent for Oldsmobile, R. M. Owen, wandered on to the stand with his backer, Roy Rainey, and announced that sales had been so good that Rainey was interested in starting another agency for Owen, in New York. They proposed ordering 500

159

Above: an Oldsmobile 33 convertible coupé of 1933. Two extra passengers could be carried in the 'dickey' or 'rumble' seat behind the driver

Below: a parade of American cars led by a 1932 Oldsmobile convertible coupé

cars, but Ransom Olds commented: 'Why not make it a thousand cars, boys, and get some notice?'

Rainey and Owen agreed, and a contract was signed the same night.

Their publicity campaign seems to have been crude, cheap and effective: They started out by doing stunts with the cars on Fifth Avenue to attract attention. They got themselves arrested for speeding, upset a bicycle policeman, and made the car so talked about that people began to look into the matter seriously. That year 750 cars were sold in New York City, and the factory had to announce a waiting list.

Soon, too, the little tiller-steered Oldsmobile became the first car to be immortalised in a popular song: 'Come with me Lucille in my Merry Oldsmobile' crooned the harmony songsters of the day. The tune, written by Gus Edwards and Vincent Bryan, was re-recorded in the 1920s as a giveaway gimmick for a new Oldsmobile model by the Jean Goldkette Band with Bix Beiderbecke on cornet, and this waxing is now one of the rarest jazz collectors' items in existence, less than

half-a-dozen copies having survived.

The best thing, though, about the Oldsmobile was that it was designed for the non-mechanically minded customer, for whom the instruction booklet was suitably reassuring: 'Don't confess that you are less intelligent than thousands of people who are driving Oldsmobiles. We make the only motor that 'motes'. . . . Don't drive your Oldsmobile more than 100 miles on the first day. You wouldn't drive a green horse ten miles till you were acquainted with him. Do you know more about a gasoline motor than you do about a horse?'

By applying cycle industry methods of standardisation and production, Olds was able to step up output of his gas buggy on an impressive scale. At the Detroit Automobile and Sportsmen's Show in early 1903, he announced that the car had ceased to be a luxury, and had now become a utility. Within ten years, he predicted, the average car would weigh 700–800 lb and be small, compact and simply constructed. As if to prove him right, sales of Oldsmobiles rose to 4000 for the year, and the Oldsmobile works was claimed to be the world's biggest automobile factory. Engines were still supplied by the Dodges and Leland and Faulconer, bodies by the C. R. Wilson Body Company on Cass Avenue—both the latter companies were soon also supplying the newly founded Ford Motor Company.

The Oldsmobile assembly process, which used jigs and machine tools to build up the complete vehicles in progressive steps was the first tentative step of the motor industry towards the moving production line. *Automobile* wrote in December 1903: 'The motors are passed, step by step, down the assembling bench towards the testing department which is in the next room, a new piece being added at every move with clocklike regularity.'

A few months later, the Detroit *Free Press* visited the Olds Motor Works: 'Rows upon rows of special machinery are humming and buzzing away, bewildering the onlooker with their number. A great expanse of floor space stretches away before the visitor, along which are arranged these ingenious devices, each with its own peculiar work to do. Some bore out the cylinders, each machine making two cylinders at a time; some finish the connecting rods and shafts; in fact every step in the process of turning out the finished machinery of a modern car is carried out by a group of these beautiful machines. The finishing and enamelling of the bodies, the upholstery of seats and cushions, and so on, are carried on in a large separate part of the plant. One little imagines, as he looks at the swiftly running car on the street, the immense amount of detail and careful manipulation that have been necessary on the hundreds of parts before they have all been brought together and adjusted to form this engine of commerce and pleasure.'

Sales in 1904 reached 5000, but Ransom Olds was

Below: the advertising blurb for this 1935 Eight Sport Coupé reads '. . . The all-weather coupé "that has everything!" Interior matches exterior Oldsmobile streamline beauty. Fisher No Draft Ventilation and the solid-steel "Turret-Top" Body by Fisher. The friends who go along? Always comfortable in that wide and roomy rumble seat'. There is not much one can say after that!

soon given cause to remember that he owned only 5 per cent of the company, for Samuel Smith decided that it was time the company (of which son Fred was now secretary and treasurer) ought to be getting into the lucrative field of high-powered luxury cars. Which was not at all what Ransom Olds wanted, so he decided it was time to retire. 'We had done so well by that time,' he recalled, 'that I thought I had about all that I needed, and rather than hamper the ideas of the rest of the group I sold out my stock and decided to take a long vacation.'

That was in August 1904; and while Olds was holidaying in Northern Michigan with his family, he received a telegram asking him to return to Lansing.

'As I stepped off the train, I was met by an old friend who handed me an interesting looking paper. Reading it, I found that a group of my friends had

organised a half-million dollar company, of which I was to be the head, and within three hours had raised the money to finance it. Of this, I was to have a controlling interest, $260,000.' And thus the Reo was born, and at first built vehicles of a fairly similar type to the Oldsmobile.

Soon the rival companies were neighbours, for in the summer of 1905, Samuel Smith, attracted by the offer of a 52-acre site subscribed for by the Lansing Businessmen's Association, decided to move Oldsmobile back to its (and his) home town.

As yet, there was little divergence from the pattern laid down by Ransom Olds. The standard 'curved-dash' model was still available, with its tiller steering that enabled tyro drivers to determine which way the front wheels were pointing; but now there was also a 'Touring Runabout' version with wheel steering and a dummy bonnet, priced at $750, plus a 20 hp flat-twin model with five-seated touring coachwork, which cost $1400. There was also a 'Coach', a forward-control 11-seated shooting brake-type vehicle, with a 16 hp vertical-twin engine; this vehicle cost $2200.

The Curved-dash Olds was still listed the following year, but it now looked a poor old-fashioned thing, and was available at no extra cost with 'straight-dash' bodywork, a futile attempt at updating. There were two new car models, the Model L 'Double-Action Olds', and the 26/28 hp Model S.

The Double-Action had a vertical-twin two-stroke engine of 20/24 hp rating, and like the Model S, broke new ground for this marque by adopting a three-speed sliding-gear transmission and a shaft-driven rear axle; it cost $1250 complete with four-seated coachwork.

The Model S, priced at $2250, had a four-cylinder engine, the company's first, while for lovers of the grandiose there was an 18-seated wagonette with a horrifying rear overhang, for which Oldsmobile considered the old 16 hp vertical-twin and two-speed

epicyclic transmission were still adequate.

This ambitious marketing programme was pushed through despite the advice of Roy Chapin, who had taken over as sales manager in 1904, and raised the output of Runabouts to 6500 in 1905; and the high-priced models began to build up losses. Equally, though, the Runabout was clearly on the wane. Fred Smith was a great one for inventing slogans for the Oldsmobile Runabout, and had coined the phrase, 'Nothing to watch but the road'. 'The idea is good,' commented an owner, who was obviously fed up with the glacier-like performance of his Oldsmobile, 'but I get darned tired of watching the same piece of road.'

By early 1906, Oldsmobile was in debt, its cash reserves depleted. Roy Chapin and his friend Howard Coffin (Oldsmobile's newly-appointed chief engineer) were among those who resigned at this time.

But the company continued with its Alice-in-Wonderland bigger-and-bigger production programme in the face of convincing financial proof of the total error of such a course. 1908 saw the introduction

Top: the two-door Oldsmobile 70 of 1938 was powered by an eight-cylinder engine and was regarded as a somewhat prestige model by the public

Above: a 1954 Oldsmobile two-door convertible

Right: a four-door model of 1940

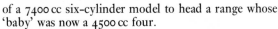

of a 7400 cc six-cylinder model to head a range whose 'baby' was now a 4500 cc four.

The inevitable takeover that year left Billy Durant in charge, and Oldsmobile one of the less healthy components of the new General Motors group, a position that was not helped by the new management's insistence on repeating all the mistakes of the Smith regime on an even bigger scale. A truly colossal car appeared in 1910 in the shape of an 11,569 cc six, which carried its 11 ft 6 in wheelbase aloft on 42 in wheels, which gave the car such vertiginous height that a double-stepped running-board was essential. One of these cars raced the famous 20th Century Limited railway express from New York to Albany—and won—after which the model took the name *Limited* in honour of the event, though 'unlimited' might have been more appropriate.

After 1912, however, there were reassuring signs that the days of the behemoths were numbered, for the biggest in the range was now a mere baby of 6997 cc; refinements such as compressed-air starters and four-speed transmissions were available, while Delco electric starting and lighting were standardised in 1914.

A low-priced four was added to the range in 1915, to be joined in 1916 by a 4-litre V8 which combined low cost with high efficiency; its side-valve engine had aluminium pistons, a definite innovation at that period.

The 1916 season saw Oldsmobile produce the millionth General Motors car, one of their new 2900 cc sixes; but after the Armistice the V8 was the prime offering, though a stop-gap ohv four using the same 2.8-litre engine as its sister marque, Chevrolet, was launched in 1921, only to be swept away, like the V8, in 1923.

The one model which replaced them was a 2774 cc six with a Buick-like radiator, which was intended to appeal to a slightly 'sportier' class of customer than other GM marques attracted.

'The impulse to sit behind its wheel, step on the accelerator and drive out into the open—through valleys, up steep hills and to buck up against most any obstacle of travel seems to come with the first view of the Oldsmobile Sport Touring,' carolled the sales literature.

'Some manufacturers have neglected their open cars and cater principally to closed-car buyers. But not so with Oldsmobile, who, realising that there are many who prefer open-car freedom, has kept abreast of the times with fine appointments of comfort, beauty and convenience in the Touring Car. . . . The Touring Car is beautiful and graceful from all angles. Its body is hung close to the ground and passengers enjoy comfort from sitting down deep in the cushions rather than on them. . . . Performance—fleetness of acceleration when in traffic, or starting from a stand-still, and power that virtually removes the hills from the highways—is in such abundance in this latest Oldsmobile Six that everyone who has driven it marvels at the reserve that seems ever ready to meet any demand. It fulfils every letter of the creed to which it was built—"Beauty, Performance, Price—Not one but all three".'

The year 1927 saw the marque pioneering the use of chromium-plated brightwork, and introducing four-wheel braking. Sales rose from 44,000 in 1924 to over 100,000 in 1929, in which year a low-priced V8, the Viking, was launched. It was based on the LaSalle, and had a 4244 cc sidevalve power unit, but the Depression was the wrong time to launch a V8, and within two years the Viking was dead.

But Oldsmobile were still multi-cylinder minded, as the announcement of a new 3933 cc straight-eight in 1932 bore witness. The company was gradually evolving into a corporate kite-flyer for new technical advances, though there was nothing specially advanced

Above left: front-end view of the 1951 Oldsmobile model

Top right: the two-door Oldsmobile 88 of 1954

Above: the conservative lines of the F-85 model of 1963 made a pleasant change from the extravagant styling that had been a feature of American cars only a few years earlier

about the adoption of independent front suspension in 1934. The following year saw the controversial 'Turret-top' styling, which hinted at the jellymould shapes of the future, while 1938 saw the first production General Motors automatic transmissions installed in Oldsmobiles. This transmission seems to have been beset with its share of troubles, for American historians point to 1940 as being of far greater significance, for in that year, they claim, the automatic became reliable.

There were also the technical innovations, though whether all of these represented an advance in the automotive art is questionable: 'Autronic eye' automatic headlamp beam control, air conditioning, four-barrel carburettors. Many of them merely represented extra hefty chunks of electronic circuitry for the power unit to haul around, demanding a return to monster power units to maintain performance levels.

The year 1949 brought 'Futuramic' styling and a 4965 cc 'Rocket' V8, heralding the descent into the styling abyss followed by so many contemporary American marques, which plumbed bottom with such disasters as the 1958 Dynamic 88 Starfire Coupé (it was all Starfire and Jetfire in those days, though there was the token attempt at building a compact, the 3523 cc V8 F-85 of 1961).

The old sporty image was revived with the 1962 Cutlass version of the F-85, while even more performance—110 mph—was promised the following year by a turbocharged Jetfire version of this car. It is perhaps hardly coincidental that the following year the V8 was shelved in favour of a Buick-based V6.

But the real breakthrough for Olds came in 1966, when they announced their first chain-drive model since the demise of the curved-dash runabout; but there could not have been a greater contrast between the two concepts, for the new Tornado used short silent-tooth chains to drive the front wheels—through Hydramatic transmission.

Not surprisingly, it was a big car, with a 6965 cc V8 engine, yet it aroused much acclaim at a time when technical innovation was apt to be sniped at with the old 'unsafe at any speed' parrot-cry of the Nader-raiders. Engine capacity was upped to 7456 cc in 1968.

Oldsmobile, like all US manufacturers was affected by the energy crisis in the 1970s, and one of their models for 1978 was offered with a diesel engine option, and the Oldsmobile 88 Royale with the 5.7-litre V8 diesel would return an average fuel consumption of nearly 30 mpg. Oldsmobile sold 55,000 of these cars in the United States in 1978 in an increasing fuel conscious market.

For 1979, the Toronado was trimmed down outside and given more room inside. It lost almost two feet in length and some 900 lb in weight, to gain a 3 mpg improvement in fuel consumption. The optional, 5.7-

Top left: the Oldsmobile Omega of 1973; note the unusual front-end styling

Top right: one of Oldsmobile's best-known models was the Toronado; this is the Custom version of 1972

Above left: the Omega hatchback coupé of 1973

Above right: the Oldsmobile 88 Royale of 1979—yet another example of 'downsizing', the 88 was over 6 inches shorter and 400 lb lighter than the 1977 version. It was available with a six-cylinder, 3.8-litre engine, 4.3, 5.7 or 6.6-litre V8 petrol engine, or a 5.7-litre diesel engine

litre GM diesel engine (now equipped with a fast cold start system to overcome one of the diesel's major drawbacks, lengthy cold start procedures) gave even better results. The Toronado was one of twenty-six models in the 1979 range. The other lines were the compact Starfire, with the 2.5-litre four as standard, the Omega, Cutlass, Eighty-Eight and Ninety-Eight. A 3.8-litre V6 was now the standard engine for Omega, Cutlass and the Eighty-Eight. Among Oldsmobile's other 1979 engine options was a new 4.3-litre V8 diesel. The GM diesels were available on nineteen of the twenty-six Oldsmobile models and these engines met all emission regulations without the use of costly catalytic converters or exhaust gas recirculation. It was indicative of the ever tightening grip of the legislators, however, that even the inherently 'clean' diesels would soon have to recirculate their exhaust gases, and GM would have considerable problems in meeting some requirements.

During 1979 the introduction of an all-new, front-wheel-drive Omega (for the 1980 model year) ousted the Starfire and put front-wheel-drive technology, of two quite different sorts, at the top and bottom of that year's range. The new Omega was 750 lb lighter than its predecessor and, at the other end of the scale, the Toronado shed another 111 lb.

Changes to the range during 1980 were evolutionary rather than revolutionary. 1981's fuel economy improvements were gained with the aid of low-drag brakes, higher-pressure tyres, continued downsizing of cars and engines and extensive use of a new, four-speed, overdrive automatic transmission. The largest gasoline engine was now just five litres, a far cry from the $7\frac{1}{2}$-litre gas-guzzlers of the late 1960s.

For 1982 the big news was front-wheel-drive for a new addition to the Cutlass line, the Cutlass Ciera, although the rest of the Cutlass range continued with rear-wheel-drive. There was also a new, 4.3-litre V6 diesel engine and a new, 3-litre petrol V6, all of which helped Oldsmobile to notch up another 'best ever' year for the all-important fleet average fuel figures. Since 1975 Oldsmobile's average rating had risen from around 15.6 mpg to 25.3 mpg and the figures were no longer only important to satisfy the Environmental Protection Agency. The American motor industry was in deep trouble, chasing a shrinking market and suffering at the hands of the imports, but Oldsmobile looked like a survivor. In 1981 a new manufacturing plant, of almost one million square feet, was opened near Lansing, to produce up to 1600 of the new diesels every day by the time it reached full capacity, in 1982. It was an illustration of Oldsmobile's formula for riding out the industry's latest crisis and a sure display of confidence from the oldest name in the business.

Below: the 1980 Omega Brougham was some 750lb lighter than the 1979 model and put front-wheel-drive engineering at both ends of the Oldsmobile range

Right: the 1982 Cutlass Supreme Brougham Coupé was one of the rear-wheel-drive Cutlass variants, distinguished by the strange shovel nose

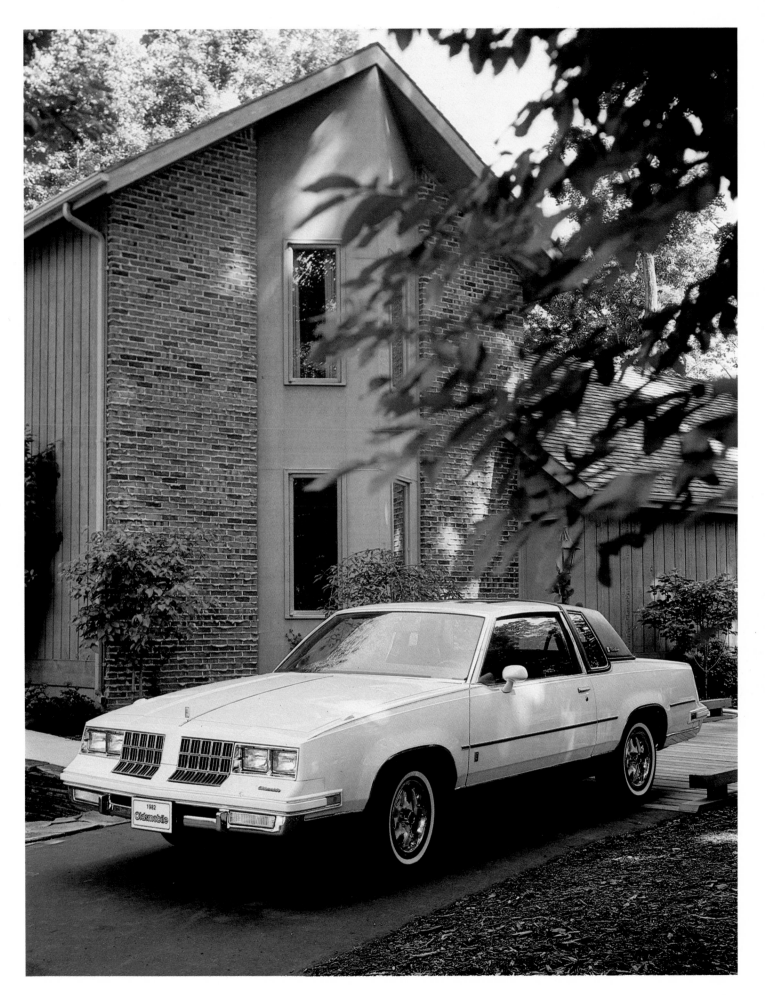

Packard

Until the 1954 merger with Studebaker, Packard was the only independent American luxury car manufacturer

ONE OF THE GREATEST NAMES in car building in the history of the United States, Packard stood for fine engineering, long life, great 12-cylinder luxury cars, early racing success and, in its last years, technical innovation. Clearly identified by their yoke-shaped radiators and fluted hoods, Packards projected an aura of prestige and excellence (especially in the years between the two World Wars) that was unmatched by any other make in North America. Indeed, in most of the years from World War I until its merger with Studebaker in 1954, a span of more than thirty years, Packard was America's only entirely independent auto company dedicated exclusively to the manufacture of the finest possible cars. For this reason, and also for its accomplishments in the design and production of aircraft engines, Packard was the only company in the United States whose work could be favourably compared with that of England's Rolls-Royce organisation.

From 1899, when the first Packard car was completed, until the last one was made in 1958, the company produced 1,610,890 automobiles. Its largest production in one year was 109,518 in 1937, approached, but not equalled, by the best post-World War II year in 1948, in which 104,593 Packards were sold. Less famed was Packard's production of trucks, amounting to 43,484 units from 1908 to 1923. Begin-

ning with its Model 905, a V12 offered to the US Government before the nation entered World War I, Packard was a designer and maker of aviation engines until the end of World War II. This work was first directed by Colonel Jesse G. Vincent, who came to Packard in 1910. The Government was not interested in the Model 905, but it made Vincent and Packard important partners in the programme to develop a special aircraft engine that produced the Liberty V12 (which was later to power such record-breaking cars as *Babs* and the *White Triplex*). In 1930, Packard announced its development of the first aircraft diesel engine, and in World War II it performed miracles of both precision and volume in converting the famous Rolls-Royce Merlin engine for production by Packard in the United States.

However, Packard was a car company first and foremost, upholding—until its last hours—the traditions of excellence that dated from its very founding. The creator of the Packard car was James Ward Packard, whose New York and Ohio Company, in Warren, Ohio, was a maker of electrical equipment at the turn of the century. Like many engineers of his time, he was intrigued by the new-fangled motor vehicle and first had bought a French De Dion Bouton tricycle and then, in 1898, one of the first production cars made, in nearby Cleveland, Ohio, by

Below left: a 1903 Model C, which had a top speed of 40 mph and cost $3000. An example of this type was driven from San Francisco to New York in 61 days by drivers Fetch and Krarup

Below: a 1908 type 30 touring model

the flamboyant Alexander Winton. Driving the fifty miles home to Warren, Packard suffered numerous troubles with his new car. When he sought satisfaction from Winton, the rebuff he received was enough to start him working on a car design of his own. With the help of his brother, William Doud Packard, and two top-flight men he hired from Winton, he produced his first car in the next fourteen months. It ran for the first time on the streets of Warren on 6 November 1899.

This first car, appropriately named the Model A, had the high wire wheels, tiller steering and single-cylinder engine, mounted under the seat, that were all typical of such early American cars as Ford, Cadillac and Oldsmobile. Unusual was its automatic spark advance, a Packard invention. Packard had no trouble selling this first car (for $1250), and set up an automobile division before the turn of the century to start producing Packards. He exhibited three cars at the first New York Show, in 1900, and in 1901 began equipping his cars with steering wheels, among the first in America to do so. From the A, he progressed to the Models B, C and F by 1902, still of the simple single-cylinder design that Packard favoured. He felt that four-cylinder cars just had four times as many things to go wrong.

Packard's jump not only to four but soon to twelve cylinders was the inspiration of Henry B. Joy, a

wealthy Detroit manufacturer who went to the New York Show in 1901, looking for a producer of horseless carriages to buy. Stopping at several agencies, Joy, and his brother-in-law, T. H. Newberry, chanced on the Ohio-built Packard and liked it. Joy bought one and, after driving it in Detroit, he negotiated, with Newberry and seven other associates, to buy a controlling interest in The Packard Motor Car Company (as it had been reformed in 1900). Although James Packard remained president of the firm when the Joy group took control, he decided to remain in Warren when the company's plant was moved to Detroit in 1903. He kept that post until 1909, staying as board chairman until 1912. He had kept his electrical equipment firm in existence separately and this ultimately became the Packard Electric Division of General Motors. According to Packard legend, James Packard was the man

Top: the first V12 built by Packard in 1915

Centre: the Packard V12 that achieved a speed of 149.87 mph on Daytona Beach in 1919. The official land-speed record at that time was 124 mph, but the 14,830 cc Packard's speed was never officially recognised

Above: a 1912 six-cylinder

who endowed the young auto company with the advertising slogan that became world-famous: 'Ask the man who owns one'.

Henry Joy, an energetic individual who fought hard on behalf of the new auto industry for good roads and freedom from arbitrary restrictions, also put Packard on a new road. Completed in 1904, the new Packard plant in Detroit was the first designed for car production by a young architect, Louis Kahn, who would become famous for his work in this field. The first four-cylinder Packard, the Model K, appeared in 1903, and was the work of a French designer hired by Joy, Charles Schmidt. In the same year, Packard set up the first factory school in auto engineering, with regular classes for employees, and soon expanded it to give a one-month course in car maintenance and repair to Packard owners and chauffeurs. In those early years, Packard also developed a sales policy, unusual in the United States, that would distinguish it in later years. It tended to establish factory-owned distributorships and dealerships in key locations, instead of selling through independent dealers, as most others did. While other companies were paid for a car when it left the factory, Packard often did not collect until, much later, a retail sale was made. Larger amounts of capital investment were needed to work this way, and also to make many more parts of the car in Packard's own factory to keep its standards of quality as high as they had been in the past.

In 1904, designer Schmidt produced the Model L

Above: a 1928 Packard 526 convertible coupé, powered by a 6.3-litre 106 bhp straight-eight engine

Packard. This was historic, being the first Packard car to have the characteristic yoke-shaped radiator, with fluted hood corners, that was visible in all but the very last cars to bear the Packard name. It was also the first to show another Packard hallmark, indented hexagonal designs in the centre of each hub cap, later typically painted red. Becoming more and more prominent as a maker of luxury cars, Joy added a six to the Packard line in 1912. In the meantime, the fours had shown sparkling pace in competition, beginning with the special *Grey Wolf* built on a Model K chassis in 1904. This clocked 77.8 mph that year to set records at Daytona, and was placed fourth overall in the first Vanderbilt Cup Race in 1904.

Alvan Macauley, who formed the Packard car in his own image, came to the company as its general manager in 1910 and moved up to its presidency in 1916 when Henry Joy resigned; he was upset because his associates had voted against selling Packard to the men who created the Nash Motors Company instead. Joy, Macauley and engineer Jesse Vincent had been the architects of the car that was to put Packard on the map of motoring for all time, the sensational Twin Six of 1915. While others were debating over four, six and eight cylinders as the proper number for a luxury car, Packard leapfrogged them all with a 12-cylinder engine, introduced in May 1915 for the 1916 model year. Although not the first such engine, the Packard twelve was the first of its type to be built in large numbers for cars. So successful was it that almost half

the firm's 1916 output of 18,572 cars was accounted for by twelves. That was double the previous year's production, and the sales and profits (more than $6 million) doubled too with the Twin Six launching.

Built through the 1922 model year, the twelve kept its original dimensions of 76.2 × 127 mm for 6950 cc. Although it had only three main bearings and a slender crankshaft, the L-head engine had roller tappets and could rev smoothly to 3000 rpm, which was its maximum. It drove through a multi-disc clutch to a three-speed gearbox (little needed because it could accelerate smoothly from 3 mph in top gear) and a 4.36:1 rear axle. Prices ranged from $2600 for a touring car to $4600 for the Imperial Limousine on the long 135 inch wheelbase. During this first incarnation of its Twin Six, Packard made 35,046 such cars, beautiful big automobiles which were favoured by tycoons, by royalty, and even by Presidents. Warren G. Harding was the first US President to be driven in an automobile to his inauguration—in a Twin Six Packard.

Just before the US entered World War I, Packard built two special racing cars, both with V12 engines specially designed for aviation use. Both were driven by Ralph DePalma, the smaller one with a 299 cu in engine to successes in 1917 and 1918, and then to sixth at Indianapolis in 1919. Built strictly as a record-breaker, the larger car used the Model 905 aero engine, ahead of a central seat and tapered tail, to set a flying mile record of 149.9 mph at Daytona in 1919. Even more impressive was an average of 92.71 mph for the standing-start mile, a figure that stood as a US unlimited record for more than thirty years and was not bettered officially by a European car until 1929. These racers, Enzo Ferrari wrote, helped inspire him to make his own twelve-cylindered cars: 'I had always hankered after a 12-cylinder engine, recalling early photographs I had seen of a Packard that had raced at Indianapolis . . .' continued Ferrari. 'Just after the war, I had had occasion, too, to see the 12-cylinder engines of the magnificent Packard automobiles of high ranking US officers.' Thus did the Twin Six tradition take firm and fruitful root in Italy. Packard's last racing entry was a team of special six-cylinder 2-litre cars for Indianapolis in 1923, which proved to be too new and undeveloped to complete the 500 miles

Top: a Packard Single Six tourer 525 of 1927

Centre: a 645 phaeton of 1929

Above: another 645, this being a 1930 tourer now in the Sylvester collection

on the Indianapolis Speedway.

The Speedway entry of a six was significant because Packard's first new post-war model, the first to issue from an expanded and improved plant in 1921, was a six. This was the Single Six, followed to market in June 1923 by the most important Packard of the 1920s, the Single Eight. This replaced the V12, and brought to volume production the classic in-line eight, a type which Duesenberg had pioneered in the US in much smaller numbers. It had, at first, the same bore and stroke as the six, 85.7 × 127 mm, giving the eight a displacement of 5860 cc and an output of 84 bhp, only 6 bhp less than the Twin Six in its final form. It had a cast-iron block with side valves, opened by short rocker levers, mounted on an aluminium crankcase that was fitted with nine main bearings. The otherwise-conventional chassis featured four-wheel brakes with a mechanical linkage, being among the first models from a major American maker to have braked front wheels. A four-speed transmission also came into use on the new Packard eights.

After the business slump of the first years of the 1920s, car sales rose again by the mid-decade, and Packard, now with a new plant behind its spotless reputation, consolidated its position as the number one luxury car in the United States. In 1923, Packard had a slight production lead over Cadillac at the 22,000-car level; in 1926, it built 34,000 cars against Cadillac's 27,489. By the standards of the day, Packard's in-line eight was smoother running than the V8s that were favoured by both Cadillac and Lincoln, and hence kinder to the enclosed bodies that came into use during the '20s. Output kept climbing to the 50,000-car level in 1928, the year when Packard stopped building sixes and placed all its confidence in straight-eights of

north of the city of Detroit during the year 1927.

This proving ground was the womb from which emerged a wider range of Packard cars to meet the challenge of the 1930s. At the top of the range was a completely new 67-degree V12 measuring 87.3 × 101.6 mm for 7292 cc, another Jesse Vincent creation. It had four main bearings and a deep-sided iron block with aluminium heads, and delivered 160 bhp at 3200 rpm. On this new Twin Six chassis, the finest coach-builders of the day, such as Dietrich, LeBaron, Brunn and Rollston, made some of the handsomest cars of all time, automobiles that served as definitions of the 'classic' era in American motor history. However, not many could afford these cars, priced between $4000 and $6000 in those depression years, and only 5744 were made before Twin Six production ended in 1939 not long before the war began in Europe.

Early in 1932, Packard had introduced another car at the low end of the economic scale, the Light Eight, selling for less than $2000. Although a pretty car, with a unique curved-bottom interpretation of the classic

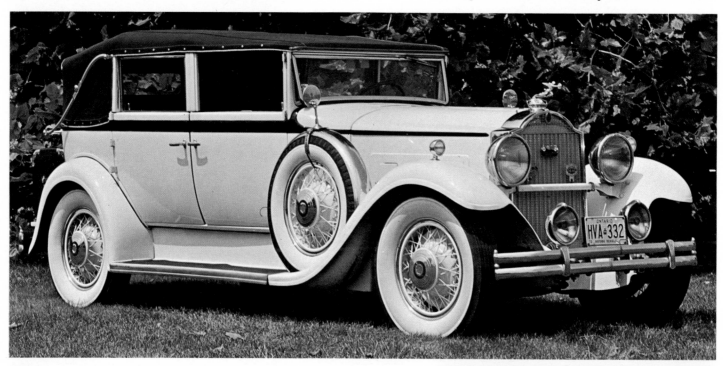

different bore sizes to suit car weights and price classes. This policy was inaugurated on 1 August 1928 when Packard chose to launch what it called its Sixth Series cars showing, by this designation system used until after World War II, its contempt for the conventional model year changes engaged in by other manufacturers, and at the same time making life difficult for those who would unravel the story of Packard cars.

In those years, Packard came closest to making a sports car, with the Speedster Eight models of the Sixth and Seventh Series. They had large-bore engines with enlarged manifolds, a higher compression ratio and a high-lift camshaft, delivering a sporting 145 bhp at 3200 rpm in 1929–30 trim. Only 220 Speedsters in various body types were built, showing that the type's guaranteed 100 mph top speed held little appeal to the traditional Packard buyer. Special Runabout bodies, built on this chassis by Packard's own custom body shop, were tested for 250 miles at speed by racing driver Tommy Milton at the company's 2.5-mile test track, part of the remarkable proving ground it built on 500 acres

Above: now in the Bruce Cole collection is this superb 833 cabriolet of 1931

Right: a 1934 twelve-cylinder coupé sport in the Du Monte O. Voight collection

Packard grille, the Light Eight failed to catch on and was merged with the main line, simply as the Eight, in 1933. Packard was still the sales leader by a clear margin among the luxury makes (in a shrinking market) when it decided to protect the heart of its range with a completely new car, moderately priced for Packard and in the medium-price range for the industry at large. George T. Christopher was hired from GM to set up the superb new plant to make the car that was announced, in January 1935, as the

Packard 120. It was named for its 120 inch wheelbase, and was sprung independently at the front wheels for the first time according to a design by research engineer Forest MacFarland. With four-wheel hydraulic brakes, a genuine Packard in-line eight under the proud hood, fresh teardrop-fender styling and a price tag in its cheapest business-coupé form of only $990, the 120 had powerful appeal to the many people who had only dreamed of owning a Packard before. When, two years later, a six was added to the new line,

Top: a 1932 Packard roadster model 900

Centre: a 1938 sport coupé Packard, now in the Conron collection

Above: another 1934 twelve-cylinder car, a coupé roadster

Packard production set the all-time record figure for the year 1937.

Between the 120 and the Twin Six, the straight-eight Packard tradition had been kept alive during the 1930s, against tremendous economic odds, by the Senior Series models carrying 160 and 180 designations. One of the most attractive and memorable bodies built on this chassis was the graceful Convertible Victoria styled by Howard 'Dutch' Darrin for the 1940 and '41 seasons, best known simply as the Packard Darrin, a worthy contemporary of the first Lincoln Continental. The lifetime of the Senior 180 Packard in the West was ended during World War II, when dies for its body and chassis were sold, at modest cost, to the Soviet Union, which had always shown a liking for Packards. Made to cement wartime relationships, this deal accounted for the post-war appearance of Russian ZIS models that looked identical to the pre-war Packard Senior 180 models which had been so successful.

Alvan Macauley made this sale because Packard had introduced a very handsome new body for its Clipper model, unveiled in March 1941, on a 127 inch wheelbase as a competitor to Cadillac in the upper-medium-price class. Its tapering forms were subtle and delicate, flowing back from a high, narrow grille. This was the style with which Packard resumed production after World War II, with both six and eight-cylinder engines. The car was a good one, and the market was

173

ready, but little Packard could not get as much steel as the bigger firms, not even as much as the politically well connected Kaiser-Frazer firm, and production in 1946 was less than one third of the goal of 100,000 cars. In the basis of the existing body, a new shape with full pontoon fenders was styled and introduced as the 1948 model, a husky-looking Packard that sold well in its own country and elsewhere.

Under new direction at the top, George Christopher in 1948 and Hugh Ferry in 1949, Packard's fine engineering staff produced its own automatic transmission, the Ultramatic, highly efficient with a direct-drive clutch in addition to a torque converter. A completely new body style for 1951 was attractive, but

of the car. These excellent new ideas, with an improved Ultramatic and new series names, topped by the Patrician, gave sales new life in 1955—a good year for the whole industry—but they sagged again in 1956, which turned out to be the last year in which genuine original Packard cars were made, due to the Studebaker merger.

The Packard name survived two more model years, 1957 and '58, on facelifted Studebakers, the appearance of which was such that we may be grateful that only 7431 in all were made, including 588 wide-mouthed Packard Hawks in 1958. The last blow fell in 1962 when the Studebaker-Packard Corporation eliminated 'Packard' from its name. Packard, for whom the

Below left: a 1941 Packard 120 Sedan

Below right: with typical 1940s American styling is this '48 eight-cylinder Clipper

trailed three years behind the industry pacesetter: General Motors. Under a new head, James Nance in 1952, radical changes were made in Packard, the car and the company. In June 1954, a merger took place between Packard and Studebaker, and three months later the '55 Packard appeared. It was completely reskinned over the lower body, and powered (belatedly) by a new V8 engine offered in two bore sizes to give displacements of 320 and 352 cu in. There was a radical new suspension, too, the invention of William Allison, which used long torsion bars to link the front and rear wheels together to reduce ride pitch and offered also an automatic levelling system for the rear

Above: the last 'real' Packard was this 1956 Clipper

Right: what would Ralph Nader have said about this 1940 Packard interior, complete with steering column ready to impale!

years between the two great wars were so very successful in every way, never really reached its stride again in the late 1940s and '50s. Unlike other makers, it had not used the 1930s and the war years to build up its own styling and marketing skills, the qualities which, for better or worse, were to spell survival in the Atomic Age. It may not, after all, have been a time in which any Packard car could really have felt at home, so the company's demise may have been for the best.

Pierce-Arrow

From its modest beginnings, the Pierce-Arrow company became one of the most envied makes in the history of American motoring

Top: the twin-cylinder, 15 hp, Pierce-Arrow roadster of 1904

Above: a four-seater Pierce-Arrow tourer of 1906

'THE SERIES 80 OWNER is never embarrassed by having his car mistaken for any other make. Everybody recognises a Pierce-Arrow.'

It conjures up a concept worthy of an H. M. Bateman cartoon, that mid 1920s advertising slogan: 'The man who mistook a Pierce-Arrow for Another Make'. For this would, in the eyes of the wealthy Americans who formed the Pierce-Arrow's clientele, have been a social gaffe of the very worst kind; the Pierce-Arrow was the chosen car of every American President from William Howard Taft to Franklin Delano Roosevelt, and almost certainly the majority of the Four Hundred had at least one Pierce in their motor stables.

Yet the car which symbolised such an atmosphere of sybaritic snobbery had sprung from truly humble origins. In 1865, George N. Pierce had set up in business in Hanover Street, Buffalo, New York, making bird cages, squirrel cages and similar wire products and, eventually, the company's skill in wire working led to the manufacture of bicycle spokes and hence to complete cycles. Comfort and speed were the hallmarks of the Pierce cycles, which boasted shaft drive, cushion frame, sprung forks and freewheel in their most popular models. It was natural therefore that, at the dawn of the motor age, Pierce should take up the new locomotion with enthusiasm, if not initially with success. Their first car, built in 1900 to designs supplied by the Overman Steam Car Company, was hardly a world beater. For one thing, it was apt to strip its rear-axle gearing at the slightest provocation. So the company turned to petrol, acquiring a de Dion-type tricycle built by Diamond. This $2\frac{1}{2}$ hp machine proved more practicable, but its passenger seat, mounted above the single front wheel ahead of the handlebars, promised some fairly violent upsets. Perhaps this was the reason that the board of directors decided to convert the Diamond to a four-wheeler. This proved successful, and the production of motor cars was contemplated. The man they called in to do the design work, David Fergusson, was an Englishman from Bradford, Yorkshire, whose grounding in automobile engineering had been colourful, at least, for he had come to America as part of the entourage of Edward Joel Pennington and his partner Baines, in 1899, when that pair of rogues arrived in New York to sell 'war motors' to the United States Government.

The Government failed to place the order, Pennington and Baines went their separate ways, and Fergusson was left to fend for himself. He found a job at the E. C. Stearns Company of Syracuse, New York, where he began work on a petrol car. However, at that stage, the Stearns Company thought there was more future in steam and, hearing of the Pierce quadricycle, Fergusson applied for the job of designer where he

175

Right: in 1919 Pierce-Arrow produced this four-seater touring car. It was available with several engine options ranging from 48 hp to 66 hp

Above: a 1909 Pierce roadster, an example of which can be seen in the Harrah Museum

soon made his presence felt by the Pierce management.

Fergusson began work on the first true Pierce car in February 1901. Known as the Motorette, it was a $2\frac{3}{4}$ hp de Dion-powered Stanhope buggy which appeared to have borrowed design points from just about every popular vehicle of the day.

Nevertheless, it ran so successfully, so impressing the Pierce board—and, just as importantly, their nation-wide network of cycle dealers—that the decision was taken to go into quantity production of the design. During the 1902 season, 25 $2\frac{3}{4}$ hp Motorettes were delivered, plus 125 of a new, more powerful $3\frac{1}{2}$ hp

model, which could boast the feature of a reverse gear (to go backwards with the $2\frac{3}{4}$ hp, the driver had either to use a favourable camber or get out and push!).

The quest for power and speed continued, with the development of a twin-cylinder 15 hp model called the Arrow late in 1902. This really broke away from the buggy image, with a long bonnet, wheel steering and a five-seater tonneau body plus, at $2500, big-car prices, too. Nevertheless, a total of 50 of the new Pierce Arrows were built during 1903, and one of them took fourth place in the October 1903 New York–Pittsburgh reliability trial, winning a gold medal (however, one of the old tiller-steered Pierce Stanhopes fared even better, coming in second in this demanding and prestigious event).

In fact, the gold-medal car represented a considerable advance over the original 15 hp model, which had obviously been inspired by the de Dion (suppliers of its power unit), having a low-slung frontal radiator and a rear-hinged crocodile bonnet; the later 15 hps had honeycomb radiators and *Roi-des-Belges* coachwork, retaining only the column gear change and tubular chassis of their predecessor.

The old single-cylinder Stanhope, which was apparently popular with doctors, continued in production until 1906, by which time this thoroughly outdated vehicle had been reduced in price from $1200 to $900. It was apparent by 1904, though, that Pierce were firmly committed to a multi-cylinder future. For that was the year that Fergusson (who was to remain Pierce's chief engineer until the beginning of the 1920s) introduced his classic Great Arrow four-cylinder, a 24/28 hp 3770 cc model on the fashionable Mercédès lines, with a pressed-steel frame, a sure sign that the marque was swinging away from its cycle origins (although the four-cylinder Pierce motor cycle was one of the great designs to be seen during pre-World War I days).

The next year saw two more big four-cylinder Pierce Great Arrows (the two-cylinder was now discontinued), a 30 hp and a 6135 cc 40 hp. It was, too, the year that saw the marque's outstanding victory in the very first Glidden Tour, a 1000-mile trial 'to establish before the whole world the identity of the best touring car obtainable'. Percy Pierce (son of George N.) drove a standard 28/32 Great Arrow carrying as passengers his parents, his fiancée and mechanic George Ulrich, and earned 996 points out of 1000; the car was voted

Top: the six-cylinder 12.7-litre Pierce-Arrow 66-A-1 of 1913

Above: the 66-A-5 Pierce-Arrow of 1918; it was powered by a six-cylinder engine

Right: an example of early Pierce-Arrow advertising; the car is a 1924 80 sedan

as commercially practicable'. And in 1906, increasing demand for their products compelled a move to a brand-new purpose-built factory on Elmwood Avenue, Buffalo, on a 44-acre site which had formed part of the 1901 Pan-American Exposition.

An experimental six-cylinder model was entered for the 1906 Glidden Tour, and the first production six appeared the following year. Thereafter, the four-cylinder models were gradually phased out, until in 1910 only sixes were available. The company and the cars had taken the inevitable step of adopting the Pierce-Arrow name in 1909, in which year they claimed: 'We believe that every Pierce Arrow car is today running and giving satisfaction to its owner, except in the case of cars that have been put entirely out of business by a collision'.

The 1909 range consisted of 36 hp, 48 hp and 66 hp sixes, of 5686 cc, 7423 cc and 10,619 cc respectively. The biggest six was the latest development of the 1907 model and, for 1910, it was uprated to 66 taxable horsepower and given a swept volume of 11,700 cc. Separately cast T-head cylinders gave the 66 engine a curiously archaic look, but with sales varying between 66 and 206 a year, this behemoth was successful enough to warrant a further inflation of swept volume to 13,514 cc in 1912, in which year the gargantuan 66

the most successful by a majority of the contestants (a condition of the event), and took time off midway to take part in a hill-climb up Mount Washington. The enormous amount of publicity resulting from this victory boosted sales—and the marque proved it had been no freak performance by winning the Glidden Tours three times in a row (in 1906, 1907 and 1908) as well.

Incidentally, the 1905 Pierce Great Arrow *Roi-des-Belges* tourer had body panels cast from aluminium, a method of construction that was to be a distinctive feature of the company's products for the next fifteen years. Although a wood framework was used, the cast panels resulted, claimed the manufacturers, in a lighter, stronger body—it also facilitated the production of elaborately curved contours without panel beating.

Also available in 1905 were three closed Great Arrows—the Landaulet, the Suburban, and the Opera Coach—bodied by the leading coachbuilder Quinby, all three were priced at $5000, against the $4000 of the open model. The Opera Coach, which was a sort of station bus, had seating for eight, and looked somewhat like an opera box on wheels.

By now, the George N. Pierce Company was a major power in the American motor industry: one of their directors, Charles Clifton, was president of the Association of Licenced Automobile Manufacturers, which claimed to control the production and sale in the USA of 'all gasoline automobiles which are accepted

rode on a wheelbase of 12 ft 3½ in. Together with the 1916 Fageol, the Pierce-Arrow 66 could claim to be the biggest-ever American production car; its total production of 1638 over ten years must represent some kind of record, too. In later years, many of these Pierce 66 models found their way to Minneapolis, Minnesota, where Fire Chief Walter Ringer had discovered that it was possible to create a fire engine very cheaply by lengthening the chassis with channel steel, bolting the existing rear axle to the frame and fitting it with sprockets to drive a new dead axle by chain. His lead was followed by other fire depart-

ments, and quite a few Pierce-Arrow 66s ended their days as fire engines, lasting for upwards of 20 years in this guise.

In 1913, Pierce-Arrow decided to adopt a new marketing policy: from that point on, there would be no annual model changes. Instead, a 'Series' designation was introduced, which changed only when radical alterations to the specification were made. Pierce-Arrow claimed this move was made because their cars were so perfect that there was no point in introducing a new model each year, but in fact the 'Series' concept fitted the Pierce-Arrow production methods perfectly. These were the exact antithesis of mass-production, for Pierce-Arrows were built in batches of a single model. For example, they would turn out several hundred 38 hp cars, then a similar amount of 48 hps and finally several dozen 66 hps, with scant attempt at rationalisation of parts between the three models. Typically, Pierce-Arrow started numbering with the 'Second Series'.

The Second Series introduced a design feature which was to become the Pierce-Arrow hallmark, the 'fender headlight'. Mounting the headlamps in housings on the wings was a novel concept, and one which the company patented in 1912; it was possible, as an optional extra, to have conventionally mounted lights instead, but few owners chose this alternative, which was offered until 1932.

The last 66 was produced in the spring of 1918, after the model's best year of production, in which 301 had been turned out. At the same time, the 38 hp was dropped, and a new 47 hp introduced, known as the Fifth Series, with four valves per cylinder, and cylinders cast in pairs. This lasted little more than a year, and then a revised series with monobloc power units appeared. More importantly, the 1920 Pierce-Arrows were the first with left-hand steering, right-hand steering having been retained long after most American makes had abandoned it, partly out of Pierce's innate conservatism, partly because it was more convenient with a chauffeur-driven car to have the driver on the pavement side so that he could quickly dismount to open the rear doors for his passengers to alight onto the sidewalk. Steel bodies

were now predominant, too, the cast-aluminium construction having also had its day.

Indeed, there were ominous signs that the Pierce-Arrow policy of aiming at the upper-crust market was losing its potency. Sales began to slide, and in an effort to reverse the trend, the company brought out a 'cheap' model, the Series 80 (its high-priced running mate, the Series 36, had the dubious distinction of being much sought after on the second-hand market by the prohibition-busting 'rum-runners', as its engine had just the right qualities of silence and reliability that they wanted to power the boats used to bring bootleg hooch ashore past the watchful eyes of the Federal agents!).

The Series 80 introduced four-wheel braking to the Pierce-Arrow range, and its moderate price (starting from $2895) and refined engineering combined to make this a best-seller in Pierce-Arrow terms. A more powerful engine was available from the end of 1927, and this was used in the Series 81 which succeeded the 80 for 1928. Unfortunately, the styling of the Series 81 was entrusted to one James R. Way, whose trendy Art Deco ideas did not go down at all well with the Pierce-Arrow clientele. He even committed the appalling solecism of putting the Pierce-Arrow name on the radiator, which had been one of those things which is never done, like wearing suede shoes with evening dress. The customers did not like it, and the slipping sales proved it.

The Model 81 was hastily interred. At the same time, work was proceeding on a straight-eight successor to the Model 36, which was beginning to show its age. Then, frightened by the company's falling revenues, the shareholders voted that Pierce-Arrow should be taken over by the prosperous Studebaker Corporation. It was a disastrous mistake with serious consequences.

While Studebaker ownership did not diminish Pierce-Arrow quality, it demeaned it: to the typical Pierce-Arrow owner, accustomed to buying his car from a bespoke dealer, it was highly *infra dignitate* to do business with the new 'dual distributorships' which sold Pierce-Arrows alongside cheap Studebakers. It was as though they had gone into a cut-price grocer's to buy champagne.

Top: the streamlined Silver Arrow of 1933; it was a superbly built machine fitted with a V12 engine producing 235 bhp

Above: some idea of the size and quality of Pierce-Arrow cars can be gauged by the way this 1930 coupé 8 dwarfs its lady driver

It was a pity, for the new 5998 cc straight-eight of 1929 was an excellent car, a fact reflected in sales of 8000 for the season; even at the height of the Depression, in 1930, 7000 cars were sold. Now, Pierce-Arrow began development work on a radical new model, a V12, which made its bow in 1932, in 6522 cc and 7030 cc forms, with prices starting at only $3900. The Mormon Meteor, Ab Jenkins, took a 1932 roadster with a prototype 7571 cc V12 engine on Salt Lake Flats for a record attempt, and set up an unofficial American 24-hour speed record of 112.9 mph. The following year, he took a stock V12 on to the flats and made the record official with a 117 mph average, breaking 14 international and 65 other records for Pierce-Arrow. He subsequently upped the 24-hour figure to 127.2 mph with a modified Pierce-Arrow, but even the excellent publicity accruing from these record runs could not help Pierce-Arrow revive sales, which had crumbled to 2692 in 1932.

A consortium of Buffalo businessmen had bought Pierce-Arrow back from Studebaker in 1933, but they might as well have saved their money. The addition of hydraulic tappets to that year's V12 made no difference to the sales graphs, nor did the exciting Silver Arrow designed for the Chicago World Fair of 1933, with futuristic full-width styling and a streamlined rear end

with a tin rear-view 'dormer window' cause more than a ripple of excitement. Ten were built, with a $10,000 price tag but, although a 'production' Silver Arrow was subsequently offered, this was no more than a fastback version of the standard sedan.

After only a year of regained independence, there were rumours that Pierce-Arrow was seeking new mergers, and some financial independence, there were rumours that Pierce-Arrow was seeking new mergers, and some financial reconstruction was already being undertaken. Sales for 1935 were down to 1000 cars, yet at the end of the year, three outstanding new models, which were advertised as 'the safest cars in the world', were launched. These were the Model 1601 eight and Models 1602 and 1603 twelves, and their advanced specification included huge vacuum-servo brakes, strong X-braced frames, anti-roll bar at the rear, quadruple headlamps, reversing lights, dual tail-lights, tinted safety glass, overdrive, crankcase emission control, freewheeling and many luxury items. It was too good a package to offer at $3195, and the company began building trailer caravans as a sideline to try and bolster its finances. However, it was too late. Pierce-Arrow struggled on through 1937 and into 1938, and then a creditor demanded that the company should be liquidated to pay back the $200,000 he was owed. The firm was declared insolvent and its assets, worth nearly $1 million, auctioned . . . to realise only a paltry $40,000. The Seagrave Fire Apparatus Company purchased all the engine-making plant to produce Pierce-Arrow power for its fire engines; the last Pierce-Arrow to leave the plant was sold to the company's chief engineer, Karl Wise. But there was one last twist to come to the story.

When Pierce-Arrow was wound up, the Pierce-Arrow Buffalo Parts Company was formed to look after the sales of the company's spares. When they decided to dispose of their remaining stock in 1941, the very last Pierce-Arrow was constructed out of a melange of 1930s components. The sum of its parts were averaged out as '1934' for registration purposes.

It was a curious end for a marque which in its heyday could count orders for cars with diamond-studded tonneaux and gold-plated brightwork

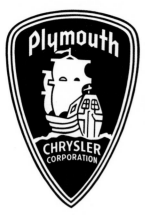

Plymouth

Plymouth, claimed the makers, symbolised the honesty, strength and determination of the Pilgrims

IT WAS THE SUMMER of 1928 and Walter P. Chrysler was very much the man of the moment in the American motor industry. Having brought the company which bore his name to fourth position in the sales charts within two years of its founding, he was now in the process of buying the Dodge Brothers Company for $170,000,000 in stock and $59,000,000 in assumed interest payment on Dodge bonds. Furthermore, even before the deal had been formalised, Chrysler was already planning to bring out a new low-priced model to try and gain a foothold in the lucrative Ford/Chevrolet market sector. The first production example of this car, which was to replace the old four-cylinder Chrysler 52 (itself based on the Maxwell, the Chrysler's progenitor) rolled off the production line in great secrecy on 11 June 1928: on 16 June the news was leaked in a newspaper article, which stated that the car was to be called 'Plymouth'.

What's in a name? 'Plymouth,' claimed the article, 'symbolises the endurance and strength, the rugged honesty, enterprise, and determination . . . of the Pilgrim band who were the first American colonists.'

The car's first public showing was at the Madison Square Garden in New York the following month. 'Give the public something better, and they will buy,' said Walter P. about the new car. His publicity department was not so restrained:

'An absolutely new development in motor car style . . . new slender profile chromium-plated radiator . . . long low bodies . . . new type beaded crown fenders . . . moulded edge running boards . . . generous room for 2 to 5 passengers, according to body model . . . luxurious deep upholstery and appointment detail such as you expect only in cars of far higher price . . . beautiful bowl-type head lamps . . . new 'Silver Dome' high-compression engine, for use with any gasoline . . .

smooth speed up to 60 and more miles an hour . . . characteristic Chrysler acceleration . . . unbelievable smoothness of operation—at all driving speeds . . . new type Velvet-Power engine mountings . . . body impulse neutraliser . . . new type shock-absorbing spring compensators give exceptional riding comfort . . . New type spring shackles—reduce noise, wear, attention . . . Chrysler light-action internal expanding hydraulic four-wheel brakes—no other car of this price possesses this feature.'

And the price range—$670 to $725—though not earth-shatteringly low, was attractive enough to lure 58,000 buyers before the year was out. The new car created attention wherever it was shown—in Chicago, 30,000 people crowded into the Coliseum to see the Plymouth—and demand was so much above expectation that a new factory had to be hurriedly erected on a 40-acre site in October, to be ready for use early in 1929.

The new plant had a daily capacity of 1800 cars, and by May 1929 a total of 1000 cars a day was leaving the factory. Small wonder that *Time* magazine claimed that Chrysler had 'gone into the low-priced field with the throttle wide open'.

Not unexpectedly, sales of the 1929 Plymouth U, which had a slightly larger engine than its predecessor, were up on 1928 figures, though by only 50 per cent, not quite such an advance as one would have expected, considering that the 1928 figures were based on just five months' trading. Prices were down—$655 for the coupé, $695 for the sedan—a trend which continued as the Depression began to hit car sales. As the low-priced model in the Chrysler/De Soto/Dodge/Plymouth range, the marque led group sales, and in 1930 it was announced that the marketing activity was to be rationalised, and that in future dealers selling other

Chrysler makes would also sell Plymouths, instead of there being four separate dealer organisations. This gave Plymouth extra sales outlets, while continuing price cuts brought the marque within striking distance of its two rivals Ford and Chevrolet. In March 1930, sweeping price reductions were announced, with the four-door Plymouth sedan now $625, the same as its Ford and Chevrolet equivalents, though the coupé, at $590, was $90 more than the Ford, $25 more than the Chevrolet (the Willys Whippet was cheaper than all of them, but somehow it didn't seem to count).

The 1930 Plymouth U was a well-equipped car, with the option of a radio—it was only three years since Philco had manufactured the first commercially-produced car radio—as well as an electric fuel gauge, hydraulic shock-absorbers and a fuel-pump replacing the old vacuum-tank feed.

Meanwhile, at the Chrysler Corporation's new Highland Park research centre, Fred M. Zeder and his technicians were working on an all-new Plymouth. The two-year programme of research, testing and re-tooling culminated in the appearance, in June 1931, of the Plymouth PA, available in eight different body styles ranging from $535 to $645, and boasting such advanced features as free-wheeling, a double-dropped frame giving a low centre of gravity, 'floating power' engine mountings, constant-mesh transmission for easy gear-changing and automatic vacuum-operated ignition advance and retard.

When the third car came off the line, Walter Chrysler climbed into the driving seat and set off for the Ford office in Dearborn. He spent a couple of hours touring the Engineering Laboratory with Henry and Edsel Ford, then took them out to see the new car. The Fords, it was said, were 'delighted' when Chrysler took them for a demonstration run, then presented them with the car and went home in a taxi, but one wonders

Top: a 1934 Plymouth two-door tourer; it was powered by a six-cylinder engine. These were marketed in Britain as Chrysler Kews

Above: the four-door, four-seater Plymouth PA sedan of 1931

whether the delight remained as the Plymouth began to take sales from the Model A Ford, especially in prestigious areas like the environs of New York.

By now, Plymouth was headed by an ex-Ford man, Fred Rockelman, who had been summarily dismissed in March 1930 because he had disagreed with the cavalier treatment which Ford's right-hand man, 'Cast-Iron Charlie' Sorenson, was affording the company's dealer force.

Under Rockelman's leadership, Plymouth began an aggressive advertising campaign which emphasised

the marque's advantages over its price rivals: 'Look at all three! But don't buy any low-priced car until you've driven the new Plymouth with Floating Power'.

It was dog-eat-dog with a vengeance; but times were desperate. The Chrysler Corporation had its own special formula for beating the Depression: a bank building in Detroit was hired, and staffed with unemployed tellers, then Chrysler transferred its own cash from other banks to meet its own cheques written for employees and suppliers. Salaries and expenses were cut and cut again in the 1931-2-3 period, though one thing that Walter Chrysler would never stint was finance for research.

Thus in 1932 the new Plymouth PB was endowed

Left: front-end view of the Chrysler Kew (née Plymouth six-cylinder)

Below left: two Plymouths of the early 30s: a 1931 PA (*above*) and a 1930 four-cylinder

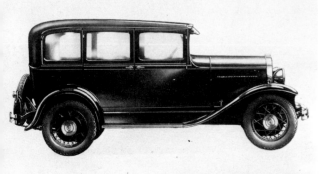

with a rigid X-braced chassis, an oil filter and 'centrifuse' brake drums with cast iron fused to rims of steel to dissipate heat. Then, following a $9 million research and development programme, the 1933 Plymouth PD, the marque's first six-cylinder model, was launched. The price of the car was quite remarkable—it cost just $495—and it boosted output from 1000 to 1200 cars daily.

Another $9 million was spent in research and development of the next new Chrysler model, the 1933 PD, which had a 70 hp six cylinder engine, yet sold for

Above: Plymouth's P8 model of 1939; this is the four-door sedan version

only $495. Incidentally, during the 1930s the Plymouth name was not used on the British market, where the cars were normally known as Chrysler Kew or Wimbledon sixes, the Kew being a small-bore export-only model. A novel feature of the 1933 models was the Chrysler automatic clutch, which was equipped with a vacuum servo which withdrew the clutch whenever the throttle pedal was released. 'The mechanism embodies what is known as an inertia compensator,' confided *The Motor*, 'which ensures that there is no lag in operation, and that the clutch takes up without delay. The free wheel is controlled by a lever on the dash, which may take up any one of three positions. In one the car is controlled in the

coupé, and rear seat passengers could now elect to have a radio loudspeaker all their own, fixed to the back of the front seat, which presumably nullified the effect of all that safety padding.

The front end of the 1939 Plymouth was different again, with horizontal slots and headlights in the wings representing the first step towards the 'full-width' styling of a couple of years later. The concealed scuttle ventilator now incorporated a rain trap to prevent the interior of the car steaming up in wet weather, while other aids to the good life included a steering-column-mounted gearshift and power-assisted convertible hoods.

Still on the accident-prevention trail, the Plymouth

Below left: the Plymouth Fury two-door coupé of 1957 used a V8 motor of 5720 cc

normal manner. In the second position the free wheel is in operation, and in the third both automatic clutch and free wheel operate.'

By now, Plymouths had a more streamlined radiator grille, but styling was always more conservative than on the Chrysler and DeSoto marques, and the Plymouth was never infected by the controversial Airflow styling of its big sisters.

The millionth Plymouth was produced on 10 August 1934: it had taken just six years to reach this impressive total, despite the Depression. By now, the marque had acquired coil-spring independent front suspension: the more radically-styled PJ of 1935 also had the improved weight distribution, anti-roll bar and 'Chair-Height' seating which had been introduced on the previous year's Chryslers.

For 1936, the Plymouth P-2 also offered rubber-insulated body mountings and a choice of ten different coachwork styles. For only $40 more than the standard sedan, one could buy a curious model which was, perhaps, designed for unsuccessful doctors, for it could be converted from passenger car to ambulance to hearse in a matter of seconds . . .

Styling for safety was a feature of the 1937 P-4, whose instrument panel incorporated recessed controls and a rounded lower edge raised well above knee height. There was a well-padded roll across the top of the front seats to cusion back-seat passengers in case of an impact, and door handles curved inwards so that clothes could not catch in them. There were now blower units and defroster vents to direct air over the windscreen.

So far, the radiator grille of the Plymouth had been gently raked backwards: for 1938, the trend was reversed, and the fencers' mask grille now stood aggressively erect, giving the cars a somewhat fore-shortened look, as it was set well ahead of the axle. Among the body styles available was a rumble seat

management must have been convinced that, if you could not persuade drivers to keep to arbitrary speed limits voluntarily, you could at least irritate them into complying with the law. To which end, the 1939 Plymouths were fitted with a 'safety-signal' speed-ometer, a device which sounds capable of reducing the most rational driver to gibbering insanity within a fairly short distance. At speeds up to 30 mph, the Safety-Signal flashed a green light, between 30 mph and 50 mph it flashed amber, and over 50 mph it flashed red.

Anyway, this preoccupation with safety won Ply-mouth their second design award in 1940, in which year 'rotary door latches' and sealed-beam headlamps became standard; the vacuum-operated windscreen wipers now pivoted from the bottom, rather than the top, of the screen, the better to cope with the divided vee-screen which had made its debut on the 1939 models. And Plymouth were proud to announce that they were the only low-priced car producer to offer a seven-passenger sedan in their model line-up.

Apart from minor styling changes, the main new features of the 1941 Plymouths were directed at improving the convenience of operation. Thus the battery was relocated under the bonnet, where it was easier to check its condition, the boot had a counter-balanced lid so that it was possible to use both hands for loading and unloading, and door stays were fitted. More radical changes were made on the 1942 models, which were destined for a short production life as Plymouth switched over to war work.

The 1942 Plymouth 14C had full-width styling, with bonnet and wings an integral whole; the doors curved outwards at their base to cover the vestigial running boards, and now the interior light came on automatically when the doors were opened.

It was a modified version of this model, the 15S, which formed the basis of production immediately

Left: the two-door Plymouth Belvedere of 1957

Centre left: Plymouth entered the American 'compact stakes' with their Valiant model. This is the four-door version of 1962

Bottom left: the unusual Plymouth Fury two-door hardtop coupé of 1961

Top, from left to right: the two-door Plymouth Signet of 1966; the Road Runner of 1971 and the Plymouth Satellite Sebring of 1971

after the war; in 1948 the car acquired the new low-pressure 'super-cushion' tyres to add to ride comfort.

Estate cars made the news in the 1949 Plymouth line-up: there was a nine-passenger model called the Special Deluxe Station Wagon, with external wood trim and the second and third rows of the stalls removable to increase load space. The new six-seater Deluxe Suburban had all-steel coachwork, and a clear load space of four feet before the back seat was folded down.

High up the treacle stakes came Plymouth's description of a feature common to all the 1949 models:

'Automatic turn-the-key ignition was born to a low-priced car'. In a Detroit manger, maybe?

For the first time, three different Plymouth series were offered: the P-17 Plymouth DeLuxe on a 111-in wheelbase, the P-18 DeLuxe on a 118½-in wheelbase and the P-18 Special DeLuxe, also on the 118½-in wheelbase, a range which continued through 1950. That year, an automatic choke was standard, said to be unique among low-priced cars: the 1950 Special DeLuxe, with amendments to the brightwork, was also available in some export markets as the DeSoto Diplomat or the Dodge Kingsway.

Above: the powerful Plymouth Barracuda hardtop two-door coupé of 1970 continued the sophisticated styling of earlier models

But in 1951 the old order suffered a shake-up. Plymouth had lost their third place in the US market to Buick, largely, it seems, because of their conservative styling, and the new models were given a mild face-lift and named Concord, Cambridge and Cranbrook. Minor technical changes included electric windscreen wipers in place of the contrary old vacuum wipers, plus Oriflow shock absorbers with 'sea-leg' mountings. This range continued throughout the 1952 season, with the addition of overdrive as an optional extra plus new two-tone paint schemes.

Flush-sided coachwork and one-piece wraparound windscreens were adopted on the 1953 Cambridge and Cranbrook—the Concord was dropped from the model range. Hy-Drive torque convertor transmission became available, and two-door hardtops acquired a curious design of front bench seat divided a third of the way across, instead of down the middle so that two people could be seated in the front yet still allow access to the rear seats.

There was a further change of image for 1954, with restyled Plaza, Savoy and Belvedere models forming the lineup, with the options of power-assisted steering and two-speed PowerFlite automatic transmission. And on 25 March, the Chrysler Corporation revealed that an experimental gas-turbine engine had been successfully tested in a Plymouth hardtop—an American industry 'first'.

Larger engines were fitted to the late 1954 Plymouths, but a more fundamental power unit change was on the way. The 1955 models could be had with a new Hy-Fire V8 engine, which was available in two displacements, with power outputs of 157 bhp and 167 bhp; the larger engine could also be ordered with a four-choke carburettor, which boosted output to 177 bhp. Air-conditioning was now available as an option.

Power units were larger still on the 1956 models, which featured push-button operation for the Power-Flite automatic transmission, plus vacuum-servo braking. And the biggest engine of all was fitted in the new two-door Fury hardtop, with its gold-anodised aluminium side trim: one of these cars took the flying mile stock car record at Daytona with an officially-timed speed of 124.01 mph.

And experiments with gas turbine engined Plymouths continued: in 1956 a four-door jet sedan made the first transAmerican crossing by a vehicle of its type.

The new year was only a few days old when, on 27 January 1957, the 10-millionth Plymouth rolled off the lines: sales that year were among Plymouth's best, with more than 600,000 cars produced, an output rate which contributed to the building of the 11 millionth

Plymouth little over two years later. Now three-speed TorqueFlite automatic transmission was available as an option, while new torsion-bar front suspension was introduced, along with quadruple headlamps.

Topping the range for 1959 was the new Plymouth Sport Fury, which could be bought with electronic fuel injection; its front seats swivelled outwards to facilitate entry and exit, a feature which could be specified on the other Plymouths of that year, which also saw the demise of the old sidevalve six after 26 years.

Walter Chrysler had launched his first car at New York's Hotel Commodore in 1925; now Plymouth used the same venue for the début of their all-new V-200 Valiant compact, on 27 October 1959: this unit-construction model featured the latest Slant Six ohv power unit, and had an alternator as standard equipment. There was a new Fury, too, the result of a multi-million dollar modernisation programme at the Plymouth factory. Its huge tail fins marked the end of an era: the following year's Furies would be shorn of these appendages, fitted instead with tail lamps which 'were unique pods, which appeared to float within concave depressions in the rear fenders'.

A new variant of the Valiant, the sporty-type Signet 200, appeared in 1962, with the option of a die-cast aluminium cylinder block, and was elected winner of the Society of Illustrators' styling award for design excellence, a fact which did not prevent Plymouth introducing an all-new bodyshell for 1963 on Valiant and Signet models.

Introduced in 1964 was the fast-back Barracuda, which had a huge, 14.4 sq ft, rear window: it was followed by V8 Valiants, an intermediate-sized model called the Belvedere and a redesigned Fury, which in 1966 was available in luxurious VIP form.

Plymouth's increasingly wide coverage of the market continued into the 1970s with the announcement of the Valiant Duster Coupé and the sporty Road Runner variant of the Satellite (née Belvedere).

In the mid 1970s Plymouth marketed the Mitsubishi Sapporo and Celeste models as a way of covering gaps in its own product line-up. In 1978, however, the situation improved when Plymouth's own sub-compact, the Horizon, appeared. It was identical to the Dodge Omni – a small, attractive, front-wheel-drive hatchback.

Excluding imports with the Plymouth name added, the 1979 line consisted of the Fury, the Horizon and the Volare. The Volare had first appeared in 1976 in coupé, sedan and station wagon forms, with a six-cylinder engine of 3.7 litres or a V8 of either 5.2 or 5.7 litres.

Right: the 1980 Gran Fury was the sort of car that compounded Chrysler's problems. It was too big at a time when people were thinking small, and even a downsizing for 1982 into the earlier Aspen mould was really only a gesture

Below: a better Plymouth, the 1982 four-door Reliant. This was Plymouth's K-car incarnation, first seen in 1980 and generally improved in successive model changes

As Chrysler slipped from tenth place in the 1978 list of America's top 500 companies to a lowly seventeenth in 1979, recording in the process an all-time, all-industry, record loss of $1.1 billion, Plymouth waited for the new cars which could mean make or break.

Chrysler did a good job on the K-cars and, by the time they reached the market for the 1981 model year, they were widely regarded as very fine cars. The Plymouth versions, two and four-door saloons and a five-door station wagon, were known as Reliant and they replaced the Volare. They were all-new, front-wheel-drive cars, powered by a new, transversely mounted, 2.2-litre four, or the 2.6-litre, Mitsubishi-built, Silent Shaft four. The new 2.2-litre engine also found its way into the popular Horizon, which otherwise continued essentially unchanged for 1981. The Colt-by-any-other-name Plymouth Champ offered a twin gearstick, eight-speed transmission, on everything down to the 1.4-litre basic engine and had opened a few eyes as to just how good a really small car could be. The other Mitsubishi-built Plymouth, the attractive Sap-poro, underwent a few subtle changes without losing its distinctive character. The big Plymouth, the Gran Fury, plodded on for another year, as a reminder of where Chrysler had gone wrong over the past few years.

A year later, for the 1982 season, the Gran Fury took a step in the right direction, albeit without any real engineering achievement, being reborn as yet another derivative of the ageing Volare line of yesteryear. The Champ and the Sapporo remained at the popular end of the Plymouth line, the Champ now coming in five-door hatchback shape to add further glitter to an already attractive package. The Horizon was still going strong, with little changed but the paintwork, and the Reliant looked set to capitalise on a solid first year by changing nothing but the ride and the sound insulation.

Like that of its sister, Dodge, the success or otherwise of Plymouth meant more than just the life or death of a badge; by it, Chrysler itself would stand or fall. Yet again, Plymouth was having to live up to the claim of its namesake's founders and emulate the strength and determination of the Pilgrims.

Pontiac

An Indian chief in the age of the motor car

THE PONTIAC MARQUE name dates back to 1893, when young Edward M. Murphy founded the Pontiac Buggy Company in Pontiac, Michigan, a town which had taken its name from a mighty Indian chief who, 150 years before, had banded the Ottawas, Chippewas, Pottawattomis and Miamis into a powerful confederation. When, in 1907, Murphy went into motor-car manufacturing, however, he called his new company Oakland, and it was not until the middle

Below: the six-cylinder Landaulette of 1929

Bottom: this is the six-cylinder roadster version of 1925

1920s that the Pontiac name was used on a car, when General Motors had taken over.

The Oakland had pioneered Duco cellulose finish and four-wheel braking in a medium-priced car, and it was as a low-priced running mate for this successful model that the Pontiac was launched at the January 1926 New York Auto Show. 'The Chief of the Sixes' was an all-new design by Ben H. Anibal, formerly chief engineer of Cadillac, to the specification of Al R. Glancy, General Manager of Oakland. The Pontiac, however, proved to be a cuckoo in the nest, for it was so popular that it toppled the Oakland from favour. Sales of this $825 side-valve 3064 cc six totalled 76,742 in the fitst year of production, 140,000 in 1927 and 210,890 in 1928; by 1931, the Oakland was dead.

Shortly after the launching of the Pontiac, it was apparent that the original factory in the centre of Pontiac township was too small, and a 246-acre site on the northern edge of the city was acquired for expansion. The new buildings incorporated an extensive area of glass roofing to provide the maximum natural

illumination, which earned the factory the nickname of the 'daylight plant'.

The success of the Pontiac is all the more remarkable when it is considered that this was—and still is—the only marque to be created (rather than acquired) by General Motors and survive more than a couple of seasons.

Only 90 days after the ground was broken on the new

keeps the interior of windows and windshield safely fog-free. And in appearance it sets the new style— visibly identifies a car as modern'.

You would find it difficult from that surfeit of fulsomeness to realise that just ten years earlier most of the cars on the roads of the world had been open tourers, in which 'serenely confident young ladies' would have had to have dressed up like aviators to avoid those unkind breezes . . . yet now they demanded total protection from the elements.

The year 1934 saw a slightly more positive technical advance, in the adoption of Dubonnet-type independent front suspension, which followed a design which had been launched at the Paris Salon four years earlier. Commented *The Motor*: 'There is a coil spring for each wheel, enclosed in a cylinder which is hinged to the chassis frame. The stub axle on which the wheel turns is carried by a trailing arm which is journalled in the cylinder and is fitted with an interior projection engaging with the coil spring. An extra link is also used to steady the system against brake reactions. A unique feature of the Dubonnet plan is that all the steering gear is on the frame, so that it is totally unaffected by up-and-down wheel movements'. With their genius for trivialising technicalities with infantile names, the Americans rendered the Dubonnet suspension into 'knee-action springing'.

All-steel 'turret-top' bodywork was another feature of the 1934 Pontiac line, while for 1935 they acquired

factory site, cars were leaving the finished building, an occurrence which was regarded as something of a miracle by the construction industry. Not only that, but the factory was linked to a new Fisher Body plant by a closed-in overhead bridge, which eliminated the usual problem of having to bring in bodies by truck.

For 1930, the Pontiac was redesigned, and fitted with an ohv 3277 cc six-cylinder engine which it had, among many other features, in common with the Marquette, a none-too-successful light-six recently introduced by Buick, another General Motors company.

While the Marquette was shortlived, though, the Pontiac continued to flourish. The last Oakland had been a V8 based on the Oldsmobile Viking; for 1932, this model, too, became a Pontiac. Here, however, even the magic of the Pontiac name failed to do anything for this 4104 cc flop, which was allowed to fade away unmourned.

Its successor was a complete contrast, the first American straight-eight to sell at less than $600. Its 3654 cc power unit developed 77 bhp, giving a top speed of almost 80 mph. It helped Pontiac sell 89,000 cars and gain fifth place on the American market; the new eight even supplanted the six-cylinder Pontiac for a while.

Then, in 1933, a new general manager, Harry J. Klingler, took over at Pontiac, and it was decided to reinstate the six-cylinder model, which had only been suspended for a short while.

The straight-eight featured, in common with other General Motors models, hinged quarter-lights in front and rear windows, a simple innovation which was hailed as a great technological breakthrough: 'Not a hair out of place . . . this serenely confident young lady has just stepped from her car. She has no fear that her hair was tousled or her gown ruffled by unkind breezes, for her car has Fisher No Draft Ventilation, latest and greatest contribution to personal appearance and comfort—to health and safety. No Draft Ventilation, in any weather, provides fresh air without chilling drafts on any passenger. In stormy weather it

'Silver Streak' styling and radiator grilles which followed the vulgar contemporary vogue for looking like a meat safe. In Britain, those who preferred more conservative coachwork were well catered for by the English concessionaires, whose managing director, Kaye Don, had just retired from motor racing after a tragically unfortunate accident in the Isle of Man had resulted in the death of his mechanic. This

Below: this car is Pontiac's 6–27 model of 1926 and is to be seen in the Harrah Museum

Below: the soft-top, two-door Pontiac cabriolet sport of 1933 was powered by a V8 motor

company offered from their Berkeley Street show-rooms: fixed-head sports coupé (£350), two-door touring saloon (£360), drop-head coupé (£370), four-door touring saloon (£370), foursome English-built drophead coupé (£470) and sedanca coupé, also English-built (£495), all on the 28 hp six-cylinder chassis. Eight-cylinder 33.6 hp versions of the same vehicles cost between £15 and £30 more.

Although the marque did not exhibit at Olympia in 1935, Pontiac organised a display of their range at 5–6 Eastbury Court, on the Hyde Park side of the exhibition. *The Motor* seemed quite impressed: 'These cars have extremely pleasing lines, following the latest American practice in regard to radiator grilles, wing and head design. Very smooth riding is provided by the combination of knee-action front suspension and long semi-elliptic springs at the rear. The softness of the springing is adequately demonstrated by the way in which the car can be rocked when stationary, yet on the road it stiffens up in a surprising manner to give quite a pronounced sense of security.

'The engines are of the side-valve type, rubber mounted to damp out vibrations; the transmission is taken by a single dry-plate clutch of large diameter to a three-speed gearbox with a very simple and light gear change.'

There was little change in the appearance of 'The Most Beautiful Thing on Wheels' for 1937 but then, the American industry had just had its second best season ever after the boom year of 1929, and 'it is not the habit of the industry to make daring innovations in the midst of a good buying cycle. Such innovations are considered to be better saved for the day when car owners must be prodded to buy new cars'.

It seems, however, that the Silver Streak's lucky streak was far from exhausted, for there were to be no major changes to the specification for some years; sales doubled in the 1935–36 season, calling for further enlargement of the factory to meet demand.

Left: the four-door Pontiac 6 Landau Sedan of 1928

For 1938, there was the option of a column-mounted gear-change (which was standardised on the following year's cars), while the coupé had a curious sideways-on rear seat which folded away into a cubbyhole at the back of the passenger compartment when not in use.

There was, however, a new look for 1941 in the shape of the new Torpedo range, which had twin-choke

193

carburettors allied to larger engines than the previous year's models; apart from the cheap Torpedo, which retailed at less than $1000, there were also the Streamliner and Streamliner Chieftain, all available with six- or eight-cylinder power unit.

Pontiac produced 330,061 of these 1941 cars, an achievement which made them the largest manufacturer in their price bracket, and the fifth largest in the American industry.

It was this range, little altered, which was to form Pontiac's output after the war, while the company launched an ambitious expansion programme, aimed at raising production by up to 50 per cent. The iron foundry was enlarged, the engine plant redesigned to take more machines for more production, a new rear axle manufacturing building and facilities for heat-treating steel forgings for increased strength and durability were some of the facets of this scheme, as

Below: a Pontiac cabriolet two-door convertible of 1948; it was fitted with a V8 engine and was also available with several other body variations

Bottom: a Pontiac Eight convertible of 1951

was a new warehouse holding parts for obsolete models. This contained an automatic plant for electroplating brightwork.

In 1949, the General Motors group carried out a corporate restyling programme throughout the product range, and Pontiacs emerged lower in appearance, using bodyshells that had much in common with the contemporary Oldsmobiles. The X-frame chassis was redesigned, too, and there was now the option of Hydramatic transmission: but engines were still L-head sixes and eights.

Fastback versions of the Pontiac range were offered under the name Streamliner, while in 1950 the Catalina Hardtop Coupé was added to the line-up.

Harry J. Klinger moved on in 1951 to become vice president in charge of vehicle production for General Motors, and was succeeded as head of Pontiac by Arnold Lenz; but Lenz died tragically in the following year.

His replacement, R. M. Critchfield, lost little time in launching Pontiac on the most ambitious enlargement and modernisation programme undertaken since the marque's foundation. Already the 1951 Silver Anniversary car range had been nationalised, with the demise of the Streamliner fastbacks: now there was a new car-finishing building and a completely modernised engine plant which began production of Pontiac's first all-new engine design for many years. This was a V8 unit which was standardised on all 1955 models.

A new top-of-the-range model, the Series 28 Star Chief Eight, had been launched in 1954, available with Convertible, Custom Catalina, De Luxe Sedan or Custom Sedan coachwork, while the old six and eight-cylinder models continued virtually unchanged.

In June 1954, Pontiac produced its five-millionth car since the marque's inception in 1926, and the following year the company recorded a new record production of 581,860 cars: it had already nudged ahead of Plymouth to become fourth best-selling American car.

The 1955 models with the new 180 bhp ohv Strato-Streak V8 engine had revised styling in the current General Motors idiom, with dog-leg doors and wraparound windscreen: the old straight-six lingered

Right: the ultra-powerful Pontiac GTO of 1968; it was available with a V8 engine with power options ranging from 269 bhp to 365 bhp

Below: the Pontiac Le Mans four-door hardtop of 1968

on in the Pontiac Laurentian and Pathfinder Models produced by General Motors of Canada, which were based on Chevrolet mechanical components.

There was another change of general manager in 1956: this time the incumbent was Semon E. ('Bunkie') Knudsen, at 43 the youngest general manager in the General Motors organisation, who proceeded to cultivate the currently fashionable 'youth image' for the Pontiac products. A new engineering group was set up, headed by E. M. ('Pete') Estes, and new models were developed. A new, larger V8 engine, the Tempest, appeared on 1958 models: in its most powerful form it came complete with fuel injection and Super Hydra-Matic transmission. But the first real fruits of the Knudsen shake-up (Bunkie's father, incidentally, had been Henry Ford's right-hand man before joining GM) came in 1959, with cars such as the Pontiac Catalina, which threw off much of the chromy

Right: the V8-engined Pontiac Grand Prix model of 1969

vulgarity of its immediate predecessors, presaging the cleaner style of the 1960s. The knee-cracking dogleg door aperture remained, however, allied to a 'Vista-Panoramic' windscreen; as well, there was a wraparound rear window.

Then, in the autumn of 1960, came the all-new Tempest compact, with an oversquare four-cylinder engine mounted in a unit constructed body/chassis shell. The three-speed gearbox was mounted in the rear axle, a curious slice of automotive *deja vu* which harked back to the pre-World War I era when engineers were less concerned about having such a mass of metal dancing about between the rear springs. After all

the fins and chrome of the Fifties, the styling of the Tempest looked quite bland, apart from a curious falling line to the side moulding of the body which made the rear end look as though it was sagging. Or, as General Motors put it: 'Unique in conception and fresh in styling, the Tempest became an immediate success and was recognised as the outstanding engineering achievement of the year'.

Bunkie became history in 1961, moving on to become general manager of Chevrolet, and Pete Estes took over Pontiac, which continued to expand, achieving third place in US sales the same year. Unlike the top two places, which have been disputed between Ford and Chevrolet ever since the Depression, third place in the American sales league is regarded as somewhat of a hot seat: Pontiac, nevertheless, managed to hang on to it throughout the sixties, continuing to expand both sales and facilities.

In 1964 three new construction projects were inaugurated, which added 1½ million square feet to the Pontiac factory: they included a 180,000 square foot addition to the foundry, containing core-making machines, water-cooled cupolas and a new finishing room. There was also a service parts warehouse, which covered an area of 1,070,000 sq ft under one roof, plus an 800 ft × 330 ft storage and shipping building,

designed to speed shipments of components to other Pontiac assembly plants.

Pete Estes continued to follow in Bunkie's footsteps, moving on to become general manager of Chevrolet in 1965; his successor at Pontiac was John Z. DeLorean, formerly the company's chief engineer.

Before the launch of the 1966 models, Pontiac

Below left: front and rear view of the 1971 Pontiac GTO Judge

Below: 1972 Pontiac Grand Prix V8 model

announced that an all-new overhead camshaft engine would be standardised on the next season's models, claiming that this was the first time that such a power unit had been used on an American passenger car. At which, Duesenberg, Stutz and Wills Sainte Claire might have been permitted a posthumous protest . . .

Not that the old V8 hadn't been a mighty performer,

Opposite page, top: the fast and powerful Pontiac Firebird Trans-Am coupé of 1971

Opposite page, centre: front-end view of the purposeful Pontiac Firebird 400 model of 1970

Left: the two-door Pontiac Grand Ville cabriolet of 1971 was powered by a V8 engine of 7642 cc

for it had powered the first of the muscle cars, the Pontiac GTO, which had shamelessly borrowed its nomenclature from the classic Ferrari model, though there were doubtless few in the executive offices at One Pontiac Plaza who could have told you that GTO stood for *Gran Tourismo Omologato* in its original application.

Car and Driver waxed enthusiastic over the Pontiac GTO: 'Ferrari never built enough GTOs to earn the name anyway—just to be on the safe side, though, Pontiac built a faster one!' And to the more chauvinistic American commentators, who felt that the ability to exceed 100 mph in a straight line was the prime qualification for a sporting car, the GTO seemed to justify all the superlatives heaped on it: although they did admit that the rear axle was apt to hop about like a maddened hare when the brakes were applied hard.

But, like a retired weightlifter, the Pontiac GTO began to lose its muscle under layers of affluent adiposity during the latter 1960s, although in 1968 *Motor Trend* had awarded the model its Golden Calipers trophy for the Car of the Year, stating that it was 'so successful in confirming the correlations between safety, styling and performance'. Among its features was the Pontiac-developed Endura shock-absorbing bumper.

By now, there was another sporty Pontiac. This was the Firebird, launched in January 1967 and aimed at 'the youthful sports car market'. It offered a choice between the ohc six and the big V8, and contributed to Pontiac's best-ever production figures of 943,253, for the 1968 season. That year the 'specialty cars'—Tempest, Firebird and GTO Grand Prix—exceeded those of the 'conventional line', while the next year the Grand Prix tripled its sales compared with the 1968 model, reaching 105,000 units and winning the *Car Life* Car of the Year Award.

February 1969 saw another general manager for the company. F. James McDonald replaced John DeLorean, who had followed the by-now traditional path to the top job at Chevrolet. McDonald had been works manager of Pontiac from 1965–68, and then spent a year at Chevrolet as director of manufacturing.

In 1979, in addition to the famous Firebird range which included the Formula, Firebird and Esprit models along with the top of the range Trans Am, Pontiac produced seven other models. The Bonneville/Catalina, Le Mans, Grand Prix, Grand Am, and Phoenix were all large to full size sedans and coupés available with engines ranging from the 3.8-litre Buick V6, to the V8s of 4.9, 5.0, and 5.7 litres.

Following the demise of the Astre in 1978, the Sunbird (a coupé or sports hatch) became the smallest Pontiac, and was available with a 2.5-litre, four-cylinder, crossflow engine at one end of the scale, or the 5-litre V8 at the other.

Despite the energy crises of the 1970s demand for Pontiacs, with their reputation of quality and high performance, continued unabated and, with Alec C. Mair as general manager, the company seemed well set for the 1980s.

For the 1980 model year, Pontiac introduced the

Right: although the 1979 Firebird Trans Am was still a car in the muscle-car mould, pollution regulations had robbed it of much of its former sting and left it with more sedate performance

Below: the unusually-styled Pontiac Grand Am of 1974 was a luxury four-door model and had a V8 engine of 7453 cc

Right: the 1981 Bonneville was the last of the full-sized Bonnevilles and was replaced by the Model G, which was a variant of the smaller Le Mans

Below: the 1980 Phoenix was Pontiac's first car of the 1980s and like almost everyone else's first car of the 1980s it was a front-wheel-drive offering

new, 210 hp, turbocharged version of the 4.9-litre GM V8 engine as an option for the Firebird. The car with this high performance package was known as the Turbo Trans Am Firebird. The normally aspirated 4.9 V8 became the basic engine for the Trans Am. Elsewhere in the range, GM's 3.8-litre V6 was the basic engine for the 1980 Le Mans, Grand Prix, Catalina and Bonneville variants and the 3.8 was also available as a performance option in the Sunbird, which featured the 2.5-litre four-cylinder GM motor as standard. Pontiac were doing quite well as the hard times approached again. The popularity of the Trans Am range in particular continued to soar and almost 120,000 were built in 1979.

Pontiac, in common with most of its competitors, joined the swelling ranks of the front-wheel-drive compact builders when they introduced the Phoenix, in hatchback and sporting saloon guises, in April 1979. The Phoenix had the 2.5-litre four as standard equipment but was also available with the 2.8 V6. Manual transmission was standard and auto became an option. GM's new 5.7-litre diesel engine was another development prompted by the industry's commitment to meeting federal fuel consumption requirements. The 1980 Bonneville, in fact, was claimed to give better fuel consumption than 28 smaller imports and a better cruising range than 95% of *all* imports. 'Full-sized' Pontiacs, the Catalina, Bonneville and Bonneville Brougham, shed weight and became more aerodynamically efficient, while remaining '1979-sized'.

In May 1981 Pontiac progressed one step further on the road towards providing a car for the future, with the introduction of the attractive, all-new, sub-compact, front-wheel-drive J2000. Within the industry the J configuration had come to signify 'world car' and the J2000, offered as two-door coupé, three-door hatchback, four-door saloon or station wagon, was distinctly European in style and mechanical content,

although the front-end styling was unmistakably Pontiac. The standard engine was a transversely mounted, 1.8-litre straight four. With 46.2 hp per litre, this engine had one of the highest volume efficiencies of any GM engine—at a time when it was still not uncommon for the larger V8s to produce a leisurely 25–30 hp per litre. Efficiency was now the vogue word; it was no longer quite so fashionable to talk about outright horsepower.

As with the Sunbird, a four-speed manual transmission came as standard with the J2000, but now with an overdrive top ratio. All of a sudden the tables had turned and it was the automatic transmission which was more usually the optional equipment—albeit more as a sop to the all-important EPA fuel consumption ratings than to cater for any change in driver attitudes. In the same way, suspension design was slowly dragging itself out of the cart age and emulating long-established European standards. The J2000 was fairly typical of the new American cars in having independent suspension by MacPherson struts and lower wishbones at the front, with rack and pinion steering, and 'double-crank trailing-twist axle' with trailing arms and variable rate coil springs at the rear. Another exciting car revealed by Pontiac in May 1981 and scheduled for production in 1982 was a mid-engined, two-seater sports car in the Fiat X1/9 image.

Pontiac took other lessons from overseas competitors, initiating more stringent pre-delivery inspections and 'salesperson product training programs' in an obvious reply to the methods widely used by Japanese and European franchises but largely eschewed by domestic producers.

The Pontiac range was now ready for the 1980s. The J2000 was intended to appeal to traditional buyers as well as to those buyers with what Pontiac called 'new values'. It was a very important introduction indeed at a time when the industry as a whole was on its knees.

Right: with the 1982 J2000 range, Pontiac moved into the 'world car' movement while retaining a distinctive Pontiac look, thanks to the traditional front end styling

IT WAS IN 1878 that Thomas B. Jeffery, an Englishman who had emigrated to America, began manufacturing bicycles. Before long, the Gormully & Thomas B. Jeffery manufacturing company was one of the biggest in the industry, with branches at Boston, Washington and New York, and the main factory on North Franklin and Pearson Streets, Chicago. By the 1890s, there was even a branch factory in the centre of the English cycle trade, Coventry, and the company, whose products were marketed under the trade name 'Rambler', was rivalling the Pope-Columbia group for supremacy in the American market.

Jeffery was a prolific inventor, and pioneered the beaded-edge clincher tyre on the American scene; in the 1890s, the company claimed 'Rambler bicycles for man, woman or child are safest and most luxurious—G & J Pneumatic Tires Make Them So'. An added touch of luxury was the spring frame, which was promoted as having some therapeutic value, and a pseudo-scientific treatise by one Dr Tooker (*Bicycling for Girls from a Medical Standpoint*) was sent free with the company's catalogue. Another invention of Jeffery's was the 'railway velocipede', a pedal-powered vehicle for permanent-way inspectors.

In 1897, Jeffery began work on a motor carriage, which was built in the machine shop of his Chicago factory. Nor unnaturally, cycle practice was followed in its construction, with a tubular chassis and wire wheels. The tiller-steered buggy, with its curious lozenge-shaped coachwork, was obviously unfitted for series production, a fact betrayed by such minor considerations as the flywheel of the rearward-pointing horizontal engine being between the driver's feet.

By 1900, Jeffery had two cars ready to show to the public. The work of his son, Charles, the vehicles had tiller steering and twin-cylinder engines. One was bodied as a stanhope, the other as a runabout, and they

Rambler

Rambler's history is confused by the many models it encompasses

Above: a 1902 Rambler two-seater runabout fitted with tiller steering

Left: this 1904 Rambler, was one of the most popular models ever built by the Thomas B. Jeffery Company of Kenosha, Wisconsin; it featured a twin-cylinder, 25 hp engine. Note the wicker picnic baskets mounted on both sides; these were offered as optional equipment

were shown at the International Exhibition and Tournament in Chicago and at America's first national motor show at the New York Madison Square Garden. Reaction to these cars, which in the summer of 1900 completed a round trip from Chicago to Milwaukee, must have been favourable, for Thomas Jeffrey sold his interest in Gormully & Jeffrey and bought a factory in Kenosha, Wisconsin, which had formerly belonged to the Sterling Bicycle Company, where Charles began work on further prototypes. The first of these, the Model A, appeared in the following year. A more finished design than its predecessors, Model A had the engine in front under a bonnet whose sides were formed by the elements of the gilled-tube radiator. Unusually for that date, the car had left-hand positioning of the steering wheel.

In the summer of 1901, Charles Jeffery completed a second experimental car, the Model B, a refined version of the Model A, which had, if anything, even more 'European' features than its predecessor. Old Thomas B. Jeffery, though, thought that these twin-engined runabouts were too radical in design for the American market, which was still demanding gas buggies. So, the Model C was developed.

The Model C was a crude and spidery tiller-steered machine with a single-cylinder 12 hp engine under the seat, driving the rear axle via a central chain, and started by a crank beside the driver's seat that seemed to have strayed from a barrel organ. Finished in Brewster green with red striping, this first production Rambler sold for $750, and went on the market in March 1902, in Chicago. Soon it was joined by a de luxe version, the Model D, costing $825 with 'hand-buffed leather top, rubber side curtains and storm apron'. Together, these cars sold 1500 units in the first year of production, putting Rambler in the 'big league' of production, along with the Curved-Dash Olds and the Locomobile Steamer.

As 1902 progressed, so the design of these cars became more substantial: the cycle-type wire wheels were replaced with wooden artillery wheels in mid year, and a clip-on *dos-a-dos* seat was available to convert the

Far right: the Rambler Cross Country model of 1912 was powered by a four-cylinder engine. This particular example can now be seen in the Harrah Museum in Nevada

Below: in 1911, an estate agency used this photo as part of a publicity campaign to sell property. The car on the right is a Rambler Tourer

strictly-two-seater Rambler into an uncomfortable
four-seater. A contemporary photograph shows that a
determined family motorist could squeeze two small
children into the lid of the frontal luggage locker to
boost carrying capacity to six! Another worthwhile
addition to the specification was the fitting of mud-
guards, while the 1903 Model E boasted wheel steering
and a 15 hp engine. Sales of this and the better-finished
Model F totalled 1350.

A clumsy looking tubular radiator distinguished the
1904 Model G, although as the engine was still under
the seat, the impressively louvred bonnet was a total
fraud (or perhaps the louvres were for keeping the beer
and sandwiches cool on picnics). Nine different models
were offered that year, of which the most popular was
the Model L, with side-mounted wicker baskets and a
surrey top. Sales were up to 2342. From 1904 to 1908,
Ramblers featured throttle operation by what seemed to
be a subsidiary steering wheel.

The year 1905 saw the adoption of a more-
rounded—but still ugly—pattern of radiator and bon-

net, plus the addition of an 18 hp twin-cylinder engine, with twin chains driving the rear wheels. The presidential accolade was afforded to one of these cars when Theodore Roosevelt rode in a Rambler Surrey Type Two in the Rough Riders' Reunion Parade at Louisville, Kentucky, on 4 April 1905. That model, complete with roll-down storm curtains, cost $1650.

The first closed Rambler appeared in 1906 in the shape of the Model 16, priced at $3000, and whose cooling system seemed to be something of a physical marvel: 'Every attention is paid to comfort and convenience, and a radiator is provided whereby the desired temperature may at all times be attained'. As the limousine came in, though, so the old surrey-topped tourers disappeared. Ramblers were moving up in the price stakes, a fact reflected in the drop in sales for 1906, down to 2765 compared with the 1905 total of 3807.

The slack caused by the change in image was only temporary: in 1907, Rambler announced their first four-cylinder model, the 40 hp Model 25, and they sold 3201 cars. By now, the mid-engined cars had acquired bodies which hinged upwards for ease of access to the mechanical parts.

In 1908, Rambler spent considerable sums on image-building public-relations exercises, such as the spending of $25,000 on enamelled road-direction signs (on which the Rambler logo was bigger than the directions) in the states of Wisconsin and Illinois, and the presentation of silver watch fobs to all owners who had driven their Ramblers more than 15,000 miles. Over 200 were enrolled by the summer of 1908, when any owner planning a long tour was still considered newsworthy enough to be featured in the company's house magazine. Realising the publicity value of famous personalities riding in their products, the company also published photographs of Buffalo Bill Cody and Mark Twain in Rambler four-cylinder cars, which they described as 'dignified, silent, comfortable and reliable'. A sporting model, the 34A, was added to the line-up. It had exaggeratedly flared oystershell front wings,

Above: in 1950, the Rambler name was revived, after a period of 37 years, and given to this 'compact' model produced by Nash Motors

Right: the 1955 Rambler Country Club two-door coupé. The Country Club name was also a revival from the early days of Rambler history

and the performance potential of the Rambler car was given in a news story that recounted how an irate Rambler owner had chased a horse-thief for thirteen hours from Kankakee, Illinois, finally capturing him in Rennsalaer, Indiana. Sales were up again, to 3597, but slumped again the following year to 1692. However, at the 1909 Chicago Motor Show, attended by 200,000 people, more Ramblers (160) were sold than any other make. A major advance on the 1909 Ramblers was the option of a detachable spare wheel, the first time that such a fitting had been available on an American car.

The company was obviously determined that 1910 was going to be a better year for sales, but cloaked the fact in the proud statement that for 1910 production would be limited to 2500 cars 'to assure maximum

Left: a cutaway of the in-line, side-valve, six-cylinder engine used to power the revived Rambler models produced by Nash and Hudson in the 1950s; the engine was of 2.8-litres capacity

Above: the four-door Rambler Classic sedan model of 1966

quality'. That they were still desperate for customers was demonstrated when one client traded in six cows for his Rambler. Once again, however, the firm was hitting the headlines, with President Howard William Taft riding in one of the very first 1910-model Ramblers in November 1909, when visiting the hamlet of Rambler, near Augusta, Georgia.

There was a bitter blow on 21 March 1910, when Thomas B. Jeffery collapsed and died while on a European tour. Three months later, the company was incorporated under Wisconsin law, with capital stock of $3,000,000.

By now, Rambler had left the old gas-buggy image far behind, and the 1911 models, which sold over 3000, were substantial cars with some clever mechanical

details, like a locking petrol tap 'to prevent the use of the car without the consent of the owner'. The model 63 coupé had a 'steering column that may be adjusted at any angle to suit the comfort of the operator'; this car seated four, three facing forward and 'one had a commanding view of the road behind'.

The company stressed the safety built into their products: 'Each car is required in test to come to a full stop within fifty feet at 18 mph'. Comfort and durability were important, too. The use of big wheels and tyres 'provide not only added comfort, but tests have shown that tyres even an inch larger in diameter and half an inch greater in width will last twice as long'. In 1912, three Model 73-4CC Ramblers—the CC stood for 'Cross-Country'—covered 320 miles in one day, from Chicago to Toledo, on a company demonstration.

Sales for 1912 were 3550; for 1913, they rose to 4435, and in that year Rambler standardised electric lighting, with the sidelamps faired into the scuttle, and offered a 10,000-mile guarantee with each car. The cars were not the whole story for 1913, for early in the year Rambler introduced a range of trucks under the Jeffery name,

which proved so popular that within twelve months commercial-vehicle production had out-stripped cars by more than 1100 units.

For 1914, the cars were known as Jeffery, too, and the company was pioneering mass-produced four-wheel drive with the famous Jeffery Quad truck. The change of image seems to have been the right move, for in 1914 the Jeffery company built 10,417 cars and 3096 trucks. The fact that the purple-penned Ned Jordan was helping to market the company's products may have had something to do with it, as well.

The production of cars had tailed off again when Charles W. Nash resigned from General Motors in 1916 and bought out the Thomas B. Jeffery Company. It picked up again immediately after the takeover, but the Jeffery name was dropped for all time in the summer of 1917, to be replaced by the Nash image and superscription.

However, the Rambler name was revived, 37 years after its decease, for the new 'compact' introduced in 1950 by Nash Motors, and was used as a model name for some years—after the merger between Nash and Hudson which created American Motors in 1954, some Hudsons were also called Ramblers (or vice versa).

It was soon patently obvious, however, that the Rambler name had far more pulling power than that of either Nash or Hudson, and by 1955 Ramblers were outselling all other models in the combined range, and had become virtually a separate marque—by 1956,

three-quarters of the group output of 104,199 cars were Ramblers.

A new Rambler series appeared in 1956, powered by a 120 hp ohv six-cylinder engine. The ugly, typically 1950s lines of the latest bodyshell were accentuated by eccentrically applied two-tone paint schemes, applied in a broad side flash which curved down to the rear wheel arch and simultaneously swooped up and over the rear window pillar. There was a new pillarless 'hardtop sedan', which was also available as a station wagon, said to be the first time a car had combined 'the appeal of the station wagon and the hardtop con-

Top: the fastback Rambler Marlin model of 1965

Above: in 1954, the Nash and Hudson companies merged to form American Motors. Typical of the AMC models was this Rambler Ambassador 990 station wagon of 1965

year, Rambler became a separate marque once again, and the old habit of labelling a Rambler by the Nash or Hudson names died. So, too, did the Nash and Hudson cars, as the 1957 models gave way to the '58s.

In any case, the Hudson Hornet and Nash Ambassador lines had become virtual dead letters long before: out of 118,990 cars built in 1957 by the three components of American Motors, 114,084 had been Ramblers. That year, too, a more powerful Rambler option was added to the line, in the form of a new 190 bhp V8 engine. There was a limited-edition, 255 bhp Rambler Rebel with a 327 cu in version of this power unit. Only 1500 or so Rebels were built, distinguished by a colour scheme of silver with 'gold anodised spears'.

Now that they had the corporate roost all to themselves, Ramblers blossomed forth. More than 100 improvements were made to the 1958 models, although the utility of some of the changes is questionable: the bodyshell underwent a major face (and posterior) lift, with a new radiator grille, marginally less vulgar than the last, quadruple headlamps, and lethally pointed tailfins. Other changes included a 'step-on' parking brake and a deep-dip rust-proofing system, with all bodyshells immersed in a 15,000 gallon tank of primer before painting.

Sales rocketed, with 186,227 Ramblers sold, resulting in a profit of $26 Million. The best-selling model was the 127 hp six-cylinder Super Cross Country station wagon, while there was a new de luxe Rambler Ambassador range (reviving an old Nash model name) with a 270 hp V8 engine and a new production version of the Rebel pillarless hardtop, with a 215 hp V8.

The compact Rambler was growing up into a big car, with 108 in wheelbases on the standard models and 117 in on the Ambassadors. So, a new 'compact compact' appeared in the range, on a 100 in wheelbase. It was a case of *déjà vu*, for the new model was simply a revival of the old Rambler which had been discontinued two years earlier, with a body shape which, in its essentials, dated back to 1953. Renamed the Rambler American, this 'new-old' model was a great—one could

vertible', a statement of dubious validity since the hardtop sedan was not a convertible!

Another 'unique feature' whose merits were mainly existent in the eyes of the publicity department was featured on station wagons: 'a roll-down rear window which eliminated the irksome upper tailgate found on competitive wagons'.

It was in 1956 that the two-millionth unit-constructed car rolled off the Kenosha production line, a record achieved since 1941, when the Nash 600 had been announced, with its 'unitised' body-shell.

The AMC group's concentration on the Rambler line was the result of the passionate belief of George Romney, president and chairman of American Motors, that the compact car was the car of the future. Romney had joined Nash-Kelvinator in 1950 as general manager, having made a name for himself during the war as manager of the Automotive Council for War Production, which co-ordinated the activities of the American motor industry to maximise the output of military material. It was Romney, too, who had been responsible for the re-introduction of the memorable and respected Rambler marque name.

During the mid 1950s, it looked as though Romney's promotion of the compact concept had been an unlucky gamble, as American Motors reported four consecutive years of heavy losses. In 1957, despite a loss of $11,833,200 on sales of $362 million, there were signs that there were good times around the corner. That

From top to bottom:
1963 Rambler 440
four-door sedan;

1966 Rambler Rogue
two-door coupé;

1970 Javelin coupé;

1975 AMC Pacer
with a straight six
engine

hardly say immediate—success. Available in any body style you liked, as long as it was a two-door sedan, the American sold 42,196 in the 1958 season.

Rambler were still marketing that ugly little motorised roller-skate, the Metropolitan, built by Austin in England, but this was really outside the mainstream of events.

Rambler's rapid rise up the sales charts had been aided by a recession in the American economy in 1957–58 but, although the nation's financial troubles were passing in 1959, Rambler sales continued to rise. Indeed, in 1959, Rambler became the most successful 'independent' motor-manufacturing company in the history of the American automobile industry. A total of 368,464 cars was sold, net sales amounted to $869,849,704, and profits of $60,341,823 were recorded. Yet, in direct contrast to the normal custom of annual model change, the 1959 Ramblers were little altered from the previous year's models, except that a two-door station wagon was added to the American range. Rambler claimed: 'the high resale value of the Rambler American is indicative of the buyer's preference for simplicity and economy'.

Just in case the buyer wanted something other than simplicity and economy, however, the V8 Ambassador Series 'incorporated the luxury, comfort and performance of larger US cars with compactness of design'.

The 1960 models had only minor styling alterations (although a four-door sedan was added to the American range) and again sales records were broken, with an output of 434,707 cars, making Rambler fourth in the US sales league. Sales passed the billion(US)-dollar mark for the first time, reaching $1,057,716,447, with profits of $48,243,361.

To cope with the increased demand, the Lakefront plant at Kenosha was added to the production facilities as part of an expansion programme aimed at reaching an annual production of 600,000, although the restyled 1961 models only sold 372,485. Among the innovations was a convertible version of the American, claimed to be the only such model with unitary construction, and the cheapest convertible on the US market. The new Americans were even more compact than their predecessors, with 5.2 in cut off the overall length and 3 in off the width. All Custom Americans featured AMC's new light-alloy ohv six-cylinder engine, which was an option on Super and Deluxe versions of this model. Every Rambler now had a guaranteed-for-life-in-the-hands-of-the-original-owner ceramic-coated silencer.

As a further sales inducement, prices were cut on all 27 models in the 1962 product range, almost half of them by more than $112. Standard equipment was improved, with the addition of dual-circuit brakes, all-season Dowgard cooling, galvanised rocker panels and reduced lubrication requirements.

Rambler continued to offer advanced technical features during the 1960s, with the option of disc brakes in 1965, but as the decade drew on, it seemed as though the marque name was once again losing its potency. New cars like the Javelin were launched under their own names, with the Rambler tag becoming less and less prominent, until in 1970 it vanished from all cars sold in the North American continent.

In February 1975, AMC introduced the Pacer, a significant car that represented a brave departure in American automotive design. The Pacer featured outstanding all-round visibility by any standards, which was quite exceptional for an American car. However, although 'compact' in length, it suffered excessive width and a feeble power to weight ratio.

Following the debacle of the Pacer, which was never popular, AMC was deep in trouble; the Gremlin was basically a shortened version of the Hornet and hardly the car to see the company into the 1980s with any style. The investment for the much needed new models proved a heavy burden, and when the new models appeared in 1977—the AMX hatchback and, more important, The Concord—AMC was the sick man of America's four major manufacturers. At one stage they were reduced to cutting the price of their new models for 1978 by six per cent, and many critics expected the company to go to the wall during the course of that year. American Motors just managed to hang on, however, and the introduction of the AMC Spirit for 1979 seemed to be a good omen for the company.

AMC needed more than another model launch. Discussions with possible partners of 'world market' strength had started in 1977; in 1978 AMC began negotiations with Renault and in January 1979 agreement was reached on a 'substantial association' with the French company, whereby each would market the other's products in addition to its own. AMC would distribute the small, front-wheel-drive LeCar in the USA and Canada, and Renault became exclusive

Below: a 1979 Concord, one of the new cars AMC were banking on to help the company survive into the 1980s. The Concord was available as a sedan, hatchback or station wagon, with a six-cylinder, 3.8-litre engine as standard, and was mechanically simple, with wishbone front suspension and a live rear axle located by semi-elliptic springs

distributors of the AMC Jeep in France and certain other countries. By 1979 AMC had over 800 Renault franchises, growing to over 1300 by January 1981.

More importantly, Renault provided $150 million in financing, aimed at production of Renault-designed front-wheel-drive cars at Kenosha from 1982 onwards; Renault purchased 1½ million ordinary AMC shares at $10 a share, and other stock (maturing over five years) for a further $45 million. They also made available up to $50 million in other, working capital, credit arrangements. At this stage, Renault could convert its holdings to own approximately 22.7% of ordinary AMC stock. Over the next two years the holding would grow, until, in theory, Renault owned more than 50% of AMC. In fact, following a further $220 million investment in September 1980, Renault owned around 46% of AMC by 1981.

With this new marriage, 1979 was a record year for the corporation. Reported earnings (before extraordinary tax credits) were over $68 million—138% up on the previous year and 38% ahead of the peak of twenty years before. Net sales were a record $3.1 billion, which represented sales of 415,199 cars and Jeeps, worldwide, on top of the success of other company interests.

Much of this was attributed to the ability of LeCar to meet the new demand for economical, small cars, but the AMC Jeep also did well, recording a sales increase of 15% in spite of a general downturn in the market, attributable to energy worries. The Jeep CJ, with a new four-cylinder engine, was the first conventional four-wheel-drive vehicle to better 20 mpg in EPA tests. Furthermore, the newly introduced Eagle, the first American-built four-wheel-drive car (as opposed to wagon) was an outstanding success. Production of the Eagle was doubled in December 1979 to 400 units a day, as the Pacer was discontinued, a little earlier than planned. The Eagle was offered in saloon and station wagon guises, all with independent front suspension. With the Concord continuing as the company's best seller and the Spirit finding a steady market, the future looked bright.

Top: the 1981 Jeep CJ Renegade is recognisably descended from its wartime namesake but was an altogether more sophisticated device. By 1981 the off-road market was in recession but Jeep had survived tougher times than these

Above: the 1981 Eagle wagon, four-wheel-drive, four cylinders, and four-speed

Left: Renault's 1981 Le Car gave AMC the all-important base in the small car market

AMC established a lead in consumer relations in 1971 with the introduction of its Buyer Protection Plan —amazingly, the industry's only full warranty since 1976. In October 1979 the scheme was extended to include an optional three-year, or 36,000 mile, 'Service Security Plan' on major components. From 1980 all AMC cars were given Ziebart factory rustproofing, with a five-year warranty against rusting through. The days of 'planned obsolescence' were drawing to a close.

The heady financial results of 1979 were short-lived. Towards the end of the year, Jeep sales had shown a slight fall, although Spirit and Concord sales increased. In 1980, however, AMC, like the rest of the industry, struggled against recession, fuel shortages and the market inroads made by the imports. AMC contributed a net loss of almost $200 million to the American industry's staggering 1980 deficit of over $4 *billion*. The four-wheel-drive, off-road, market all but collapsed and, but for the timely emphasis on small cars, AMC might well have gone with it. In fact, AMC's market share rose from 2 to 2.3% and the 18i, a slightly larger car with more 'traditional' styling, was added to the Renault range offered in the USA. Eagles for the 1981 model year were given a 2.5-litre four-cylinder engine as standard, with a new 4.2-litre six option, as were the latest Spirits and Concords. Eagles were further improved during 1981 by the addition of Select Drive, which allowed two- or four-wheel drive to be chosen by a dashboard switch.

For 1982, Select Drive was a standard fitment on Eagles and a five-speed manual transmission was offered as an option on all AMC cars and most Jeeps.

In spite of the whole industry's financial problems, AMC looked ahead with guarded optimism. New paint facilities had been opened in Toledo, the Kenosha plant was much modernised and new working systems, with group involvement not unlike that found in Japan, were initiated. As the youngest of the 'big four', AMC was perhaps showing itself to be the most ready to accept change, and that seemed to be the most certain road to ultimate survival.

Top: the 1981 Spirit Liftback had chunky lines not unlike the Eagle's, and a long list of standard equipment

Above: the 1981 Concord four-door sedan came with a choice of four- or six-cylinder engines but by now the design was growing very long in the tooth

Left: for the 1982 Eagles, Select Drive, giving the choice between two- and four-wheel-drive, became a standard fitting. This is the sporty SX/4 liftback model

210

IN SIXTY-FOUR YEARS OF car manufacturing in North America, the Dutch name of Studebaker came to stand for cars of quality at moderate prices, light and economical engineering design, adventurous styling— and persistent financial trouble. The last-mentioned may not be entirely fair: the Studebaker Corporation did not go out of business in March 1966; it simply stopped making cars then. For, in spite of several years of fine sales success (it registered more than 200,000 cars in both 1950 and 1951), Studebaker never quite mastered the art of consistently earning money in the making *and selling* of automobiles.

In one sense, the Studebaker enterprises scored the ultimate success: they were successful makers of the product that made obsolete the vehicle on which their prosperity had been founded, that is, the horsedrawn wagon. For the Studebakers were wagonmakers in the New World, to which Peter Studebaker came, from Holland, to be the founder of the clan in 1736. Two of his great-grandsons, Henry and Clem, set up shop in South Bend, Indiana as the H and C Studebaker firm

Studebaker
From horse buggies to supercharged supercars

in 1852 and, in March of that year, built their first wagon for sale. With capital from another brother, John, they expanded their business to equip the Union Army in the Civil War. By 1875, they could claim to be 'the largest vehicle house in the world'. Twenty years later, at the dawn of the automobile age, the Studebaker Brothers Manufacturing Company was making 75,000

Below: front-end view of the 1923 Studebaker saloon

horse-drawn vehicles a year.

At the turn of the century, Studebaker was naturally called on by budding auto tycoons to supply chassis for their vehicles, and this led, eventually, by stages, to true Studebaker cars. Instrumental in urging this was young Frederick S. Fish, John Studebaker's son-in-law and the company's legal counsel. He developed its automotive activities in parallel with the profitable wagon-building line, which Studebaker did not discontinue until 1921. In 1902, twenty electric Studebaker runabouts were made, officially the company's first cars. Then, in co-operation with the Garford firm, gasoline-powered Studebaker production began in 1904, first as a single-cylinder and then, in 1905, with the addition of more expensive four-cylinder models.

Finding these cars unsuited to its reputation for large volume and low prices, Studebaker looked for more promising autos and found them in 1908 in the range of a new Detroit company that made Wayne and EMF cars, for which Studebaker became the sales agent. A new nameplate, Flanders, appeared on a smaller car in 1910, and the large and costly Garford was dropped after 1911. That was the year that saw the Studebaker Corporation formed, on 14 February, from the combined assets of the Studebaker and EMF companies. Fred Fish held the presidency of the new company. The other trade names were phased out in

Above: the remains of a Studebaker wagon of the 1800s

favour of the Studebaker name, and engineering was placed under Studebaker direction, although still done in the old EMF facilities in Detroit.

From all this confusion emerged, in 1914, a Studebaker line of just two cars, the Four and the Six, both with cylinder dimensions of 3.5 in × 5 in, giving 192 (3146 cc) and 289 cu in (4736 cc) displacements, respectively. On a 108 inch wheelbase, the smaller car cost $1050, while the Six, with its 121 inch wheelbase, was priced at $1575. These cars had pressed-steel front fenders and axle housings, and one-piece cylinder-block castings. They were tough, well tested cars that carried the company to record auto production of 65,885 in 1916.

Under a brilliant new chief engineer, Fred M. Zeder, and a new president, Albert R. Erskine, the line was completely overhauled for the 1918 model year. In 1920, the four was dropped and replaced by a six, known as the Light Six, of 207 cu in (3392 cc). The rest of the range consisted of the 289 cu in (4736 cc) Special Six and the 354 cu in (5801 cc) Big Six. These engines developed 45, 55 and 60 bhp, respectively, at a modest 2000 rpm. Zeder left Studebaker in 1920, but the cars he created lived on with little change to sell increasingly well. The high-water mark in registrations came in 1925, when the company put 107,732 cars into service. Its total production that

Above: 1915 Studebaker four-seater tourer

Below: a four-door Studebaker saloon of 1928 vintage

year, including trucks, was 134,664 units. Others, though, had grown much faster: from its third-place industry ranking in 1912, Studebaker had dropped to eighth in order of production volume by 1926.

Under the capable Albert Erskine, called by historian Maurice Hendry 'probably the most dynamic leader the company ever had', Studebaker sought to introduce smaller cars that would sell better both in the US and abroad. Their first such entry, the $975 Erskine, was announced for the 1927 model year after tests on the new Studebaker Proving Ground at South Bend, only the second such facility in America, after GM; it lasted only a little more than two years. Then, in 1932 and 1933, the Rockne six was offered, from $585 up, named after famous gridiron coach, Knute Rockne. Although it did not survive, its L-head engine did, and it powered some other Studebaker models up until 1950.

The South Bend company acquired an aggressive new chief engineer in Delmar G. 'Barney' Roos in 1926. Five years earlier, Roos had held the same post at Pierce-Arrow, the Buffalo, NY maker of luxury cars, which fell on hard times and was bought by Studebaker in 1928. Although South Bend held control, and there was some engineering co-operation between the two firms, they remained essentially independent, and Pierce-Arrow was sold again by a troubled Studebaker in 1933. In the meantime, Roos and Erskine had launched a straight-eight Studebaker, the President 8, in 1928, and renamed the sixes the Dictator and Commander, as pretentious an array of model names as the industry has ever seen. Smaller eights for the Dictator and Commander were introduced in 1929. By 1930, all these eights had crankshafts supported by no less than nine main bearings.

Top: a 1923 Studebaker convertible; note the plain disc wheels, an unusual feature in days when spoked wheels were the norm

Left: Studebaker's six-cylinder 3½-litre engine of 1926; this particular example was photographed in a Brazilian museum where it was undergoing restoration

Below: a 1929 Studebaker Erskine convertible; this model was named after Albert Erskine, regarded as one of the most dynamic leaders the company ever had. The Erskine cost $975

Many laurels in record-breaking and long-distance demonstrations were won by Studebakers in the late 1920s, and when the Indianapolis rules were liberalised to let in stock-based cars in 1930, this was an open invitation to the racing enthusiasts in South Bend. After private sallies in 1930 and '31, a factory team of five cars was entered in 1932, using modified President 8 components. They placed an impressive third, sixth and thirteenth, with two not finishing. All five were also entered, less successfully, in 1933 with streamlined bodies. In spite of these efforts, Studebaker registrations plummeted to only 36,242 in the depression year 1932. Unable to meet its debts, Studebaker declared bankruptcy in 1933, and among the court-appointed receivers were Paul G. Hoffman and Hardold S. Vance. The former had been a successful distributor for Studebaker before joining them in 1925, and the latter had worked his way up through the manufacturing ranks. They sold Pierce-Arrow, dropped the big President 8, brought out new sixes with the Rockne engine and, by 1935, had Studebaker on its feet again.

Vance as board chairman and Hoffman as president gave Studebaker firmer and more distinctive product and marketing policies. To give them the style they sorely needed, they hired Raymond Loewy as a consultant in 1936. The immediate pre-war models, the 1941 line especially, show crisp, sheer lines that more than match those of such classics of the same era as the Cadillac 60 Special and Lincoln Continental.

Top left: an eight-cylinder Studebaker competing in the 1929 Brooklands Double Twelve event

Below: a publicity photograph of the 1931 Studebaker saloon

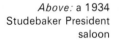

Above: a 1934
Studebaker President
saloon

Top right: a four-door
Studebaker Commander
of 1938

Centre right: the unusual
flowing lines of the 1934
Studebaker Land Cruiser
saloon

Right: front-end view of
Studebaker's
Commander model;
these cars were powered
by an L-head six-
cylinder engine

Since 1935, Studebakers offered independent front
suspension with a transverse-leaf spring and optional
overdrive. The conspiculously inappropriate 'Dictator'
model name was at last dropped in 1938, and in the
following model year Studebaker was moved irrevo-
cably into the American small-car market with the
introduction of the $700 Champion. Powered by a
164 cu in (2687 cc) six, it weighed only 2330 pounds on
a 110 inch wheelbase.

Sparked by the spunky Champion, Studebaker car
registrations were above the 100,000 mark in both 1940
and 1941. From this plateau, it would step out again
after World War II, in which Studebaker built trucks,
aeroplane engines and the Weasel personnel carrier,
which it also designed. Its war contracts totalled
$1.2 billion in value, putting the company in an ex-
cellent position to finance a new post-war model,
and was the first manufacturer to place a new model on
the market. The '47 Studebaker was a landmark in the
history of auto styling, the first large-volume production car to blend its front fenders completely into the
body and combine that with a true straight horizontal
grille. Interiors were handsome, pull-out door handles
were novel and practical and the Starlight coupé, with
its four-piece wraparound rear window, was as adventurous as anything the auto industry has done since.
Playing a key role in its design, which was at the

time publicly credited to Raymond Loewy, was Virgil M. Exner.

These new cars were powered by L-head sixes, including the Champion, Commander and the new Land Cruiser on a 123 inch wheelbase. They sold well with little change through 1949, when registration of 199,460 cars gave Studebaker 4.1 per cent of the market, its highest modern penetration. The same share was held in 1950 with a new coil-spring front suspension, an automatic transmission with direct drive in high gear and a new aeroplane-style pointed nose from the Loewy studios. Registrations that year reached the all-time high of 268,229 cars; total sales were 335,000 units and earnings were nearly half a billion dollars. This was the legacy of the able Paul

Above left: a four-door Studebaker of the 1960s

Above: the heavily tail-finned Studebaker Commander two-door of 1958

Left: the Studebaker Daytona coupé of 1964

Opposite page, top right: a Studebaker Daytona 283 coupé of 1966

Opposite page, centre: a diagram of the supercharger fitted to the 289-cubic inch V8 engine which powered the Golden Hawk of 1957. The supercharger was driven through a variable-rate pulley which, claimed Studebaker, produced maximum power during acceleration, while permitting normal fuel economy at cruising speeds

Hoffman, who had left Studebaker in 1948 to become the administrator of the Marshall Plan.

A short stroke, high-compression overhead-valve V8 engine was introduced in 1951, the last year of the 'spinner' nose. That year, Bob Bourke at the Loewy office in South Bend was working on a new design he hoped could be built as a one-off special, a sleek, low coupé. Its low nose and clean lines won the favour of Studebaker management, headed by president Harold Nance, and the coupé was scheduled for limited production in 1953. Its lines were also adapted to four-door and two-door sedan models for '53 and a station wagon for '54 (the previous body series had no wagon, but did have a convertible, which the new

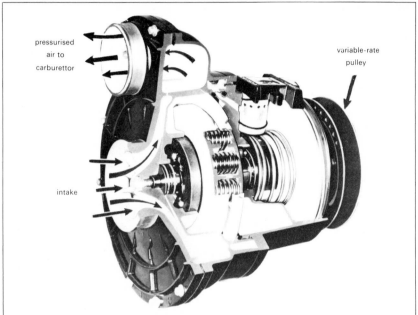

pressurised air to carburettor

variable-rate pulley

intake

range lacked).

Known as the Starliner, the new coupé was a winner, recognised the world over as one of the most beautiful cars ever made. Studebaker featured it in its brochures and advertising, and buyers flocked to get it —only to find that various problems caused a three-month delay in production. Studebaker's share of the

market fell instead of rising, dropping under the two per cent level in 1954. Exciting future plans, such as the unit-body car with all-independent suspension and 120° V6 engine that Porsche had designed for Studebaker, were out of the question. Deeply in the red, Studebaker merged with Packard late in 1954. This began four turbulent years, the first two under

Above: one of Studebaker's most popular models was the medium-sized Lark; this is the four-door version of 1964

James Nance, struggling to become a 'big' car maker as Studebaker had once before, with Pierce-Arrow under Erskine, and the second two years under a management agreement with Curtiss-Wright.

New life was given the Starliner coupé in 1956 with restyling as the Hawk, in four varieties. In 1957, a supercharger was optional on the Golden Hawk, an exceptionally capable car for its day. More vital to Studebaker's health was the new Lark of 1959, created by new president Harold Churchill by slicing the nose and tail off a normal sedan to devise the first of the compact cars with a miniscule investment. Registrations more than doubled, to 133,382 cars, and Studebaker-Packard earned $29 million in 1959; this was its last good year.

Nerve and ingenuity kept Studebaker alive through the early 1960s. Another president, Sherwood Egbert, sought salvation in sporty models. For 1962, Brooks Stevens created the GT Hawk at his request, while Loewy stylists were designing the much more radical Avanti. Problems in crafting its glassfibre body delayed production of the Avanti, which had been introduced in mid 1962, and the sliding roof of the '63 Wagonaire station wagon developed embarrassing leaks. Egbert had tried but failed to ignore the lead time normally demanded by the auto industry. In the meantime, he had at least so diversified the company that half its sales (and all its earnings) came from non-automotive business.

It fell to Byers Burlingame, named president in November 1963, to wean Studebaker away from cars. In December, he announced that the South Bend plant would be closed and production continued only at an assembly factory in Hamilton, Ontario, Canada,

Above: the most spectacular model ever produced by Studebaker was the Avanti; designed by Raymond Loewy, it was introduced in 1962 and had a glassfibre body, disc brakes on the front and an optional supercharger

Left: the interior of the Avanti

with Chevrolet engines from the 1964 models onward. Some very tasteful restyling was managed, first for the 1964 cars and then again in '66. Disc brakes were a Studebaker innovation in the US on 1964 models, standard on the front wheels of the Avanti and optional on the others. Only 26,073 of these '64 Studebakers were registered in the US, and the number dropped to half that the following year. When the announcement came in March 1966 that Studebaker would stop making cars altogether, there was, as planned, minimal resistance from its 450 remaining dealers in the US.

The shovel-nosed Avanti coupé, the most spectacular auto ever made by Studebaker, survived the collapse. It was rescued in 1965 by a South Bend dealer, Nathan Altman, who formed a new company to produce it, only slightly changed, as the Avanti II. Otherwise, only memories remain, of Big Sixes, EMF, Starlights and Starliners, of the glory days of Studebaker automobiles.

THEY CALLED THE STUTZ the 'car that made good in a day', but Harry C. Stutz had been designing cars for fourteen years or so before the first vehicle to bear his name appeared. He started with a crude gas buggy in 1897, then progressed to the low-built American Underslung of 1907, in which the chassis was hung below the axles. Stutz later went into component manufacture, and one of his specialities was a robust three-speed transaxle unit, which combined a gearbox and final drive in one casing.

To prove the quality of this back-axle assembly, Stutz built a racing car—in five weeks—and entered it in the first-ever Indianapolis 500 in 1911. The car,

Stutz
Stutz made some of the most classic cars ever produced

driven by Cal Anderson, finished eleventh, and the marque's reputation was established. The company producing the Stutz car was known as the Ideal Motor Car Company, and its factory was in Indianapolis. In 1913, the corporate name was altered to the Stutz Motor Car Company of America.

There was little remarkable about the first Stutz cars, which were powered by 6.3-litre Wisconsin engines, although the marque continued its sporting career, achieving fourth and sixth places in the 1912 Indianapolis 500, first and second places in the Illinois Trophy at the Elgin racetrack, and third place in the Milwaukee Grand Prize.

In 1914, however, the archetypal Stutz, and one of motoring history's most legendary models, was born. It was the Bearcat, whose name is symbolic of the whole bathtub-gin-swilling, charlestoning, vo-de-o-doing atmosphere of the early 1920s (although by that time, the Stutz Bearcat was becoming a little passé). The original Bearcat aped the Mercer Raceabout formula of massive engine, minimal coachwork—bonnet, wings, two seats and a bolster fuel tank were deemed adequate—and proved remarkably popular,

Above: one of the best known of all American sports cars was the Stutz Bearcat speedster of 1914; it was powered by a T-head, four-cylinder engine producing 60 bhp at 1500 rpm

with sales rising from 759 cars in 1913 to 2207 in 1917.

One reason behind the fame of the Stutz at this period was the success of the White Squadron of racing Stutzes in the major races of 1915, although these cars, with their specially built sixteen-valve Wisconsin single-overhead-camshaft engines of 4851 cc, were far from being standard models. The White Squadron cars were third, fourth and seventh at Indianapolis, first and second at Sheepshead Bay and won the Point Loma, Minneapolis and Elgin events, while the team's leading drivers, Earl Cooper and Gil Anderson, were first and third in the National Drivers' Championship for the year.

In 1916, Cooper came second in the Vanderbilt Cup, and the following year won a 250-mile race at the Chicago Board Speedway. The year 1919 saw Eddie Hearne take second place at Indianapolis, but the White Squadron cars were now past their best, and faded from the scene (although one of them has survived, in New Zealand).

On the road, too, the Stutz was breaking records: when a dissatisfied owner took his car back to the supplying dealer, protesting vehemently that this totally gutless new 1916 Bearcat was no match for the smaller-engined Mercer Raceabouts on the streets of New York, the Stutz publicity department handed the 'dud' over to that curious character Cannonball Baker, who had a seemingly insatiable urge to thunder across the USA from Atlantic to Pacific in high-powered cars, and announced that he would use it to break the Trans-American record which was then held by a motor cycle.

Break the record Cannonball did, taking eleven days, $7\frac{1}{2}$ hours to complete the trip. On one memorable day, he put 592 miles into 24 hours, and the car finished unscathed except for a broken shock-absorber bracket.

Although the Stutz company was seemingly riding high, Harry Stutz resigned in 1919 and founded the HCS motor company, also Indianapolis-based. The HCS car was an expensive assembled car whose radiator and bonnet styling (but little else) were cribbed from the Hispano-Suiza; the marque failed to make any great impression on the car-buying public, and quietly died in due course.

The Bearcat had become pansified by 1920, with such effete irrelevancies as windscreen, doors and hood. Shortly afterwards, the gearbox parted company with the rear axle and went to live in the conventional position, and Stutz began making their own four and six-cylinder power units. The company had come under the control of steel tycoon Charles M. Schwab, but there was little evidence of new thinking at the top, and the last Bearcat, the 4.7-litre Speedway Six of 1924, had little to offer, and sales continued to fall.

There was a further change of management in 1925, when Frederic E. Moscovics took over as president, and brought in the Belgian designer Paul Bastien, who had previously worked for Métallurgique in his homeland. Bastien created a car that was intended to exemplify 'safety, beauty and comfort', but the new Safety Stutz Vertical Eight could not shake off the sporty image of its forebears that easily. Its 4.7-litre straight-eight engine was endowed with a single overhead camshaft, and developed 92 bhp at 3200 rpm, enabling the car to achieve 75 mph.

The Safety Stutz had a worm-drive rear axle, which permitted the car to be built very low, while an advanced feature was the use of hydraulic four-wheel brakes (which really *were* hydraulic, operating on a mixture of water and alcohol). The car could be had with low-built Weymann closed coachwork, or as an

agressively beetle-backed speedster; crowning the handsome radiator was a mascot representing the sun god Ra, while the car was endowed with a primitive form of safety glass with wire mesh embedded in windows and windscreen!

Altogether, the new Stutz was one of the outstanding American cars, of its day and of all time, although its chances in an era when mediocrity was the order of the day seemed less than encouraging.

Moscovics relented of his decision to play down the sporty side of the Stutz, though, and entered the speedsters (known as Black Hawks from 1927) in a wide selection of races, which they duly won.

The great sporting year of the Stutz was 1928. In that year, Gil Anderson drove one of the new 4883 cc Black Hawk speedsters at 106.52 mph at Daytona to set up a new American stock-car record. Although Frank Lockhart's attempt on the Land-Speed record with the ultra-streamlined Stutz Blackhawk ended in a fatal crash, it is worth remembering that this sixteen-cylinder Miller-engined car built in the Stutz factory was, at 3.1-litres, the smallest-capacity LSR car of all time, yet achieved 225 mph on one of its unsuccessful runs, faster than the 88-litre White Triplex which had just set up a new record when Lockhart crashed.

It was a Stutz, too, that raced an Hispano-Suiza for a purse of $25,000 at Indianapolis, when Moscovics bet French coachbuilder Charles T. Weymann that a 4.8-litre Stutz could beat an 8-litre Hispano in a twenty-four-hour endurance race. But Moscovics should have thought better of the challenge, for after nineteen hours the Stutz packed up with valve trouble and the Hispano collected the prize money.

It was nearly a different story at Le Mans that year, though, for Weymann entered a team of three Stutzes to challenge the best sports-tourers of Europe, and the bold venture nearly paid off, for the car of Bloch and Brisson, which finished second to the $4\frac{1}{2}$-litre Bentley of Barnato and Rubin, had lost its top gear ninety minutes from the end. It was the nearest an American car came to winning the Vingt-Quatre Heures du Mans until the Ford Mk IVs and GT40s came on the scene to win the 1966–7–8–9 events.

It was a result that fully endorsed the Stutz claim that 'the car which is safest has the right to be fastest',

Above: this superb example of Stutz's 1923 Bearcat model can now be seen in the impressive Ford Motor Museum in Detroit

220

out the entire range with perfect smoothness and ease of handling, and does not at any point give the operator the feeling of strain and overtaxed mechanism. Low centre of gravity contributes largely to the safety of the car in that overturning in case of accident is practically impossible. Also, the increased roadability is particularly noticeable in terms of absence of side sway and the greater comfort. The low centre of mass of the new car is made possible through careful engineering, which has taken full advantage of the possibilities of the worm-drive axle. With full load, the floor boards are approximately 20 inches from the road, and it is only 70 inches to the top of the deck on closed cars. This indicates the ample headroom, as well as the low construction of the car . . . Long trips may be covered with a minimum of fatigue and nervous energy.'

Such considerations were not paramount when the Sutz cars for the 1929 Le Mans race were constructed, for these were fitted with superchargers between the dumbirons, feeding the single carburettor through a massive induction pipe several feet long. The cars were 'fearsome looking beasts . . . capable of 105 or 106 mph . . . blowers are chancy things and apt to smash up engines.'

The best that one of the Stutz team could manage was fifth place. There were Stutz entries at Le Mans in 1930 and '32 as well, but none of them finished.

The design of the straight-eight was further improved for the 1931 season, with the addition of a 'No-Back' device behind the gearbox so that the car could not run backwards when restarting on hills, and a 'Variable Booster Brake' which could be used to alter the amount of servo-assistance given to the brakes. *The Motor* explained:

Above: a Stutz Black Hawk Custom Series AA tourer of 1927; it was powered by an eight-cylinder engine developing 110 bhp. The model photographed is now on view in the Harrah Museum in Nevada

Below: the 1928 Stutz BB Convertible Sedan Sotheby; it was fitted with a straight-eight engine

for the ailing Stutz had covered an impressive 1594.26 miles against the winning car's 1656.68 miles.

In January 1929, the Stutz company issued a booklet describing the attributes of the Low-Weighted Stutz, 'The wide speed range, or flexibility, of the new car is a distinct factor not only because of congested traffic conditions, but also because the car performs through-

'It is a simple matter to arrange that a comparatively light pedal pressure will produce the maximum braking effect if high speeds on good road surfaces are to be the order of the day. On the other hand, when driving in traffic over greasy roads, it is just as simple to reduce the servo action to such an extent that the full depression of the brake pedal will just fail to lock the road wheels.'

There was a new model, too, a cheaper ohc six-cylinder model marketed as the Black Hawk, introduced in the hope of revitalising flagging sales figures, as it was priced on the UK market at only £685 in chassis form, whereas the cheapest eight was £995 as a chassis—the dearest, a supercharged short-chassis variant which revived the Bearcat name was £1195 in chassis guise.

The American market was now becoming dominated by the ostentatious V12 and V16 giants from Cadillac, Packard and Lincoln, in the face of whose silken luxury a mere eight cylinders of Stutz seemed rough and uncivilised. In response the last great Stutz power unit was introduced, the DV32.

'In two-seater open form, the Stutz Bearcat is sold with a guaranteed speed of 100 mph', wrote *The Motor* in October 1931. 'The engine, which develops 155 bhp at 3500 rpm, has four valves per cylinder, these being operated by two overhead camshafts, and is the only power unit of its kind in the Show. The specification includes a nine-bearing crankshaft, centrifugal-pump circulation, forced lubrication, Schebler carburettor, air cleaner and purifier. The transmission system comprises a four-forward-speed "silent-third" gearbox built in unit with the engine, and final drive by underslung worm.'

The single ohc straight-eight and the Black Hawk Six were continued alongside this splendid new model, which rather eclipsed them with its technical specification even though it was too expensive for most customers. Indeed, only the SV16 was shown at the 1932 Olympia Show, and even then the chassis price was £1097.

A free-wheel device was optional, and became standard equipment the following year, when the SV16 also came with thermostatically controlled vents in the bonnet which regulated temperature in the engine compartment, and there was servo-assistance for the clutch. A new feature on the 1934 models was a servo for the clutch withdrawal mechanism, while 1935 models had an automatic clutch allied to a three-speed transmission. Although *The Motor* claimed cheerily that 'English admirers of the Stutz claim an affinity between this car and the high-quality British sports car', the days of the DV32 and the SV16 were numbered, and in 1935 the Splendid Stutz ceased production.

However, the company had taken out insurance in 1928 by starting to produce a curious light van, the Pak-Age-Car, with all-round independent suspension and a rear-mounted engine, but even this odd-ball machine failed to keep Stutz afloat for more than another three years, although the design rights were taken over by Diamond T Trucks.

The hallowed Stutz Bearcat name has been acquired from the Stutz family in recent years (one wonders why, as Harry Stutz broke with the company fifteen years before its demise) by a manufacturer of fearfully expensive luxury cars designed for showbiz personalities. Elvis Presley purchased four of these behemoths, which seems adequately to sum up their place in automotive history.

Left: although the Stutz company is best remembered for its sporty cars, it also made some splendid saloon models; this is the Stutz Black Hawk Six 4-litre saloon of 1929

Bottom: introduced in the early 1930s as a rival to the multi-cylinder cars produced by Lincoln, Cadillac, Marmon etc, this is the short-chassis Stutz DV32 Super Bearcat

Index

Page numbers in **bold** indicate a main reference. Page numbers in *italics* at the end of an entry refer to illustrations in the first chapter. However, most illustrations of a make of car will be found in the main section indicated in **bold**.